Essays on
John McGahern

Assessing a literary legacy

Essays on
John McGahern

Assessing a literary legacy

DEREK HAND & EAMON MAHER

CORK **CUP** UNIVERSITY PRESS

First published in 2019 by
Cork University Press
Youngline Industrial Estate
Pouladuff Road
Togher
Cork T12 HT6V
Ireland

ISBN-978-1-78205-329-3
Printed by Hussar Books in Poland
Typeset by Alison Burns at Studio 10 Design, Cork

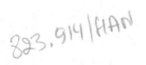

CONTENTS

ACKNOWLEDGEMENTS

The editors would like to thank their respective institutions, and particularly the School of English and the Faculty of Humanities and Social Sciences, DCU, and the Department of Humanities in TU Dublin – Tallaght Campus, for all their support of this publication. They would also like to express their gratitude to Paul Butler for supplying such an evocative cover photograph. All the staff at Cork University Press have been wonderful to work with, but a special mention must go to Maria O'Donovan for her expertise, infectious good humour and enthusiasm for this book from its infancy through to publication.

Finally, it is important to acknowledge the role of the editors' wives and families, Paula and Sophie Dang, and Liz, Liam, Marcella and Kevin, for their love and understanding, which make this type of work both possible and enjoyable.

CONTRIBUTORS

PAUL BUTLER is a photographer living in County Leitrim since 2001. He has photographed extensively within the area of Leitrim and hosted various exhibitions linked to the visualisation of John McGahern's work at venues around Ireland, including The Dock Arts Centre in Carrick-on-Shannon and The Atrium in Longford. Paul is currently working with Eamon Maher on a book which explores the theme of religion and place in McGahern's work through the lenses of photography and text.

A selection of work relating to this project can be viewed at www.paulbutler.me

NIAMH CAMPBELL is an Irish Research Council postdoctoral fellow at the University of Maynooth, and a creative writer supported by the Arts Council of Ireland. Her work has appeared in numerous publications, including *gorse* and *The Dublin Review*, and her monograph *Sacred Weather: atmospheric essentialism in the fiction of John McGahern* is forthcoming from Cork University Press.

JOE CLEARY is Professor of English at Yale University and works in the areas of Irish, postcolonial and world literatures. After receiving his BA and MA from Maynooth University, he took his PhD at Columbia University, New York, where he studied with Edward Said in the Department of English and Comparative Literature. Publications include *Literature, Partition and the Nation-State: culture and conflict in Ireland, Israel and Palestine* (Cambridge University Press, 2002), *The Cambridge Companion to Modern Irish Culture*, co-edited with Claire Connolly (Cambridge University Press, 2005), *Outrageous Fortune: capital and culture in Modern Ireland* (Field Day Publications, 2007) and *The Cambridge Companion to Irish Modernism* (Cambridge University Press, 2014). His articles have appeared in *South Atlantic Quarterly*, *Boundary 2*, *Modern Language Quarterly*, *Textual Practice*, *Field Day Review*, *Éire-Ireland* and *The Irish Review*, and he has edited or co-edited special issues of *Éire-Ireland*, *MLQ* and *Boundary 2*. He is currently completing two books: *Modernism, Empire and World Literature*, a study of how Irish, American and anti-colonial modernists helped reconfigure the world system in the period between the two world wars, and *The Unsuspected*

World: the Irish expatriate novel between the American and Chinese centuries, which explores how two generations of Irish novelists have imaginatively navigated the changing contours of the contemporary global order.

MÁIRE DOYLE studied at University College Dublin where she was awarded her doctorate on the topic of 'Love and Ethics in the Fiction of John McGahern' in 2013. She is co-editor of the essay collection *John McGahern: authority and vision*, published by Manchester University Press in 2017. Máire teaches literary criticism and creative non-fiction writing and has delivered seminars and workshops at University College Dublin, National University of Ireland, Maynooth, at the James Joyce Summer School (Dublin) and at IES Abroad (Dublin). Writing creatively, Máire has scripted and published two of McGahern's stories, 'A Slip Up' and 'All Sorts of Impossible Things', for the stage. These were performed in Dublin in 2016 and in Carrick-on-Shannon in 2017.

EÓIN FLANNERY is Senior Lecturer and Head of the Department of English Language and Literature at Mary Immaculate College, University of Limerick. He is the author of four books: *Ireland and Ecocriticism: literature, history, and environmental justice* (Routledge, 2016); *Colum McCann and the Aesthetics of Redemption* (Irish Academic Press, 2011); *Ireland and Postcolonial Studies: theory, discourse, utopia* (Palgrave Macmillan, 2009); *Versions of Ireland: empire, modernity and resistance in Irish culture* (Cambridge Scholars Press, 2006). His edited publications include: *Enemies of Empire: new perspectives on literature, history and imperialism* (2007); *Ireland in Focus: film, photography and popular culture* (2009), and *This Side of Brightness: essays on the fiction of Colum McCann* (2012). His next book, *Debt, Guilt and Literary Forms in post-Celtic Tiger Ireland*, is forthcoming.

ANNE GOARZIN is Professor of Irish Literature and Culture at the University of Rennes 2, France. Her work focuses on Irish literature as well as on the visual arts in Ireland. She teaches literature, critical theory and the visual arts at undergraduate and graduate levels and supervises post-doc and doctoral theses. She has been Chair of SOFEIR (French Society for Irish Studies https://sofeir.fr) since 2014 and she was appointed as a board member of EFACIS (European Federation of Irish Studies) in 2017. She is the author of, among other books, *John McGahern: reflets d'Irlande* (Presses Universitaires de Rennes, 2002) and editor of *New Critical Perspectives on Franco-Irish Relations* (Peter Lang, 2015). She is a regular contributor to *Études Irlandaises* and other international journals of Irish Studies.

DEREK HAND is a Senior Lecturer and Head of the School of English in Dublin City University. The Liffey Press published his book *John Banville: exploring fictions* in 2002. He edited a special edition of the *Irish University Review* on John Banville in 2006. He has lectured on Irish writing in the USA, Portugal, Norway, Singapore, Brazil, Italy, Sweden, Malaysia and France. He was awarded an IRCHSS Government of Ireland Research Fellowship for 2008–9. His *A History of the Irish Novel: 1665 to the present* was published by Cambridge University Press in 2011 and is now available in paperback.

DECLAN KIBERD is Keough Professor of Irish Studies at Notre Dame. He was for many years chair of Anglo-Irish Literature at UCD. He has published many books, the most recent of which, *After Ireland* (Head of Zeus, 2018), includes two extended essays on McGahern. He has served as a Director on the board of the Abbey Theatre.

CLAUDIA LUPPINO holds a PhD in English and American Studies from the University of Florence, Italy, and an MA in Foreign Languages and Literature from the same university. She has published articles on John McGahern, Claire Keegan and Colm Tóibín and she was the guest editor of the third issue of the *Journal of Franco-Irish Studies*. Her fields of interest and research include contemporary history, postcolonial studies and the Irish Diaspora. She is currently working on a book based on her PhD thesis, *From John McGahern to Claire Keegan: resistance to postmodernism in contemporary Irish fiction*, to be published by Peter Lang in the Reimagining Ireland Series.

EAMON MAHER is the author of two monographs on the work of John McGahern and he is Director of the National Centre for Franco-Irish Studies at the Technological University Dublin. As editor of the successful *Reimagining Ireland* series with Peter Lang Oxford, he recently edited a selection of essays from the first fifty volumes entitled *The Reimagining Ireland Reader: examining our past, shaping our future*. Currently Eamon is working with Paul Butler on a book exploring the theme of religion and place in McGahern's work through the lenses of photography and text.

SYLVIE MIKOWSKI has been Professor of Irish Studies at the University of Reims since 2003. After a 1995 PhD from the University of Caen entitled 'La mémoire et l'imagination dans les romans de John McGahern', her main topic of research has been the contemporary Irish novel. She has published *Le roman irlandais contemporain* (Presses Universitaires de Caen, 2004) and edited *Irish Women Writers/Ecrivaines d'Irlande* (with Bertrand Cardin) (Presses Universitaires de Caen, 2011), *Ireland and Popular Culture* (Peter Lang, 2014), and 'Popular Culture Today', *Imaginaires*, 2015. She has also published numerous chapters and articles, among which more recently: '*A Long Long Way* de Sebastian Barry et *14* de Jean Echenoz: la mise en crise du roman de la Première Guerre Mondiale', *Transversalités*, 2015; 'Children's Narratives in Contemporary Irish Fiction', *Études Irlandaises*, 2015; 'Gothic and Noir: the genres of the contemporary fiction of containment', *Etudes Irlandaises*, 2017; 'Résurgences gothiques dans *The Secret Scripture* de Sebastian Barry', *Otrante*, 2017. She is currently writing a book on the twenty-first-century Irish novel.

RICHARD ROBINSON is Associate Professor in the Department of English Literature and Creative Writing at Swansea University. He is the author of *Narratives of the European Border: a history of nowhere* (Palgrave Macmillan, 2007) and *John McGahern and Modernism* (Bloomsbury, 2017). He has published on James Joyce, Italo Svevo, Kazuo Ishiguro, Ian McEwan, Edward St Aubyn and John McGahern in journals such as *James Joyce Quarterly*, *Journal of European Studies*, *Critical Quarterly*, *Modern Fiction Studies*, *Textual Practice* and *Irish University Review*.

DONAL RYAN is the author of four number one best-selling novels and a short story collection. He has won numerous awards including the European Union Prize for Literature, the Guardian First Book Award, and Irish Book of the Year. His work has been adapted for stage and screen, translated into over twenty languages, and is on the Irish Leaving Certificate syllabus. In 2016 his Man Booker-nominated novel *The Spinning Heart* was voted Irish Book of the Decade. Donal lectures in Creative Writing at the University of Limerick.

DENIS SAMPSON is the author of *Outstaring Nature's Eye: the fiction of John McGahern* and *Young John McGahern: becoming a novelist*, and many articles and reviews of books related to McGahern. He has also written a biography, *Brian Moore: the chameleon novelist* and a memoir, *A Migrant Heart*, on growing up in Ireland and settling in Canada. His most recent book is *The Found Voice: writers' beginnings*, studies of Alice Munro, V.S Naipaul, Mavis Gallant, J.M. Coetzee and William Trevor. He has also broadcast on RTÉ and written for *Irish University Review*, *Queen's Quarterly*, *Dublin Review of Books*, *Irish Pages*, *Canadian Journal of Irish Studies*.

EAMONN WALL's books include *Writing the Irish West: ecologies and traditions* (University of Notre Dame Press, 2011) and *Junction City: new & selected poems, 1990–2015* (Salmon Poetry, 2015). His articles, essays and poetry have appeared widely in newspapers, journals and collections including *The Irish Times*, *Irish Literary Supplement*, *Poetry Ireland Review* and *Tracing the Cultural Legacy of Irish Catholicism*. Current projects include a study of Irish-American writing and a new collection of poetry. He lives in Missouri where he works as a professor of International Studies and English at the University of Missouri-St Louis.

FOREWORD

John McGahern: Impossible Things
Declan Kiberd

McGahern wrote his first stories and books when French letters were at the centre of the literary world and before his long and happy marriage to Madeline Green led him to take a more mellow, loving vision of the world. The commentaries of French intellectuals on human relationships tended to be bleak. Samuel Beckett (by the 1950s, a naturalised Parisian) depicted love as a function of illusion, and friendship a confession of cowardice. He followed Proust in sadly suggesting that the lives of people never quite synchronise: people merely see one another in their longing for one another. Albert Camus took up many of these themes. His characters had tough exteriors, because they saw it as a form of honour to refuse any easy sentimentality; yet that external display of an apparent numbness often masked a deep emotion.

In her perspicacious and persuasive PhD thesis on 'Love and Ethics in the Fiction of John McGahern' (UCD, 2013), Máire Doyle finds echoes of these moments in the stories of *Getting Through* or in a book such as *The Pornographer*. McGahern's earlier works had seemed rooted mainly in family and its linked emotions, whether in the expression of tenderness or rage – the pages of *The Barracks* and *The Dark* are proof enough of that. McGahern liked to joke that Ireland was a nation composed of thousands of self-governing anarchist communes, otherwise known as 'families'. The 1937 Constitution had fetishised family life as the very basis of a society, in part because it was drawn up by Éamon de Valera, a man whose early upbringing by an aunt was so lacking in warmth that, when he arrived as a boarder at Blackrock College to find all other newcomers crying nightly for their mothers, he could not understand their frustrations at all, having felt that he himself had come to live in a majestic kind of palace. Yet the Constitution which he helped to create (assisted by another Blackrock College man, John Charles McQuaid) in effect presented the family as an alternative to the social. The character named Moran in *Amongst Women* considers himself a lifelong combatant against colonial power but ultimately becomes an antagonist of the very notion of the community itself.

McGahern left his own Leitrim family to train as a teacher in St Patrick's College, Drumcondra. He taught me and my friends at St John the Baptist boys' national school (locally known as 'Belgrove' after the house which it first occupied), when we were eight years old and in second class. He sometimes depicted the life of that school, most extensively in *The Leavetaking*, but also in stories such as 'The Recruiting Officer', which describes the desolating experience of a fellow teacher in the days and weeks after he left a religious order and laicised: quite a number of the sentences in that story are taken directly from letters which he received from this man, Tom Jordan, who became a fast friend.

In the story 'All Sorts of Impossible Things', he writes of the sing-song voice employed by teachers anxious to conceal emotion from children. I remember that McGahern employed this technique very well, whether it was tables ('nine times nine is eighty one') or spellings of similar-sounding words ('blade, spade, made, fade'). He often looked absent-mindedly out the large classroom windows during these incantatory recitals and sometimes he would scratch his forehead out of sheer boredom (hence his nickname for a year or two, 'Scratchy').

A good teacher (like the one in 'All Sorts of Impossible Things'), he could seem suddenly abstracted, as if caught up in a world elsewhere, quite distinct from our classroom. Even when he disciplined the boys, it was often done absent-mindedly, as if some emotion was being summoned which was no sooner called up than blocked off. It was only many years later that I realised he might well have been reliving the experience of being disciplined by his own father. I also had the impression, even at the time, that the disciplinary element of teaching in those days was something he privately hated and despised. Years later, he confessed as much, telling me that on his first day of teaching in the town of Drogheda, he had asked a head brother whether he had any advice to offer; and the simple, singular answer was: 'Bate it into them.' McGahern was the kind of teacher I imagine D.H. Lawrence to have been, sensitive to the needs of young boys, but probably ill-fitted to some of the extra-curricular institutional demands. Like the existentialist writers and the village schoolmaster of Goldsmith, he had to learn how to put on a severe and stern act.

In March 1960 (the year in which I would have been in his class), he wrote in a letter to Michael McLaverty:

Although most of the children in the school where I teach come from comfortable homes, there is a small slum in the middle of Clontarf. This year I happen to have ten from there – eight to nine years old – and what I learn shakes me. Any scar will nearly always fester. <u>I notice how they huddle apart from the other children</u> in the playground. It is strange that while their shoes are leaking that they can always muster money for drill costumes or a shining new red tie and blue suit for First Communion – any outward show. Why I probably tell you these things is that only today I discovered that the sweaty smell of decay, nauseatingly strong from some of them, comes from their sleeping in their clothes. It is difficult to reconcile the desire to do nothing but write ('I intend to give up this scribbling,' Byron said in one of his letters), even a cushioned civil service life, with all the human suffering about us.[1]

Even though McGahern could be conservative on matters of social tact and decorum, he was keenly alert to the injuries of social class. After his dismissal from his post at Belgrove, he put a stoic face on things but wept for an afternoon in his sister's kitchen at the manifest injustice of the decision and at the fact that he was now another one of those in danger of falling out of the human community. He worked for a time as a labourer on building sites in England and later as a supply teacher in a run-down school in London. He asked the boys whether each could recall the colour of the front door of his own home. Many could not: 'That showed that the benefits of the welfare state did not reach everyone and was a sure sign of depression.'

The covering-up of emotion is a common tactic among Irish men, as is the displacement of a search for tenderness into coded forms. In 'All Sorts of Impossible Things' the bond between the two main characters is deep, unspeakable, rooted perhaps in a yearning for all the things that each man cannot have … rather like their ultimately unsuccessful hunt for hares. Each man seeks dreams of which he cannot really speak: he can speak only of having sought them.

The schoolmaster is lonely and has no wife, so his sexual frustration creates an obsession that seems to leak into everything. The publican's whiskey-drinking he sees as a rehearsal for sex, if not a sex act in itself. The agricultural instructor's wife is seen as soft and kind. In his loneliness the schoolmaster hopes that the hunting dog will comfort and console him and he in turn will cosset and comfort the bitch.

I think that McGahern himself was lonely in Belgrove as a teacher. Whenever it was my turn (it came around once a month) to wash the cups and saucers at break-time in the teachers' room, I noticed that he usually sat apart, reading a book or listening to John Arlott's cricket commentaries on a small transistor radio. A cricket-lover myself in a school filled with Gaelic football enthusiasts, I knew that this was heresy. Almost all the other teachers, like the headmaster himself, came from Cork or Kerry. McGahern was from Leitrim, appointed for his superior academic qualifications (he had an MA), but foredoomed even by them to be set apart. I'm sure that his pay as a junior master was low but he always generously bought books out of his own money to award boys who did well in the end-of-year exams. I still have a copy of *Fairy Tales of Germany* (signed with congratulations by one Seán Mac Eathairn) – he read each of the tales aloud to the class before entrusting me with the copy.

He was still a young man in his mid-twenties and, as such in that hierarchical world, frequently instructed to patrol the boys during playtime in the school yard. (It sloped and had a tendency to flood after rain, something he noted acerbically in *The Leavetaking*.) I was an absent-minded child myself and often forgot to put my sandwiches and flask in my schoolbag. My mother would invariably arrive with them at the school railings at 11.15 a.m.; Mr McGahern would come over to ask how she was and they would talk. My parents were both deeply impressed by him. Every Friday they went to see films in a picture-house in Pearse Street and often saw him emerging alone, his face haggard and thin, his body energetic and jerky of movement; and my mother would come home and say: 'That man needs a good wife.' Sometimes, I joked that she was volunteering for the role – it was only many years later, after reading his early books, that I understood how haunted this man (who had lost his own mother at the age of ten) must have been by the ways in which a mother might care for her son. But what struck me even then was the quality of his isolation.

Five or six years later, he was fired. The parish priest, a rotund and bluff man, didn't really want to get rid of him but had to: he was under orders from Archbishop McQuaid and he complained that the whole affair was 'a right schemozzle'. My father came up with a very Irish solution to this Irish problem. McGahern, unusually for a primary teacher, had no singing voice but exchanged classes with Mr Jordan, who had a fine tenor timbre, while he taught the other man's class geography. If Holy Mother Church now considered Mr McGahern ill-fitted to teach the boys catechism (whether because he had written a 'dirty' book or married a foreign lady in a registry office – it was never made completely clear), couldn't he do another exchange with Mr Jordan (a devout soul forever trying to bring his colleague back into the fold) and teach history? 'It wouldn't work', said the parish priest sadly. Primary school teachers were then, as McGahern would later wryly observe, the non-commissioned officers of the Catholic Church, often to be seen passing around collection plates at masses or holding up a canopy over the Eucharist at a Corpus Christi procession. Yet many willingly adopted these roles because they themselves had a priestly dimension: indeed, it's possible that, were it not for compulsory celibacy, quite a few of those who were primary teachers might well have become priests. McGahern's cousin, Father Liam Kelly, has more than once observed that the book titled *Memoir* was, in a sense, the mass McGahern wanted to say (but could never say) for his mother.

McGahern often cited the comment by E.R. Dodds that there is an inherent conflict between morality and religion: morality concerns the ways in which people relate, on an ethical level, to one another, whereas religion is about humankind's relationship to fate, destiny, the divine. Dodds probably developed this idea from a remark once made by W.B. Yeats about George Eliot: 'If she had more religion, she would have less morals. The moral impulse and the religious destroy each another in most cases [...] I was once afraid of turning out reasonable myself.'[2] Too often the religion practised in the rural Ireland of Yeats and McGahern was rule-bound rather than visionary. It was as if most priests functioned as the bureaucrats of a new order of regulations and by-laws, that they were in fact, as most bureaucrats are, seeking to control every human activity because they had lost faith in an over-watching God who could be trusted to set all to rights. The new order of priests, far from announcing the triumph of religion, were in many cases the sure sign of its demise. Perhaps McGahern sensed this in refusing the religious vocation which his mother had wished for him. And perhaps she understood his reservations. It is interesting that they are both buried in the same Aughawillan grave, whose headstone bears their names and the words 'national teacher'.

In 'All Sorts of Impossible Things' there is a death which seems, like so many deaths in the work of McGahern, to reenact his mother's passing – even down to the predicted detail of furniture being removed from the home in a van/cart. The mortality which sunders (or sanctifies?) the friendship of the two men shadows the entire narrative – in the healthy man's loss of hair at an early age; in the fading powers of the bitch to hunt hares; and in the sense of a landscape losing its soft charm and hardening in the arteries. Given this context, small acts of physical tenderness between men become almost sacramental, as when the teacher cuts his friend's hair and shaves him, a scene which is anticipatory of a similar act of corporeal mercy in the laying out of the body of a dead friend in *That They May Face the Rising Sun*. Here in the short story the gesture, though an act of tenderness to the still-living, seems akin to the tidying of a corpse.

Ultimately, McGahern believed, as did Scott Fitzgerald, that life was too strong and too mysterious for the mortal sons of men. Maybe the daughters of Eve understood it more fully, but for the men in 'All Sorts of Impossible Things' there can be no permanency. McGahern had himself come out of a world obsessed by examinations, qualifications and permanent appointments, but he learned quickly enough himself that even a pensionable contract could be broken by those spiritual bureaucrats who claimed access to the supernatural powers. Life in this great story turns out to be a series of short gasps, between the hunt and the downing of whiskey, and the ever-threatening ultimate examination of the dying inspector. When McGahern's own turn came to die, and he outlived the fatal prognosis by a number of years, he used to chuckle: 'I'm a brilliant student in a hopeless class.'

In his days of teaching, he used to call the summer term, often so much briefer than the autumn or winter semesters, 'a short cough'. He probably felt much the same about the short story as a form. Early in this story the doomed instructor (probably dying because of the effort he has expended in the hare-coursing) remarks that if the two friends had had to walk the twelve miles covered all at once, it would have seemed a terrible journey. 'A bit like life itself', says the schoolteacher: 'We might never manage it if we had to take it all in one gasp. We mightn't even manage to finish it.'[3] This is possibly the best explanation of why those books of McGahern filed in libraries as novels are really disguised collections of short stories: the sort of linked anecdotes which are the best that even the Tolstoys and Flauberts (and McGaherns) can produce.

INTRODUCTION

Derek Hand and Eamon Maher

The position of prose fiction – and particularly the novel form – in Irish literary culture can be quite a precarious one.[1] So much so, perhaps, that a young John McGahern, contemplating a life in writing yet-to-be, might have found the endless possibilities presented by the traditions of Irish poetry and drama more appropriate forms in which to express himself. The consequence of that precarious position for those actually writing novels in Ireland, especially from the early twentieth century onwards, is that this anxiety becomes an integral element of the stories being told: in terms of both form and content. Such self-reflexivity, such self-consciousness, can be read as either an illumination of the predicament or as a material expression or articulation of it. Certainly, anxiety can get in the way of the narrative rather than propelling it forward. One consequence is that 'struggle' becomes paramount, with narratives bearing the scars of their creation to a greater or lesser extent. For a writer such as McGahern, this is encountered again and again in his prose, which seems effortlessly fluid and precise, while actually, like the nuggets of truth that he articulates, being highly wrought and hard-won. The centrality of struggle suggests too that for John McGahern art is what fundamentally matters, its creation and its enjoyment being central to life as it is lived, and not in any way apart or removed from it.

John McGahern was particularly attracted to W.B. Yeats' great late play *Purgatory*.[2] A double-edged energy runs through the drama, with the Old Man's musings and murderous actions encapsulating the utter necessity of re-sharpening the imagination's blade in the face of utter and abject failure. Its focus on the destructive relationship between fathers and sons is of obvious interest to McGahern, but he was also perhaps drawn to how Yeats articulates the urgency of the artistic moment for both the individual artist and the community he tries to connect with. As with much of his late writing, Yeats was, on the one hand, puncturing his own pretensions to artistic greatness and on the other, attempting to spur himself on to even further achievement. In the process, both the admonishment and the challenge reinvigorated his imagination and his writing. For McGahern, the art of storytelling, of fiction writing, makes the world our own, returning what is extraordinary to the ordinary and the everyday. For him, as he expressed it so memorably in his literary credo 'The Image', 'art is […] an attempt to create a world in which we can live'.[3] It is important to stress these links between apparent opposites, the artist and her/his community, the book and its reader, the local and the universal, the day and eternity. In McGahern's aesthetic, one of these things is nothing without the other. Acknowledging this gets to the heart of his fiction, suggesting how basic and primal is the need to make the world our own in our telling of it and how it can offer us – even fleetingly – a means of assuaging the various scars and traumas in our experience of everyday life.

Understanding the nature of McGahern's commitment to art and to the art of fiction writing is central to appreciating both his aesthetic choices and the nature of his literary achievement. It has been argued that for James Joyce, 'The supreme action was writing', and that Joyce's work is not overly concerned with reflecting reality; rather, its focus is, through his fiction, with 'creating a reality which otherwise would have no existence'.[4] This is also the case for all of McGahern's writing, because he is an author who, in many ways, creates a fictional world that had never been. His stories move between England and Ireland, the countryside and Dublin, recording the everyday existence of mid-twentieth-century Irish life, giving voice to small landowners, civil servants, teachers and nurses of the fledgling Irish state. The lives being chronicled are nuanced and complicated, heroic and tawdry – lives, in short, that had not found widespread expression in Irish fiction until McGahern created that reality in his own inimitable fashion. The attraction, then, of the novel and short story was a basic adherence to description and reality. This is not to limit McGahern's work to a simply straightforward articulation of, and adherence to, some form of nineteenth-century social realism. In McGahern's novels, that struggle with form, so central to the Irish prose tradition, manifests itself in a number of ways. After his first published novel, *The Barracks*, his engagement with form becomes increasingly strained. One reason for this is that the conventional novel form of the nineteenth century needed to be abandoned because the closure it brought to narratives is far too artificial and too definitively imposing for the realities that McGahern wanted to register. McGahern's endings consequently become strange and awkward as he attempts to find a means of giving expression to a vision that precludes easy conclusions and where the action is wrapped up neatly. His novels, as they unfold, reformat themselves, reconfiguring their own boundaries and the rules by which they are to be read. The result is a liberating openness, in that the formal anxieties are never finally mastered or overcome, the coherence towards which novels move never conclusively achieved. In the end, it is the journey that is important, the 'getting through', not the destination.

The struggle emerged as well in the ways in which his writing focused on a reality that is both light and dark. Certainly the world of nature is there, to be celebrated surely, but also as an indicator of all that is utterly alien to, and apart from, the human realm. McGahern focuses on the human world of relationships, on the benign and not so benign foibles of everyday interaction. When considered as a totality, it is clear how in his writing, from main protagonists to those who exist on the margins of the plot, there are no stereotypical representative types, only the elusive complexities of people as they are: inconsistent and contradictory, at times barely conscious of the desires that underpin their actions. Such a rounded portrayal of characters can be a challenge to readers. Take Moran in *Amongst Women*, for example, and his trajectory from a controlling, domineering man, a person often consumed with a seething rage, to the figure in the final pages of the novel who is impotent and accepting of his new position. Both representations of Moran are valid; one is not more authentic than the other. And what, then, is the reader to make of the assertion made after Moran's funeral in relation to the daughters: '[…] as they left him under the yew, it was as if each of them in their different ways had become Daddy'.[5] Often with an unflinching gaze, McGahern reveals the power struggles and violence, physical and mental, at the centre of the Irish family unit. He acknowledges that beneath the façade of public decorum, of polite ceremony and social discourse, there lurks a potentially destructive force. The daughters fill the power vacuum left by their father and they remark that their younger brother Michael and their spouses resemble 'a crowd of women',[6] which represents a complete reversal of roles.

That struggle might also explain the Irish novel's fluidity when it comes to genre. Many Irish novels are never one thing – *bildungsroman*, romance, thriller, high or low – they are many things. Or, strangely, no thing. And McGahern, more so than most, might fit into that genre-less category. Evaluating his work in the round, it is possible to discern developments and trajectories over the course of his writing career. From a novel like *The Dark*, focused on becoming and growth, to a more sustained focus on being in later work such as *That They May Face the Rising Sun*, McGahern's fictional world is multifaceted and magnificently complex. For some readers, his main concerns might be masculinity, religion or emigration, and their overbearing presence in Irish life. Yet central too in his work, in its entirety (but often in a single text), is the theme of the feminine, Elizabeth Reegan in *The Barracks* being just one example of a fully imagined female protagonist. While the topic of religion is often painfully present in the work,[7] so too is the conception of religious institutions being put under pressure from a re-orientation towards individual ethical authority, with communal religious observance being usurped by an individual response to potential nodes of spirituality. In other words, what McGahern is actually delineating in his work is the progress of Ireland towards a post-Catholic reality where religion, in an institutional sense, is increasingly irrelevant. And, as in much Irish fiction, the consequences of emigration are found absolutely everywhere in his writing, from economic codes of power and inheritance, to cultural concerns and sexual mores. However, McGahern's sense of emigration is at times quite subtly attuned to the nature of the gains and losses of the movement away from the home place. He said in various interviews that for people living around Mohill, Rockingham, eighteen miles away, might as well be New York or Sicily. Even the manners and codes of conduct of those from a nearby town were often viewed as starkly different in McGahern's world. So the reality of moving to England or America might not be as traumatic or potential-filled as going a few miles down the road. Emigration in his work is tempered by the frequent act of returning: home is never easily abandoned for many of his characters. In 'The Country Funeral' and *That They May Face the Rising Sun* the return becomes paramount, a means of reinvigorating all the failures and absences that emigration has wrought. For McGahern, there is no distance between the local and the global,[8] and, perhaps, the distillation of the single day as a continual setting out and returning suggests how the rhythms of coming and going, the ebb and flow of emigration, are interconnected.

In his Introduction to *Creatures of the Earth*, McGahern argued: 'The imagination demands that life be told slant because of its need of distance.'[9] The critic too needs distance in order to perceive the work beyond that of the immediate moment of its creation and reception. This present collection was born out of a two-day conference held in St Patrick's College, Drumcondra (now part of Dublin City University) in 2016.[10] Our intention in celebrating McGahern's writing ten years after his death was to begin reassessing his fiction, acknowledging the ways in which, as Eamonn Wall says in his essay, 'we enlarge the context in which we discuss [his] work'. One hugely significant way in which we begin to approach his writing is the recognition of how personal is the act of critical reading. Returning to Yeats' *Purgatory*, it is clear that his attitude – as an author reflectively dwelling on the last things, assessing the power of his artistic impulses at the end of his life – suggests that the writer can be the harshest of all critics when it comes to assessing her/his own artistic worth and value for the future. Of course, any author becomes just another reader as the initial creative power over a text wanes and falls away. Still, in keeping with the necessity of binaries in McGahern's aesthetic vision, it is here that the importance and centrality of the reader comes to the fore. Recent scholarship has demonstrated how central was reading, and responding to reading, to McGahern's entire oeuvre.[11] It is clear now, as we have been arguing, that the view of McGahern as the uncomplicated realist, carefully rendering the world as it is, was somewhat limited. What has emerged is an image of the consummate artist in conversation and engagement with the Western literary canon. Maybe McGahern was talking of himself and his own position as a reader when he once declared that 'the best criticism surely grows out of love',[12] as does the art it engages with. Love is about openness to the other and, despite what the romantic novel might present, it is an ongoing process that needs to be worked on constantly. It would appear then that for McGahern there is a potentially productive and central role for the critic in his aesthetic.

Many of the essays in this volume mingle the personal with the critical as if that urgent need to tell stories that underpins McGahern's aesthetic is echoed in the critics who want to acknowledge and reflect their own story in their reading of his work. When McGahern visited St Patrick's College, Drumcondra to give a reading of his work in 2003, people came up to him afterwards to have him sign copies of their books. These were not brand new, but rather worn and tattered and well-thumbed. They were prized possessions to those who owned and treasured them. In the years after his death, at talks and events celebrating his work, the audience was predominantly non-academic, their interest in his writing personal and their presence at such occasions a personal testament to the work's importance for them. Not many Irish writers generate such a response. The literary critic, in many ways, has had to catch up with what readers always already knew: that John McGahern was the preeminent prose writer of his generation.

Certainly the articles gathered together in this collection are born out of a deep affection for the work. They also tease out new areas of interest and concern for readers of McGahern, deepening our understanding of his work beyond what has already been established as central. Several essays trace McGahern's developmental arc from his earliest novels and short stories to his final autobiographical *Memoir*. This panoramic view offers us a reading of his work that charts Ireland's recent history and certainly confirms McGahern's own dictum that the local is the universal in art. Undoubtedly, the anecdotes recounted in many of the novels and short stories are of the past, of an Ireland that culturally, politically and economically no longer exists. That in itself is an attraction for the present-day reader, to be offered a rendering of a world that we have moved away from. Certainly in Celtic and post-Celtic Tiger Ireland writing such as McGahern's acts as an indicator of how far the nation has come, how much distance there is between the dark past and the brighter, more enlightened present – even if everyone may not accept that the present is 'enlightened' in every respect. And yet, it is also the case that, as he said himself, 'life is the same everywhere',[13] and what is really important is not simply emphasising the differences with the past, foregrounding the break with what has gone before, but how we might read ourselves into that past. In doing so we can discover similarity and connection, recognise that our own time is not exceptional and that we are part of a continuum. In other words, the past is not necessarily something distinct from the present; it is in some ways a site of potential connection, a resource to be returned to again and again to meet the challenges of the here and now.

Like many Irish writers, McGahern is all too aware of how the failures of Irish history can weigh heavily on the communal psyche. As with James Joyce, he understands the power of the image of the writer as the secular priest of the imagination, and indeed he enacts that very moment of recognition from the religious to the secular on numerous occasions in his work: when dealing with the death of the mother in, for example, *The Leavetaking* and *Memoir*. Deirdre Madden brilliantly articulates this connection in *Molly Fox's Birthday* when she has Molly's brother Tom, who is a priest, declare:

> I suppose what's similar about being an actor and being a priest is a certain perception of time. Eternity is a priest's business. But we all live in time [...] [Theatre] exists in time – a play lasts about an hour and a half [...] but if it's any good at all it takes you somewhere outside time. And then you can see things [...] differently.[14]

This desire to see is shared by McGahern and takes on an urgency that cannot be gainsaid: 'I write because I need to write. I write to see. Through words I see.'[15] Many readers have commented on how McGahern consciously plays with time in his last novel *That They May Face the Rising Sun*,[16] though it has longer provenance in his work. Jamesie's house is full of clocks – none of which is set to the correct time. 'Who cares about time? We know the time well enough', he declares, and goes on to ask Ruttledge, '[...] Do you have any more news now before you go?'[17] Stories, tales and gossip – in short, 'news' – is what is important rather than time, because these mark development and progress. Caught between the realities of the finite and the hope of the infinite, human ceremonies and rituals, like art, negotiate the empty spaces in between.

This wish to transcend historical time and move into a space beyond time suggests that McGahern not only wants to illuminate the past and the present but also offer us images and narratives that might penetrate into the future. One of his more important gifts to the next generation of Irish writers is the many ways in which he gives validation to the real world(s) in which we live, making the local and the everyday the site of artistic possibility and potential. Yeats and the revivalists did it in the nineteenth century and McGahern does it again for the twenty-first.

One of the difficulties of dealing with any writer's work is how we are forced to negotiate not only the work itself but also the ways in which the writer in his or her lifetime positions that work and creates a context in which their art can be appreciated. Critics who approach that work are sometimes too bound to theories and ideas of a particular moment that are of little use to future generations of readers. McGahern presented, at times, an image of himself as the bluff country boy who produced a seemingly artless art. Thus, those themes of religion and emigration, and the hard, intense life of the rural scene, are rightly considered paramount. Yet his writing, especially the short stories, rendered the urban experience of the city of Dublin in the 1950s and '60s in a way that is peerless. In stories such as 'Sierra Leone', 'Parachutes', 'Along the Edges' and 'My Love, My Umbrella', he charts the lives of the middle classes, the bureaucrats and teachers, looking for a means of being in the world, of making lives in the city. McGahern is aware, even if his characters are not, of the delicate balance between the demands of the fully articulated modern, if not modernist, individual and the demands of community and family. While all of his characters struggle with negotiating this difficulty, perhaps Ruttledge in *That They May Face the Rising Sun* is one of the better examples. Ruttledge as the proxy artist figure of this community by the lake might become the chronicler of this world if given half the chance. While authorial judgment is sparse in a novel which is highly conversational as people talk and share stories and information, it is nonetheless present – as it must be. It is this, finally, which distances him from the world and the community he loves. Passing judgment betrays the easy existence inherent within this place, offering it up for a public consumption that it would hardly have wished for.

The essays gathered between the covers of this book acknowledge therefore the varied ways in which John McGahern has been read and reinforce the themes and concerns teased out in this Introduction. Each, in its own way, seeks to evaluate what exactly are the most significant aspects of McGahern's literary legacy. Declan Kiberd's Foreword speaks of a personal relationship with the writer, a relationship that dates back to Kiberd's primary school education in Belgrove, where McGahern was a teacher. Kiberd imagines how a cricket fanatic, as McGahern was, would have been viewed in that school where the overwhelming interest at the time would have been Gaelic games. He also attempts to envisage how the emerging young writer might have reacted to the life of a teacher, an honourable vocation for sure, but one that was difficult to combine with writing.

The essays of the first section deal with issues of style and show that the literary strategies employed by McGahern reveal a writer who was quite daring in many respects in terms of the risks he took, and his refusal to stand still when it came to his art. The contributors in this section carve out new perspectives and new ways of engaging with the work, challenging the reader to rethink and reassess what is already known. Denis Sampson traces McGahern's developing sense of himself as a writer, his deep knowledge and understanding of the oeuvre showing how carefully crafted was all of McGahern's writing. Richard Robinson and Niamh Campbell show the work responding to the traumas and violence of history in terms of child abuse and the fate of the Anglo-Irish Protestant community in post-independence Ireland. The essays of Sylvie Mikowski and Eamonn Wall focus on language and style. Mikowski skilfully explores the gendered nature of language, attesting to how McGahern's desire to illuminate the tensions between the masculine and feminine can be mapped linguistically, demonstrating how nuanced and charged his language was. Wall considers the intense focus on the immediate and the local, arguing that McGahern's late style gestures towards a mythic mode. What is of particular interest is the way in which each essayist suggests how problematic Ireland's present relationship is to its recent past and how McGahern's fiction embodies that dilemma while demanding that the reader respond to its many ramifications.

The second section contains essays which are concerned with McGahern's unique rendering of place, his keen use of memory and the ecological awareness that can be detected in his writing. It also points to how important the image was to McGahern's aesthetic quest. Eóin Flannery opens with a reading of the centrality of nature in McGahern's work from an ecocritical perspective, suggesting that the intense consideration of the local is best understood from this theoretical stance. Claudia Luppino makes productive links between *Memoir* and *The Leavetaking*, indicating that many of McGahern's concerns and narrative strategies remained constant throughout his career. Anne Goarzin elucidates the link between the image and the word in her enlightening discussion of the relationship between Paul Butler's photographs and McGahern's texts. Butler then rounds off the section by offering a deeply personal account of the background to his photographs, suggesting that his work is in conversation with the world of McGahern's countryside.

In the final section, Máire Doyle considers the centrality of friendship in McGahern's fiction, while Joe Cleary, using Freud's theories, ponders the ever-present rage in some of the male characters of his fictional work, a theory that he links to similar portrayals in *Memoir*. Finally, Eamon Maher focuses on sexual repression in some of the works of McGahern and the French Nobel laureate François Mauriac, and foregrounds how their Catholic upbringing impacted their dramatisation of human relationships.

The book closes with Donal Ryan's moving account of the debt he feels he owes McGahern as an artist. When he read some of his predecessor's prose early on in his career, Ryan almost gave up writing altogether, thinking that he would never be able to match the inimitable poise and wonderful array of characters he encountered in the work of the Leitrim writer.

What is clear from all these essays is that John McGahern's fictional world is never straightforward or simple. In *That They May Face the Rising Sun*, Ruttledge remarks: 'Nobody will change lives with another. Anyhow it's not possible.'[18] This is not a declaration that we cannot hope or desire change in our lives or in the world that we inhabit. But it is a recognition of our human limits. In the end we choose our own lives rather than wish for someone else's.

It is this realisation which can allow even a reprehensible and disruptive character such as John Quinn to have moments of redemption in that novel. There is mystery here as there is no final answer to the conundrums of existence.

And that is true also of reading and engaging with John McGahern's writing. Our hope in this collection is not to offer final and definitive interpretations of his literary legacy, but to open up a space where that engagement can be continued on into the future. A character says at the close of *The Leavetaking*: 'It will be neither a return nor a departure but a continuing.'[19] Stories, and lives, do not neatly begin and end but simply, echoing Samuel Beckett, 'go on'. John McGahern's art will go on, will continue to be read and enjoyed, and, indeed, loved by many readers in the years to come. The painstaking effort which went into its composition would not countenance anything other than a guaranteed posterity.

SECTION 1

Mapping Literary Strategies

Chapter 1

—

John McGahern and 'Irish Writing': From *The Dark* to *Amongst Women*[1]

—

Denis Sampson

I

From the beginning of John McGahern's career, he wanted to define his own identity as an artist, conscious of how others, especially in Ireland, would want to define it for him. As I have tried to indicate in *Young John McGahern: becoming a novelist*, he was deeply aware of how artists have to negotiate the interplay between life experience and creative work, between private and public identities, between silence and communication, between style as a definitive expression of conflicts within the self and style as an inheritance of literary traditions. He was only interested in writing 'that will last', and, of course, in writing that has lasted. The literary traditions he read for models and inspiration were, primarily, French, Russian and English, and, in particular, specific authors and books from those traditions; the few Irish writers he took time over used their material in ways that lifted them into a 'freemasonry of mental habits' outside local cultural movements.[2]

The earliest document which focuses on these issues is a letter written in September 1960, just before he began work on *The Barracks*. He is writing to Patrick Swift, the editor of *X*, who has accepted for publication a number of passages in 'The End or the Beginning of Love', his unpublished first novel. McGahern is angry because it has been rejected by publishers, apparently on two grounds: the autobiographical nature of the material in this coming-of-age novel, and the absence of plot. 'The insistence', he writes, 'that to string a few lunatic situations into a plot is more valuable and difficult than to give passion and pattern to the lives of people being eroded out of their existence in the banality and repetitiveness of themselves and their society is the maddening thing.' The conscience of a dedicated artist is revealed, a young man who has no wish to be an entertaining storyteller or a commercially successful novelist; he wants to give 'passion and pattern' to individual lives that appear crushed by social circumstances and the nature of their own character. The young writer, aged twenty-five, is outlining the sympathetic interest in lives marked by suffering, which will stay with him throughout his career – 'people being eroded out of their existence' – but it is an interest in his own, suffering, life too. Rejecting the charge of transcribing autobiographical material, however, he declares: 'THE WHOLE BOOK owes everything to my experience, the way I suffered and was made to laugh, the people I have lived among, the landscape and the books I liked, – in that way it is as auto. as I am capable of making it. […] it seems to me that the need to be an artist must remain a whole life long, and that's a hell of a long way from writing AUTOBIOGRAPHY.'[3] The fundamental task of the artist is here: to discover sources of vitality in the midst of banality, to find keys in his own experience for articulating 'passion and pattern'; in other words, the fundamental need that drives him is to redeem his own life and the lives he observes through a vital poetic style. It is no wonder he will write of *The Barracks* a short time later: 'It is not a novel but an attempt to break that form down into a religious poem.'[4]

Writing in December 1961 to another editor, the poet John Montague, regarding his response to a few chapters of *The Barracks*, McGahern comments: 'I think what you say of the need for structure true, but I think it must be unique or organic, growing out of the struggle with the material, and not a superimposed structure as in Joyce and Eliot. No matter how great that achievement, it ends in academic sterility, and I think our generation must move in the opposite direction – to survive and grow.'[5] This critical and moral vocabulary is surely significant for the creator of the woman dying of cancer, and later for the abused adolescent: banality, intellectual sterility, erosion (for example, spiritual death) versus passion, growth, an organic individual style.

These Irish-born editors, who prompted such striking early statements of clear conviction, are living in London and Paris, respectively. Both are artists – Swift a painter – who are situating themselves, not in relation to Irish society or Irish history, but in relation to international aesthetic movements. In this first period the young novelist felt less kinship with local writers than with Flaubert, Proust, Tolstoy and Yeats or with living writers such as Beckett and Auden. There were a few Irish writers, notably Michael McLaverty and Patrick Kavanagh, whose work he admired, but he had little wish to be thought of as an Irish writer, and he welcomed the opportunity a fellowship gave him to continue travelling throughout Europe and to become, as I believe was his ambition, a European writer. Much of this ambition was realised when his first novel was published. It was reviewed as a poetic novel, its style repeatedly praised for its emotional power, its 'scrupulous accuracy'. It was frequently compared to the work of Joyce in the early reviews and in later comments. It was described as a 'classical tragedy'. The prizes he was awarded for the novel marked him out as a writer of great accomplishment and promise.

II

McGahern said repeatedly that he wrote *The Dark* as if state censorship did not exist, that it had no bearing on him at all as a writer, and that he was surprised when his second novel was banned. There is evidence to the contrary: Charles Monteith, his editor at Faber & Faber, McGahern himself, and a friend, the journalist Peter Lennon, had discussed the likelihood that the publication of the novel would be a cause célèbre. Monteith had reacted with panic in June 1964 when he discovered the manuscript included an 'incest scene', as they came to refer to the episode of paternal abuse. He called for modifications. McGahern did tone down the scene, and at the end of the summer made some significant changes to 'The Pit', as the manuscript was called. The writing of *The Dark* in 1963–4 deliberately and purposefully undid the secure foundation he had created with *The Barracks*, and the risks he took with art and life at that time were unavoidable steps in self-discovery and self-definition. Simply, he needed to situate himself outside of Irish society and among the ranks of the banned. A year later, in May 1965, the author made sure to be unavailable for any interviews or comment when the novel appeared.

In the event, someone had alerted the customs agents so that the book was not even allowed into the country before it was banned. This untypical application of the law prompted an editorial in the *Irish Times*: 'Mr. McGahern is an Irish schoolteacher whose second novel this is: the first won the AE prize administered by the Arts Council. It was a novel of high promise, and Mr. McGahern is clearly a dedicated writer, not a dilettante, a follower in the manner of Joyce of a high, hard and – whatever the ultimate outcome – unrewarding calling.'[6] The editorial writer is at pains to insist that the author is not a pornographer, rather a conscientious artist.

At issue was the realistic, or naturalistic, basis of his depiction of an Irish youth: would the custodians of public morality admit that certain experiences depicted in the novel reflected a reality of Irish life? The *Times* returns to this issue in a further three editorials which refer to McGahern in 1965–6, and by February 1966 the novel has provided it with a metaphor for public debate about wider issues of the rights of citizens and what is admitted into public consciousness: 'The dark, that feeling of claustrophobia described by Mr. McGahern, is a real and pressing phenomenon. Nothing short of honesty will dispel it.'[7] Most readers will now agree with the *Times* writer, that silencing, hypocrisy and dishonesty are key social forces that the novel confronts, although equally important to the author were certain philosophical, aesthetic and spiritual concerns that shaped its style. McGahern did not break his silence or enter into public debate, but the debate that swirled around the book clarifies some ways in which his literary reputation settled at this time.

The first editorial may have been written by Terence de Vere White, the paper's literary editor, and a piece that he wrote for *Le Monde* the same week was reprinted in French in the paper. In reporting on the banning, he compares McGahern's novel to *Dubliners* and to Kavanagh's *Tarry Flynn*, a very high evaluation based on its poetic style and its scrupulous observation. Within the pages of the *Times*, however, a contrary view was expressed from a surprising quarter. John Healy, the political columnist 'Backbencher', a widely respected journalist, commented on the case: 'The *Irish Independent* wrote an editorial deploring the banning – even though [the novel] is described as unreal "in its characters, unreal in its concentration of problems within a tiny group, unreal especially in its picture of provincial Ireland today".' Healy agrees with this characterisation of the novel's portrayal of rural Irish life as unreal: 'John McGahern is a square and his world of *The Dark* just doesn't exist.'[8]

The central issue was the portrayal of Ireland, the image of the nation, and Benedict Kiely put it bluntly when he referred to 'the literature of acceptance' and 'the literature of rejection'.[9] State censorship and other forms of censorship were often used to exclude images of 'rejection' from public awareness, and, of course, *The Dark* joined a long list of banned works of literature. But there was also abroad, even in literary circles, a kind of self-censorship, an incorporation into fiction of what McGahern later called a 'censorship mentality'.[10]

A young literary critic, who was about to become a prominent voice in Irish letters, dealt with this matter more delicately than Healy. In March 1964, a reviewer of Patrick Kavanagh's *Self-Portrait* wrote in the *Times*: '[Kavanagh claimed that] *Tarry Flynn* [was] the best and only authentic account of life as it was lived in Ireland in this century (utterly true at the time of writing, but it's since been joined by McGahern's *The Barracks*).' A letter came in from Augustine Martin challenging this exclusive view of which books were 'authentic' and praising Francis MacManus and others. He added, faintly, 'I welcome the tribute to John McGahern's grievous and powerful book, *The Barracks*'[11] – 'faintly', because Martin very soon published a much-cited essay, 'Inherited Dissent', in which he took up the issue of authenticity in Irish writing and claimed that the positive aspects of a new Ireland were not properly reflected in its literature. Rather, certain writers seemed to accept unthinkingly an attitude of dissent, McGahern among them.

The 'censorship mentality' of such literary judgments rests on very fundamental feelings of piety and fidelity to an idea of the nation, or, perhaps, of rural Ireland, and to the underlying sense that 'disenchanted' writers like Joyce and McGahern betrayed its best interests. Of course, the larger premise of such critical formulations is that there is a self-contained Irish Literary Tradition, and, in Martin's view, this is what provided McGahern with his main 'literary ancestors', but insofar as the author of *The Dark* and *Nightlines* engaged with Irish material, he was deeply at odds with such thinking.

III

A Beckettian kind of silence was McGahern's first response to the banning of his novel; he remained beyond the reach of the media throughout 1965. There was a second act to the affair, however, when it became public knowledge in February 1966 that he had effectively been fired by his clerical school manager and the Archbishop of Dublin. His trade union had failed to come to his defence, and his anger at this lack of courage motivated a breaking of his silence. The story was front-page news in Irish newspapers just as he was about to leave London for New York for the publication there of *The Dark*, and he gave an interview which is worth quoting at some length. It reports McGahern's first public response and focuses on his understanding of his work in relation to his public role as writer:

> When I asked Mr. McGahern about his feelings on the dismissal in the broader context of a suspected control over creative writing he simply said: 'I think it is unfortunate that this has happened.' This, I suggested, was a rather mild reply. He referred to the confusion between publishing

and writing, and said that he considered writing a private activity. 'One writes to shape the world which one's imagination can inhabit, and one offers it to the public through one's publisher. The public is perfectly free to reject it or enjoy it. Bringing in these issues confuses the nature of the activity, which is simply reflective of the human situation through one's private world in language: it is consequently a religious activity which is keeping faith to the sources of one's own being and it is, in the pure sense of the words, a form of praise and prayer.'[12]

His reference here to writing as a 'private activity', a 'religious activity', and other remarks in which he refers to the 'beautiful and great vision of truth' of the Catholic Church 'in its origins' (although not in its 'particular interpretation' in Ireland) all raise the terms of the debate into another realm, beyond the concerns of church, state or nation. He is clearly not only defending his freedom to write as he wishes, but is asserting that art is truthful insofar as it is anchored in 'the sources of one's own being'. This is a superior form of authenticity, and morality, and he appears to connect it to an instinctive religious impulse, to the search for a visionary style. But the expression 'the sources of one's own being' might also suggest that there is a confessional and autobiographical depth to his work, and that the 'human situation' is to be discovered in the writer's own private struggle with his or her own experience. The abandonment of the autobiographical novel 'The End or the Beginning of Love' and the writing of *The Barracks* may be seen to reflect a realisation that what is most personal can only be articulated aesthetically, and this by means of masks. The writing of *The Dark* and its reception launched him into a modernist phase that lasted until the late 1970s, much of it an exploration of such issues as personal authenticity, self-consciousness and autobiography within the larger search for the 'human situation'.

His remarks in this interview of February 1966 are a journalistic version of what he will say more definitively just a few days later in New York in his first literary manifesto: 'The Image: a prologue to a reading at Rockefeller University', a compressed poetic statement, is a formal declaration of his beliefs about the genesis of art in the self, its composition, and its similarity to formal religious practice. It is the foundational document for any critical understanding of McGahern's sense of himself, his style, and the struggle to dramatise his given material.

McGahern had gone into exile from Ireland in September 1964, something he had spoken of wishing to do to various correspondents in previous years. In contrast to the ambivalent reception *The Dark* received in Ireland, and the critical discourse that enveloped it, London provided him with a certain kind of hospitality. Charles Monteith helped to open up a critical space for his work in England, aided as early as 1966 by critics and editors such as Julian Jebb, Joe Ackerley, Ian Hamilton and Melvyn Bragg. But if McGahern was alienated from Irish critical discourses, he was adamant throughout the sixties and seventies that his work should not be categorised by his English supporters as 'Irish' writing; then, as later, his criterion was 'good writing', whatever its provenance. This was especially true of his short stories, for in his earliest years he had rejected the category of 'the Irish short story', an inauthentic critical invention, as he saw it, of Seán O'Faoláin and others. Following 'The Image', his talk on Melville's 'Bartleby, the Scrivener' in Belfast in 1967 might be seen as, implicitly, another manifesto, a further effort to situate himself artistically as a 'silent' and 'religious' writer.[13]

Even though he began to return to Ireland in the early 1970s and to make moves to settle back in the west of Ireland, almost all the work of the sixties and seventies is the work of an imagination in exile, constantly searching for the 'sources of one's own being' and constantly placing him outside any narrow sense of an Irish literary tradition. 'I think it would be an insult to be called an Irish writer', he stated as late as 1977, 'if one doesn't belong to the human kind first.'[14] While he lived outside Ireland for the decade beginning in 1964, and in the decade following, he rarely gave any interviews or readings, did not write reviews or other journalism, and took little interest in contemporary Irish writing.

In December 1970 he reacted angrily to Faber & Faber's advertisement for *Nightlines* which referred to 'the great tradition of Irish short story writers'. Charles Monteith responded to McGahern's continuing irritation at this placing of his work by offering him a challenge: to edit an anthology of Irish short stories. Their correspondence registers McGahern's reasons for refusing but also indicates that he might consider an anthology of Irish writing which would focus on styles of writing and include other prose genres, such as letters and autobiography. Nothing came of this, until 1980, that is, when the idea resurfaced; he had a clear interest in such an anthology now, and in March 1981 he signed a contract for 'The Faber Book of Irish Prose'. He devoted considerable time to it, teaching a course at Colgate in 1983–4 on his selections, but of course the book was never completed. The best-known product of that effort is the lecture he delivered on *The Islandman* in Toronto in March 1984, later published with various revisions, in which the style of the Gaelic-speaking Blasket islander is made to sound like Beckett and Flaubert.

IV

It may have been the writing of 'Parachutes' in 1980, with its very recognisable setting among the Dublin literati, circa 1960, that brought his mind back to the 'innocent' period of his life before then, a time of intense observation, a time before art. The first cluster of stories in *High Ground* were written soon after 'Parachutes', stories that may be said to explore a watershed year in McGahern's own life and personal history, 1955–6. In that year, he began his independent life as an adult, he began to work as a teacher, and so he had much to learn of the world into which he had fallen. In addition to observing the world beyond the familial, or the school years in Carrick-on-Shannon, or St Patrick's teacher training college, he was called on to define his position on many fronts, in particular as a custodian of patriotic and sectarian truths in the light of which he was obliged to nurture the intellectual and imaginative growth of his young pupils.

The stories etch in the pressures of the real world of a young man's experience: finding a job, divisive colleagues, strikes, mating rituals, pragmatic manoeuvring of political figures. There is sympathy for people caught in small social dramas, with lasting consequences for the direction of their lives, but the social dramas have wider resonances in the community; the tragic and the farcical and the broadly comic light up a kind of local history, of manners and mores. They are markedly unlike the impassioned and anguished narratives of *The Dark*, *The Leavetaking* and *The Pornographer*, or earlier stories, closer to Chekhov perhaps than Beckett. Their sense of the historical moment is wry, elegiac, accepting. The understated narrative voice in these stories seems to have moved back in time, from the freighted consciousness of the 'anonymous sky' and the traumatised state of the lovesick protagonist of 'Parachutes' to a state where the absurd idea of the superior intelligence of those living on high ground, near the source of the Shannon river, can be entertained. But the self-reflexive comedy of such a notion – there is much drink taken on this occasion – is included in a sympathetic sense of how local beliefs and routines provide comfort and a certain kind of eccentric freedom.

In 'A Ballad', he experimented with a wildly comic narrative that embodied a pattern in experience which was not only traditional but perhaps primal. In some ways, this is a simple comedy of young males in the mating season, one of whom gets a woman pregnant, marries her, and in a matter of years she becomes the power behind the throne. The naïve young teacher, the narrator, observes all this in wonder. He passes no judgment; it appears to be part of his education in life. The title suggests that there is an inevitable pattern at play, a norm. The other stories reinforce this sense of a long view, of the inevitability of certain outcomes in life, perhaps a trail of unresolved conflicts, disappointments, failures, yet they are contained within a social order. Already, it would seem, McGahern had begun to make his peace with his own earlier life as a historical event, or at least as a life that was experienced in a particular way because of the culture which enveloped it.

There is a remarkable reinvention under way in these stories, a stepping back from cosmopolitan, urban, modernist, individualistic art to a concern with society, manners, morals and the art of everyday living.

V

In 1982 he agreed to write an essay on the background to *The Barracks* as a contribution to a local publication honouring a Cootehall teacher. But 'temperament took over'; he was unable to write an essay, and what resulted was the story 'Oldfashioned'. The materials in the archive indicate that the simple invitation to provide background on life in Cootehall suddenly opened doors in many directions, as if they were waiting to be opened. The 'oldfashioned tale' is part of a body of fictions, sometimes referred to in his papers as 'Around the Old Stone House', as if this may be the beginning of a novel. Notably, for some time the material of this story is organically related to 'Kelly', a story which eventually became *The Rockingham Shoot*. These two separate fictions are also related to the Kirkwood stories, eventually 'Eddie Mac' and 'The Conversion of William Kirkwood'. In a sense, all of these fictions probe the background to his youth in the barracks in Cootehall. More specifically, they are an investigation of Catholic/Protestant, Irish/Anglo-Irish relations in that community. They are a first effort on McGahern's part to write 'historical fictions' which will explore the wider culture of his upbringing, 'history' imagined in fables and parables grounded in the domestic and familial, rather than in 'national' or 'narrative' history.

The outer narrative of 'Oldfashioned' is a generalised anthropological account of social change in the village of Ardcarne, recognisably Cootehall, between the 1940s and 1970s. The barracks is seen to be a place of cruelty and obtuseness. Guard Casey may have qualities that ensure his happiness, but he is also the agent of silent forms of violence that he is unaware of. The sergeant too is an enforcer not of justice but of inherited prejudices. In this place a boy grows up – recognisably the young John McGahern. He has been deeply influenced by his brief friendship with a Protestant woman, Mrs Sinclair. He became an outsider to the culture of the village, but the fable of his relationship with Mrs Sinclair is a fable of how he became a kind of artist, his knowledge of human nature marked by her example. The woman who offers the boy a basket of apples arranged with care is the moral and aesthetic anchor of the story, apparently beyond fashion or change or history. She restored the house for her retirement, creating a garden in the middle of a wilderness, and then, after her death, it all reverted to wilderness.

VI

The evolution of the fiction through the 1980s may be keyed to the larger concerns of Irish history earlier in the century, and in the period of 'The Troubles', but it is grounded in the core material of McGahern's experience, his relationship with his father. One way of understanding McGahern's evolution towards *Amongst Women* is to note the shift in the portrayal of the father from 'Gold Watch' (1979) to the novel completed a decade later.

'Gold Watch' embodies a sense of a 'natural process' in life, the son's anguished presence in the father's house now balanced by the experience of love and marriage. The conflict between them, seen in earlier versions such as 'Wheels' and 'Korea', for instance, or, of course, *The Dark*, has now shifted away from the oppression of elemental and original authority, the father and home, towards an acceptance of generational change over the longer term. This is something the father is incapable of feeling or knowing, that it is possible for human beings to live out their life in time with some degree of calm or happiness. There is, then, a somewhat more sympathetic view of the father as an almost tragic figure, driven by unreasonable fury to control what cannot actually be controlled. He is not viewed with tenderness, however, and the son can be drawn back into his tortured and torturing ambience, but the father's wish to destroy the watch, to arrest the recording of time's passage, is contrasted with the son's wish to preserve the old watch as a thing of beauty and of continuity, connected to memory, art and the natural wheel of the generations.

The conundrum of how to embrace time's passage as a natural fact is central to 'Gold Watch'. It is not a new preoccupation of McGahern. While the 'unnatural' early death of his mother, death by severe illness, and indeed other kinds of 'unnatural' death such as by war, extreme violence, or accident, haunt his work, the notion of 'natural' death is equally present. The father is maddened by life's relentless biological progress, apparently without purpose or succour, but the son is also intrigued by the mysterious reality of time: 'I grew amused at that part of myself that still expected something, standing like a fool out there in all that moonlit silence, when only what was increased or diminished as it changed, became only what is, becoming again what was [...] time, hardly surprisingly, was still running.'[15] There is no end to time, nor is there any final revelation of meaning – McGahern artfully ends the story with this pun on the word 'conclusion': 'time that did not have to run to any conclusion'. What is certain, though, is that as human beings we participate organically in processes that govern us and are not intelligible to us: time and nature are the most common terms for such processes, history and family their local stage. In drawing the 'final portrait' of the father as a kind of historical fiction, McGahern does not neglect the larger concerns with time and nature which had been central to his work from *The Barracks* onwards.

VII

As part of this process of exploring generational change within a family, McGahern wrote a story called 'Young and Old' which dramatises the domestic crisis of 1960 when his brother Frank ran away from home, an event recounted in *Memoir*. This episode highlights some key insights into the father's personality. The narrator persuades his brother to return home, travels down the country to the house and there persuades the father to receive the boy back so he can return to school. Echoing other father–son stories, the narrator reflects: 'Anything that grew close to my father grew against him, and his instinct was to crush it; and if it grew stronger to join its strength to his, and it gave him a purity that I would never have.'[16] The observation about the father's power is interesting, for this is a story of two sons who enter into direct conflict with him, who refuse to join their strength to his, but in *Amongst Women*

Luke seems to practise a kind of 'pure' power that mirrors that of the father. The contrast with Rose and the daughters is striking, and indeed this larger familial pattern is the central mystery of power explored in the novel.

'Young and Old' does not develop far in that direction; it is closer to the earlier work in its examination of the generations and focuses on what the narrator discovers about life from his own violent confrontation with his father. Again, the incident referred to is clearly autobiographical – the young McGahern standing up to his father and threatening him with physical force: 'And when I was sixteen, a moonlit night as this, I had more sense of death (or was it life) when I slept, the table against the door, the window open on the night in case he'd try to come into the room with the gun.'[17] This remarkable passage turns aside from the narcissistic violence of the father and the retaliation by the sons to suggest that timor mortis may be a primal motivation and the origin of a need for a religious vision: 'Cathedrals were built out of such fear.' While the young brother can only see the conflict with the father in social and psychological terms, in terms of power, authority and independence, there is a suggestion of another dimension to the narrator's understanding of the father's behaviour.

A later – probably much later – school copybook with 'Grevisk' written on the outside – that being the place of the father's retirement when he left the barracks – seems to include a draft for an opening by developing this insight. 'As Moran felt the strength go, his violence spread to everything around him, in an insane resentment – and Rose, his wife, was nearest … His two sons he'd fought with and they no longer came near the place.'[18] This brief summary of the background to the action is replaced, of course, by the dramatised scene in which the daughters try to revive Monaghan Day towards the end of his life, which then moves into the extended scene of long before when Moran's colleague from the War of Independence, McQuaid, visited him for the last time, and on into the courtship and wedding day. All of these vivid scenes masterfully reveal Moran's character through his relationships with other people, but the central insight regarding his smouldering violence and resentment remains – that he is tortured by a sense of mortality and the failure to find meaning in the life that followed his early years of confidence and glory as a revolutionary.

If McGahern's first interest is in dramatising the truth of what happened in his family, the more general issue of violence against children links this interest to examples in the wider society. The violent abuse of children by priests and teachers had interested him as early as 'The Recruiting Officer'. And in 'Korea', there is a suggestion that even indirect violence, the will to kill in a context of earlier war and executions, can be absorbed by the next generation. That acute story presents a deeply disturbing view of how physical and psychological violence is normalised by war, so that personal resentments and despair can easily issue in psychopathic behaviour. Now, McGahern focused more closely on the personality of a man who believed he was justified in using violence by a higher morality. He found his subject of enquiry in Kelly, his former teacher in Knockvicar school. The passage in *Memoir* describes Master Kelly as 'tall, good-looking in a dark way, nationalistic, a Fianna Fáil member of the County Council, intellectually conceited and brutal'.[19] He is 'a member of a new aristocracy', McGahern concludes, although he harboured a deep resentment for any symbol of the old aristocracy.

While this 'Kelly' material will eventually be written as a story, and then dramatised as *The Rockingham Shoot*, to begin with it was integrally related to the Sinclair material, which was used in the central part of 'Oldfashioned'. This link from early on in the process, certainly no later than 1982, clarifies a key insight into politically motivated violence in the society at large, and is surely a response to the enveloping 'Troubles' as much as to the earlier war in which his father participated. A set of notebooks from this time makes clear that the Sinclair/Kirkwood material is directly related to the genesis of *Amongst Women* in the early eighties. In one of these notebooks, Colonel Sinclair comes to the barracks to complain about boys who stoned his car. The sergeant gets an explanation from one of the boys: 'Master Kelly said the British have no right to be in this country. That they never leave any place until they're driven out. So we made this plan.' The colonel responds: 'Thanks, Sergeant. Thanks Guards. It's a bit depressing but you see if we pressed charges we'd have the wrong people in the dock.'[20] This early dramatisation disappears from later stories, but its presence here suggests how political indoctrination and violence may be fused in the lives of impressionable children or adults. In these same notebooks, there is evidence that another story, 'The Old Man', not published until much later as 'The White Boat', is a Sinclair story of graceful acceptance of old age, something Moran is unable to do.

Another notebook includes a key early scene embedded in the Sinclair material, in which the sergeant tells his children about an ambush in which he had participated during his time in the IRA. In this story, 'Lives', an early version of the visit of McQuaid is foreshadowed. The sergeant tells the story to disillusion his son about the Sinclairs: 'The whole account glowed in the children's imagination. They were so proud of their father.' His colleague remarks: 'Even today men are proud to say they fought under you. Don't tell me that running an out of the way station is the place for a man like that.' The sergeant replies: 'It didn't bother me. Life goes anyhow. Or it is taken. And even then it seems to go on.'[21] These are the closing words of 'Lives', evidence that the sergeant does not seem to want to live in the heroic glow, that he is more quiescent now in his sense of his own and all lives passing in time.

These various explorations of the father's character and outlook, and the relationships of others to him, took place, then, in that period of time when McGahern appeared to be writing about many different characters and situations. But gaining a perspective on the father in the context of family and history took on a new urgency and called for a new narrative style. The hesitations and distractions of these years were actually preparing the ground for the novel that in the end came quickly.

VIII

There was never any question that he would construct an Irish historical novel exploring war and peace in the style of Tolstoy, or, indeed, a contemporary narrative of 'the Troubles'. 'The Morans' is a study of tyrannical domestic power and an authoritarian patriarch in the ethos of Irish Catholic nationalism. Insofar as it is interested in the evolution of Irish society between 1920 and 1970, say, the narrative is emblematic of a time and place, but it is definitively focused on the passage of time within a parent's life and in the children who become adults growing up in its shadow. It is not simply that Moran charms his daughters into a kind of uncritical loyalty and sympathy; more than that, the portrait requires an empathy for a figure who is cast more like a tragic, self-torturing figure whose life is lived largely in blindness following his early revolutionary clarity. In a telling remark in 1985, McGahern said: 'I honour my father. I have a lot of sympathy for him; he grew up in rough times.'[22] The view of the father presented in *Memoir* casts a retrospective image over all the father figures from, say, *The Dark* forward, and many of the facts in the family history given there correspond to details in *Amongst Women*, yet it was at this time also that he quoted Chekhov on allowing characters in fiction their own space; the artist must not judge them – the reader will do that.

The main work of the eighties – the stories of *High Ground*, the television play *The Rockingham Shoot*, the novel *Amongst Women*, the stage play *The Power of Darkness*, and certain commentaries that accompanied that work – established McGahern as a public figure with a distinct historical perspective and won him a new kind of fame. His entry in the mid-eighties into a public role as writer of book reviews, opinion pieces, lecturer and visiting writer at schools and universities was encouraged by the rediscovery of him by the generation of Colm Tóibín, Neil Jordan, Joseph O'Connor and others. He became available for interviews and feature articles, and, in short, the writer of silence and exile found a new voice and place in Ireland. In the years when Seamus Heaney's poetry and the plays of Brian Friel were often taken to be central to Irish writing because they incorporated an overt response to their experience of the maelstrom in Northern Ireland, McGahern preferred to remain apart from the Field Day collective, for instance, and to refrain from public commentary on political or historical alignments in Irish society.

There is no doubt that McGahern enjoyed the sympathetic acceptance and public honouring of his work in his final decades, but he guarded against the pitfalls of such acceptance: 'If a writer only sets out to reflect a particular society he will only be of interest to a historian or a sociologist. What is permanent is the spirit or the personality in language, the style, and that's what lasts.'[23] In other words, the history will be in the poetry. The image of Moran grows out of a novel of manners or an 'historical fiction' into the religious dimension as crystallised by E.R. Dodds in a formulation much quoted by McGahern, and the novelist has said that when he had written these lines he felt that it was going to work:[24] 'It was like grasping water to think how quickly the years had passed here. They were nearly gone. It was in the nature of things and yet it brought a sense of betrayal and anger, of never having understood anything much.'[25] Before he dies he will have an awakening to 'an amazing glory that he was part of', something he was unaware of 'when he was in the midst of confident life'.[26] To the incomprehension of his daughters, he takes to walking out to stand and look at the fields, 'staring into the emptiness of the meadow' as they think, failing to understand that this is his way of dealing with the mysterious relationship of man to time and nature. In this, we are not so far removed from the preoccupations of 'Gold Watch', and, in a surprising and extraordinary way, the father has grown much closer to the image of the son, standing, looking into the night sky, learning to accept the fact that time 'did not have to run to any conclusion'.

IX

In 1979, John Updike's sympathetic review of *The Pornographer* in *The New Yorker* was given the title 'An Oldfashioned Novel'. It must have struck the author as deeply ironic that this novel which completed almost two decades of experimental writing in a particular modernist style, and with modernist ambitions, should be characterised thus. The story draws attention to an important shift from the work that culminated in *The Pornographer* to a more wholehearted embrace of an aspect of his work which he was happy to call 'oldfashioned'. The contrarian impulse was always present as a measure of integrity for McGahern, and so the embrace of the 'oldfashioned' is significant for his later work.

The young writer who wished to become a 'French' artist ended with another sense of his role, in a special sense an Anglo-Irish writer who valued central aspects of Jane Austen, Thomas Hardy and George Eliot, a writer of nature whose use of the English language was schooled in English poetry. In the end, he preferred Constable to Picasso, as he told Patrick Swift in 1960. Residents of Leitrim or any other western county may feel that when he used the expression 'local' he was referring to an acceptance of them – and he was – but he was also referring to a literary style that owed much to those English writers that he liked. Mrs Sinclair is an artist who wishes to root herself back in Ardcarne while aspiring to live in Eden or Parnassus. The most wholehearted and refined expression of this 'oldfashioned' aesthetic is to be found in the book which many readers consider his greatest achievement: *That They May Face the Rising Sun*.

Chapter 2

—

'Not Even a Shadow of Violence': Undead History in John McGahern's Anglo-Irish Stories

—

Richard Robinson

In his essay 'The Solitary Reader', John McGahern recounts how as a boy he would read indiscriminately in the library of a house owned by a local Protestant family, the Moroneys.[1] The house may not have been on the scale of the Rockingham estate, but it still symbolised for McGahern a protected childhood space – a 'timeless zone of decaying, ancestral security', in Denis Sampson's words – in which the writer's life could be conceived.[2] The Moroney library can be considered a synecdoche of the reduced colony: an enclave within an Anglo-Irish enclave, a private realm in an apparently post-historical place of unworldly solitude. What emerges from this formative autobiographical experience is a seemingly benign picture, apparently lacking in any colonialist animus. The once hegemonic culture has been disarmed and neutralised. The Moroneys were poor epigones of Anglo-Irish steel and fire: William kept bees, his son Andy studied astronomy, the distant Rocky Mountains were an object of fascination. Such was the Ascendancy threat in a newly independent Ireland.

Critics have pointed to how the Big House gains in nostalgic symbolism at the very point when its political debility has been formalised. The ideology of this retrospective symbolisation can be rendered with more or less sympathy: on the one hand, the house may come to represent 'a humane order of culture and civility, a state of community beyond the circumstance of nation or class';[3] on the other, 'an image of memory, an indication of political conservatism, even an expression of cultural disdain for the contemporary moment'.[4] As Terry Eagleton has argued, the house becomes for Yeats a subject in itself, an autonomous Romantic symbol, bearing the damage of history, 'at once local and universal, rooted in one dear perpetual place yet microcosmic of an entire social order'.[5] For McGahern, a similar conception of the local and universal, of Yeats' 'dear perpetual place', ends up, at least by the publication of *That They May Face the Rising Sun* (2002), as a template of communal tolerance, in which an appreciation of old-world etiquette contrasts to the often satirised advance of grasping bourgeois values and gombeenism.[6] If McGahern's backwards look implies nostalgia, we might expect this resistance to modernity to be particularly elegiac in those stories in the *High Ground* collection whose residual Protestant protagonists are enfeebled or in the process of being assimilated into a majority Catholic state.

In the first-person fictions in this volume, such as 'Parachutes', 'High Ground', 'Crossing the Line' and 'Gold Watch', the consciousness of the first-person subject is often lacerated: there is a sense of present time being detonated by moral choice or existential revelation. The framed, impersonally omniscient mode of 'Oldfashioned', 'Eddie Mac' and 'The Conversion of William Kirkwood', on the other hand, is formally conspicuous and marks a tonal shift within the *High Ground* collection. These stories reminded one critic of sketches for an unwritten historical novel, another of 'genre pictures'.[7] This memorialising, 'period' aesthetic is not to be equated with a univocal McGahern style but with part of a deliberately varied performance. Generally, the ideological content of McGahern's form – language, narrative and genre – must be taken into account. In Fredric Jameson's terms, we may read towards a political unconscious in the text, by exploring 'the traces of history's uninterrupted narrative' and by 'restoring to the surface of the text the repressed and buried reality of its fundamental history'.[8] In what ways do these self-advertising 'old-fashioned' texts acknowledge or sublimate present conflict? To what extent are they symptomatic of absent and totalising historical forces, as Jameson suggests, and how can we unmask the anachronic narrative as a socially symbolic act, showing how readings of the past depend upon the experience of the present? We should approach these stories as expressing, consciously or not, continuing antagonisms about the present – of the 1980s when *High Ground* was published – or our present (as we may contemplate the impact of Brexit on the Northern Irish border), and as revealing a constellated and dialectical movement in the history between Ireland and Britain.

This essay traces the potentially profitable ways in which 'Oldfashioned' and the Kirkwood stories can be read with a sense of history as a 'vast unfinished plot', in Jameson's words, and in the acceptance that 'all history is contemporary history'.[9] History may be conceived of as undead. When the 'end of history' was notoriously proclaimed in the early 1990s (that is, the supposed victory of Western liberal democracy), Derrida turned to the first noun of *The Manifesto of the Communist Party*, 'spectre', to emphasise how the present is haunted by the restless spirits of those revolutionary spirits seeking historical redress. This figure of Marxian spectrality suggests that history is an ontologically open process.[10] Derrida turns to *Hamlet* to find a template for a time which is, variously, disrupted, disjointed, dislocated, disadjusted, disarticulated. Hamlet's ghost-father makes both an inaugural appearance and a revenant's return, immediately fracturing the political present, announcing 'the disjointure in the very presence of the present, this sort of non-contemporaneity of present time with itself'.[11] For Hamlet the father and the son, historical time is 'out of joint': the speech in which Hamlet utters these words is echoed in 'Oldfashioned', a story which may not be ostensibly spectral (unlike, say, 'The Wine Breath') but which is nevertheless centred on a conception of undead history, on the return of the historical repressed.

The notion of the political unconscious is particularly fitted to a reading of the Anglo-Irish class, particularly in relation to the nineteenth-century Protestant Gothic. The anxieties of a dying Ascendancy are repressed and projected into vivid, death-driven fantasies, such as those of Maturin, Le Fanu or Stoker, which continually threaten the formal constraints of realism. This sensibility is still evident in a novel such as Elizabeth Bowen's *The Last September* (1929), set during the Anglo-Irish war and shot through by figures of a moribund Gothic. A ruined mill tied to the demesne is compared to corpses 'never quite stripped and whitened to skeletons' decency', and to a crumbling House of Usher.[12] The mill is also the place where a character is grazed by an IRA bullet, so that blood is left on her lips: as Julian Moynihan has written, this provides 'its final touch of the macabre – the vampire touch, the nightmare vision of the "undead", the dead still putting on an act at living'.[13]

Bowen dramatises the 'last' days: the climacteric of decolonisation. Mc-Gahern's imagined recreation of Irish Protestants' culture in independent Ireland is of an even later remainder. The Kirkwoods and Sinclairs are historically posthumous objects of representation, depicting a dwindling, residual class deprived of historical agency. They are no longer political antagonists to be deposed. Their numbers diminishing, they represent what is left over in the after-time.[14] Derrida wonders of Hamlet's Elsinore if it is 'possible to find a rule of cohabitation under such a roof, it being understood that this house will always be a haunted house'.[15] Guard Casey's often quoted line from 'Oldfashioned', 'You don't ever find robins feeding with the sparrows', indicates that in these 1980s' fictions from *High Ground*, McGahern is also exploring the meaning of such supposedly post-historical cohabitation.[16]

'Oldfashioned'

As its title unavoidably suggests, 'Oldfashioned' is self-conscious about its belatedness in both a formal and historical sense. John Updike's review of *The Pornographer* in *The New Yorker* was entitled 'An Old-Fashioned Novel', an epithet that McGahern then re-deploys. The title slyly encodes McGahern's deliberate inhabiting of an archaic-sounding form and challenges the reader's presumption that such a form implies a commensurate ideology. The very texture of the prose may encourage the idea that, in the words of one critic, McGahern's representation of the world of the Big House is 'idealistic and nostalgic', and 'provides evidence of a romantic yearning for a harmonious social world beyond the amorphous, fragmented society of the present'.[17] In this account, 'old' historical content is transmitted in 'old' narrative, exemplifying Jameson's assertion that 'the aesthetic act is itself ideological'.[18] The narrative may be conceived of as a socially symbolic act which tries to resolve ideological conflicts or else to leave them exposed.

The specific story of the barracks guard's son, Johnny, and the Protestant Sinclairs is framed by a kind of social history, narrated in an elliptical, quasi-documentary mode. The local characters are 'placed', as if seen remotely through a bird's eye lens. Near the beginning we are told that the war was over, 'Britain had to be rebuilt' and the 'countryside emptied towards London and Luton' (*CE*, 238); near the end that '[h]ardly anybody now goes to England' (*CE*, 259). The time span of the narrative is marked out and history updated in a playful, almost folk-tale way: 'In every house across the countryside there glows at night the strange living light of television sets' (*CE*, 261). Here the present is defamiliarised both in content (the estranging glow not of the Sacred Heart but of the television) and in form (the dusty syntax of 'there glows'). The story's preoccupation with obsolescence, of which the diminished Anglo-Irish are exemplary, is thus strategically embedded in its form.

The date of the story's publication in *The Yale Review*, 1984, is significant. The title prompts us to think of the temporal 'other', of what is new and painfully present. What remains off the page is both political present time (summarising crudely, a time just after the hunger strikes, in the year of the Brighton bombing, before the Anglo-Irish Agreement of 1985, but also before the Enniskillen bombing) and a fashionably contemporary narrative aesthetic (implicitly, perhaps, some strain of self-referential postmodernism: anything but provincial realism). To read this story about the 'Anglo-Irish' – both in the sense of the extinct class, and the continuing hyphenated relationships between two countries – as unconnected to Anglo-Irish relationships in the present is to misread it. The reader must surely look for the very presence of the past. The rupture between the former IRA republican sergeant and the retired British Army colonel may be dated around 1950: it happens 'all the more finally because there was not even a shadow of violence' (*CE*, 253). The ghosts of the War of Independence, time past, continue to shadow what occurs, conditioning and making impossible the continued relationship of the Irish boy and the Anglo-Irish couple. The contemporary reader wonders about how that shadow is cast forward as well, to the violence of the future.

The colonel is a son of the manse who grew up in the Ardcarne parsonage, went to Sandhurst, became an officer in the British Army and spent much of his career in India. The portrayal of the returning Sinclairs is evidently sympathetic, though also wry about aspects of aloofness in their behaviour. The colonel's suggestion that Johnny, the academically able son of a Garda sergeant, should try for a commission in the British Army certainly lacks tact, that very quality praised in Mrs Sinclair (who acts with 'the perfect tact that is a kind of mind-reading' (*CE*, 251)). The proposal is explained by the death of the colonel's son in the war, which creates space for a new, surrogate form of affiliation. But the personal is political: a more uncharitable reading can be constructed. Sinclair's suggestion is also a blunder, an act of almost wilful historical amnesia which speaks of the British compulsion to forget its history of imperial violence. We might imagine a counterfactual future time in which Johnny did not become a film-maker but a British officer deployed in, say, Derry twenty years later, at the height of the so-called Troubles.

It seems counter-intuitive to extend a kind of readerly sympathy to the barracks sergeant, that tyrannical father figure so familiar in McGahern's work. But merely decoding parricidal animus in psychological terms is interpretatively limiting: as Deleuze and Guattari argue in the *Anti-Oedipus*, psychoanalytic decipherment of the family romance is not contained by a purely domestic antagonism in the home. McGahern's fiction indeed underlines how the foundational history of the political state – of the disappointed Law of the Father – conditions the oppression of desire and threatens to disunite the family. In 'Oldfashioned' the personal becomes political for the father, too. After turning down the colonel's proposal to make an Englishman out of the boy, the sergeant beats the ridges of the potato field he has been digging with such ferocity that the spade handle breaks: an act of displaced retaliatory violence. Any such scene staged on a potato field automatically recalls national trauma and will always struggle to be contained as a historically 'neutral' or contingent realist particular. Such is the sergeant's concern with being seen by neighbours that he pretends he is chasing a rat away from the field with his spade. It is typical of McGahern's covert and grim irony that the father's seething postcolonial *ressentiment*, calling up the ghosts of race memory and the atavistic fear of the poorhouse, must be represented with cool, almost tragicomic impersonality.

It is said of the sergeant that he 'was not a man to look for any abstraction in the sparrow's fall. If that small disturbance of the air was to earn a moment's attention, he would want to know at once what effect it would have on him or that larger version of himself he was fond of referring to as "my family"' (*CE*, 250). This reminds us not only that one particular sparrow, the son, is not being permitted to feed with the robins, but of *Hamlet* too: 'We defy augury. There is special providence in the fall of a sparrow. If it be, 'tis not to come. If it be not to come, it will be now. If it be not now, yet it will come. The readiness is all, since no man of aught he leaves knows what is't to leave betimes. Let be.'[19] By Act V, Hamlet has reached a fatalistic acceptance of his fate in the Christian eschatological design – he accepts his imminent death as the providential shaping of our ends. In contrast, the sergeant cannot passively 'let be' but rather continues to 'rough hew' the world according to his egoistic will: in his domain all others must be 'a larger version of himself'. The sergeant's following words to Sinclair adapt an English idiom from *Macbeth*: his decision not to allow the boy to join the British Army is 'the end and the be-all' (*CE*, 250), inverting Macbeth's 'the be-all and the end-all'. The father's tyrannical wish is to exercise complete control over actions by 'trammelling up' their consequences, but as Stanley van der Ziel has recently suggested, the context of the soliloquy points up the irony that 'the father's apparently sure-footed statement in fact contains the seeds of its own denial'.[20] More generally, such lurking Shakespearean intertexts emphasise that this story about time, now and to come, is for the sergeant and the colonel 'out of joint', suggesting that same concept of undead history developed in Derrida's Marxian, so-called 'hauntological' reading of *Hamlet*.

'Oldfashioned' is founded on the idea that historical animus may be repressed, covered by manners, but that it will continue to return. The wound is easily re-opened. The 'old caste hostility' (*CE*, 255), which seems to have become a historical irrelevance after independence, rises back to the surface. Unspoken meanings reverberate. The final sentence, which seems to allow the eye to rest on an untroubled pastoral scene, asks us to consider the Iron Mountains stretching 'smoky and blue' not to the north but to the 'North', a barely perceptible capitalisation which suggests the proximity of a territory as much as of a direction, as Belinda McKeon has noted.[21] That territory is one where robins and sparrows do not feed together. The political present has been displaced, but continues to haunt the text.

Johnny's film-making is analogous to McGahern's memorialising art: the comment that his films have been regarded as 'humourless, morbid, and restricted to a narrow view that was more revealing of private obsessions than any truths about life or Irish life in general' (*CE*, 259) is a pre-emptive and not so deeply encrypted form of self-commentary. It invites us to compare 'Oldfashioned' with Johnny's *My Own Place*. The film will be dull because all the people Johnny wishes to resurrect in his memory remain in the past: the camera-eye, unlike the inward eye of memory, takes in 'only what was in front of it' (*CE*, 262). The dead protagonists – the Sinclairs, the father, Guard Casey – exist only as memories and have no material trace in the present. The memory-image, which would supplant the present scene, re-populating it with ghosts, cannot be manufactured by the substitute instrument of perception. Liliane Louvel argues that it is rhythm and voice which supply what the cunningly manipulated image cannot – a 'bitter-sweet remembrance of things past'.[22] If we are to think of the story as restoratively Proustian, as this intimates, then it must be with the caveat that such a past is not stored in the archive of imagination because 'over with', but that it is potentially revenant in more disturbing ways. The reader responds not to what is whole and manifest, but to what is unconscious and occluded. History remains ontologically open: if we read the story as an elaborate confirmation that old Ireland is 'dead and gone', sealed off from the present, then we impose harmful limits on it, underestimating its knowing and unknowing displacements of revanchist energy.

The film-maker records that the paddock railings had 'long lost their second whiteness' (*CE*, 262). Before the Sinclairs' arrival, the Ardcarne parsonage had previously been 'let run wild' (*CE*, 237). Time is not teleological but successive, cyclical, sedimentary: there is painting, peeling, repainting, a second peeling; leavetakings follow and are followed by homegoings. The Sinclairs arrived against the tide of emigration to England (*CE*, 239). The retrospective view of tidal time suggests the 'vast and unfinished plot of history' which, in Jameson's terms, the present represents. McGahern's implied reader makes good temporal gapped-ness, supplying a contemporary 'shadow of violence'. This can be understood as the 'truth of life or Irish life' (*CE*, 259) that Johnny, as film-maker, is said to evade: the violence, repressed or material, of Irish history, or the violence of any history in which, after Walter Benjamin, barbarism is always concealed as the obverse or dark 'other' of culture.[23]

'Oldfashioned' insists, then, on the pastness and the presence of the past. On the one hand, the past refuses to be recaptured or resurrected. A fiction which reconstructs that dead time cannot avoid a certain performed anachronism: this is what the self-aware title acknowledges. And yet the story, unlike Johnny's film, is not dull and unpeopled. It insists on an opposite movement: that the past is not buried and over with, but continually threatens to irrupt into the present; that we apprehend, as Derrida puts it, 'the non-contemporaneity of the present time with the present'; that what is old is not dead. The telescoping of decades of mid- to late-century time allows McGahern to kill off and resurrect his characters. As the Yeatsian experience of the priest shows in 'The Wine Breath', memories of the dead are like personalised ghosts or purgatorial spirits. Although Johnny does not experience the revenant past in the same way as the priest, 'Oldfashioned' nevertheless points in its very structure to a historical pattern of tidal repetition and return: Johnny's own escape and return; Sinclair's reconstruction of his youth in the parsonage; the sergeant's retirement to a farm, joined to the Rockingham demesne, which provides an 'exact replica of the life he'd lived as a boy' (*CE*, 255). After Ireland's revolutionary history in the early twentieth century, the return of the Sinclairs initially appears to be harmless and post-historical. For the father it reawakens the spirits of Anglo-Irish enmity. For the son it is a 'closing down' (*CE*, 253) of a potential future already made impossible by unfinished history. He apprehends, after Marx, that 'the dead generations' still and always weigh 'like a nightmare on the brains of the living'.[24]

David Thomson's *Woodbrook*

For a deeper understanding of how McGahern represents the residual Anglo-Irish experience in the Kirkwood stories 'Eddie Mac' and 'The Conversion of William Kirkwood', it is instructive to turn to David Thomson's *Woodbrook*, and his rendering of the Kirkwoods, particularly as McGahern had read this book and commented on how old Willie and Andy Moroney were 'wonderfully brought to life' in it.[25] The Moroneys lived between the estates of Rockingham, Oakport and not far from Woodbrook, the house of the 'real' Kirkwoods. According to Thomson, the Moroneys were distantly related to the Kirkwoods and used to manage their estate.[26] Although the fictional William Kirkwoods, father and son, are modelled on the eccentric Moroneys of his childhood, McGahern changes their name. This may be to exploit the symbolic power of the name itself: the connotation of the Presbyterian 'Kirk' planted in the west of Ireland in the early seventeenth century in order to send its roots into the soil and remain there. The signifier 'Kirkwood' speaks in ironic contrast to the impermanence of William's eventual 'conversion'. On the one hand, then, this is a matter of nomenclatural opportunism. But the name belongs to an established Anglo-Irish family in Roscommon, inviting the reader to wonder about the ways in which the real Kirkwoods of the same locality compare to McGahern's fictional father and son. Thomson's *Woodbrook* helps to shed light on this question.

Thomson's memoir is in part the story of a chaste romance between a Scottish history tutor and the doomed Kirkwood daughter Phoebe, who dies young during the Second World War. The affair often remains curiously though powerfully implicit, suggesting the extent to which the narrator's turbulence is buttoned-up. He may admit, for example, to spending far too much time polishing Phoebe's boots. The platonic relationship stands in metonymically for the narrator's attachment to the whole family and to a now extinct Anglo-Irish culture. This seems to be consistent with a politically disengaged nostalgia which would seek to draw a veil over the brutal history of Anglo-Irish domination in the west of Ireland. However, Thomson was an undergraduate in history when he first visited Roscommon and writes throughout with the eye of a historian. He details what he calls apartheid under Queen Elizabeth I, Cromwellian massacre and the despotism of late nineteenth-century landlords. From the very first he sees how the 'physical past' is inscribed into the land and remains 'lodged in the soil and in the mind' (*W*, 10) long after his learnt academic history has been forgotten. His affection for Charlie Kirkwood (the 'Major', known as 'Daddy' even to Thomson) does not soften the account of Anglo-Irish cruelty: 'the horrid legacy we had all inherited', 'one of the most brutal systems of oppression in the history of mankind' in which, crucially, 'the sins of the fathers *can never be over and done with*' (my italics, *W*, 71). Despite local affection for the charming 'Major', he still represents a garrison class, speaks of the English as 'we' and wields 'the moral power of a dominant race long after their legal powers had gone' (*W*, 72). The house of Woodbrook is a 'remnant of one of those old social units [...] a sort of nub of life', and the custom of not paying servants, for example, is 'a survival of the old Big House polity' (*W*, 290). The idiosyncrasies of this residual polity in the 1930s are lovingly pored over by Thomson, but also shown to be ancestrally determined.

Thomson places the Kirkwoods at the end of Anglo-Irish history but his return to the dilapidated Big House is finally narrated with the immediacy of the political present. Long after Phoebe's tragically early death, Thomson revisits Woodbrook, now a 'dead weight' (*W*, 321) long since sold by the Kirkwoods. It is 1968, and the 'last vestiges of the Anglo-Irish landlord system had passed away' (*W*, 323). Although Thomson's epilogue touches on his 'sense of abandonment', a sense of the house's window opening 'into nothing' (*W*, 322), the last sentence of the book resolutely avoids the nostalgic closing of history. He refers to the so-called Troubles as being resumed, not as breaking out: 'It is as though the whole of Anglo-Irish history has been boiled down and its dregs thrown out, leaving their poisonous concentrate on these six counties' (*W*, 323–4).

Reading *Woodbrook* alongside McGahern's Kirkwood stories, what seems to be confirmed is how these texts share a surprisingly open-ended historical consciousness. On the surface, these works of personal and collective memory are trained upon a bounded period which is 'heavily' historical, in Nietzschean terms, never to happen again. But the ending of *Woodbrook* is pointedly contemporaneous, just as the last sentence of 'Oldfashioned' has a present-time dissonance. In both cases, history can be figured as 'lightly' recurrent, potentially resumptive: a repressed history which is perpetually present. This sets the pattern for the way we may read 'Eddie Mac' and 'The Conversion of William Kirkwood', paired stories which dramatise an equal and opposite movement – between appropriation and expropriation, alliance and disunion, homemaking and leavetaking.

'Eddie Mac' and 'The Conversion of William Kirkwood'

The beginning of 'Eddie Mac' briefly hints at the Bowen-like rituals of the Kirkwood family. Mrs Kirkwood's lifestyle involves tea parties and visits from other Anglo-Irish families; she sits in the library, looking out the window 'on the lawn and white paling and the winding avenue of copper and green beech' (*CE*, 263). Throughout 'big house' is insisted upon as a hoary old appellation, twice repeated (*CE*, 264, 274), and elsewhere referred to as the 'big Georgian house' (*CE*, 266), 'the huge house' (*CE*, 269), and 'the house [which] was too big for all of them' (*CE*, 271). When Mrs Kirkwood dies, we are told that the 'formal heart of the house, perhaps the heart of the house itself, stopped' with her (*CE*, 265). Her alliance with Kirkwood has rescued the family from bankruptcy. A kind of matrilineal power is conferred upon her by Eddie Mac, who has a grudging respect for the old lady's 'bit of iron' (*CE*, 277), in contrast to his attitude to the males.

The story begins with Eddie's sporting triumph as the star Gaelic football player and ends with his abandoning of the pregnant Annie May: he absconds to those northern British cities where he could 'stay lost for ever and victory could be found' (*CE*, 278). This continued gambling for individual 'victory', at the expense of others, is an index of damaged masculinity – of the waning power of former 'heroes' embittered by what they see as their own feminisation. Eddie's father too had disappeared. Eddie is conforming to a recurrent pattern: the second victory which he hopes to find, presumably in interwar, depression-era industrial cities, is likely to be played out as farce.

Eddie's attitude towards the Kirkwoods, bee-keeping nurturer or star-gazing scholar, is scathing: they are 'perfectly useless' (*CE*, 269, 273), 'both fools' (*CE*, 268). As Belinda McKeon has written, Eddie espouses an attitude to the landed Protestants which reinforces a distinction between his practical function and their 'useless' aesthetic ornamentality.[27] They lack the sort of virile mastery which he might respect. The gentle son is 'the last of the Kirkwoods' (*CE*, 289), hardly an expropriating landlord or an agent of the agrarian terror. He is no longer worthy of the name of ancestral villain and, homosocially, no longer a suitable antagonist. It is tempting to describe the enmity between Eddie and the Kirkwoods in terms of caste hostility, as if Eddie represents the active agency of an emergent nationalist myth which will dispose of the now historically redundant, emasculated Anglo-Irish masters. Eddie's violent treatment of a young bullock indeed suggests such seethingly aggressive potentiality.

However, we note that Eddie is equally derisive about the dancers standing up 'like fools for the Soldier's Song': here, the description of 'the national anthem beat[ing] stridently in the night air' (*CE*, 267) reminds us that, in this interwar story, Eddie's lack of patriotic ardour is a mark of his individualism, and perhaps of his grudging but continuing dependence on the social unit of the Big House. 'He had nothing against the Kirkwoods but they were fools' (*CE*, 277): a political agent would have something against the Kirkwoods, whereas Eddie does not appear to be *consciously* animated by historical, class-based hostility. We may see the antagonism differently: not so much between the male victor (Eddie) and the 'neutered' men (Kirkwoods), but between those now on the wrong side of history. Such is the 'uselessness' of the Kirkwoods that Eddie has taken over the running of their farm, and eats in the kitchen with them. He sees himself as tethered to spending 'faltering years' with the family (*CE*, 276): 'They'll be on the road before long […] and we'll be with them if we are not careful' (*CE*, 269): both 'them', the Anglo-Irish, and 'us', those who have worked for or served in the Big House, live in historical times out of joint. Eddie's abandoning of Annie May, whom he correctly foresees as being accommodated in a newly patched-up family, is of course heartless and cowardly. But our disapproval of Eddie's moral coarseness should not cast him as an ingrate to the Anglo-Irish, as if he should have known his place in the old semi-feudal arrangement. His individualism allows no loyalty to the new Ireland. Although Eddie's stealing of the Kirkwoods' cattle is not politically willed, it may be regarded as a symbolic form of historical redress for Anglo-Irish expropriation – a crime welling out of the political unconscious, explicable by centuries of history.

'The Conversion of William Kirkwood' ends, like 'Eddie Mac', with abandonment. At the beginning of the story there is an act of mending and solidarity between those who, in their different ways, have been left behind or cast off: the landowning Protestants, the Kirkwoods, who remain in their Big House, and their servant, Annie May, who has been left with Eddie Mac's illegitimate child, Lucy. This becomes a reconstituted type of family, despite class and religious difference. At the end of the story William Kirkwood, now converted to Catholicism, is engaged to marry Mary Kennedy, the daughter of an affluent local family, in a match which will suit them both. Mary's economic motives are clear: having seen 'the big stone house' she thinks it 'no mean setting' (*CE*, 297) and resolves to love William. The text seems to enact a subversive reversal of colonialist stereotypes, with Kirkwood now assuming the role of the subaltern or colonial mimic subsumed into a clericalist Ireland moving towards ethno-cultural homogeneity.[28] Kirkwood 'had become such a part of the people' (*CE*, 287): now it is only religion which seems to be the mark of difference. It is intimated that this new ad hoc alliance will lead to the assimilation of the Anglo-Irish residue by the rising Catholic bourgeoisie, a dispensation which will result in the expulsion of Annie May and Lucy. The story is ambiguously poised: sitting in the cold of an empty house from which mother and daughter are absent, William finally wonders 'whether there was any way his marriage could take place without bringing suffering on two people who had been a great part of his life, who had done nothing themselves to deserve being driven out into a world they were hardly prepared for' (*CE*, 300). The ending seems to be modelled on that of other first-person fictions in *High Ground*, in which McGahern exploits the moral indecision of his characters, and suggests how the future of the short story is implicit but unknown.

In this case, though, such formal open-endedness is chimerical: William's marriage will surely bring suffering. His disempowerment is such that he cannot or will not resist the Kennedys – that he will, in effect, cast out Annie May and Lucy. For Denis Sampson, it means that William, in abandoning his protector role, has indeed been converted to 'a male form of blind and violent behaviour' which now disregards 'the importance of preserving moral independence'.[29] To Belinda McKeon, this ending represents a new kind of equality which, in replacing the old world of manners, foreshadows future violence.[30] Narrative closure is far from being equated with the end of Anglo-Irish history. Viewed as a part of the continuum of history, this is a new kind of 'settlement': a compromise which still entails native victims 'being driven out' (*CE*, 300) even when the ancestral agents of aggression are themselves etiolated. William has been presented as a type of harmless eccentric and his gentleness seems to continue that of his nurturing father. It is difficult to associate the last Kirkwood with Anglo-Irish expropriation. Yet hints of recidivist mastery are introduced: by putting on military uniform William seems to perform his proper historical role, as if his mother's family of British officers, the Darbys, had 'gathered to claim him' (*CE*, 283). Kirkwood has a 'jutting Anglo-Irish jaw' (*CE*, 297) and turns out to be a crack marksman. Seeing him on horseback, people mutter: 'Put one of them back on a horse and it's as if they never left the saddle' (*CE*, 283). All of a sudden the 'perfectly useless' Kirkwood alarmingly threatens to become a fitting scion, another Major Gregory: 'Soldier, scholar, horseman, he.'[31]

William's conversion to Catholicism, first suggested by helping Lucy with her catechism studies, is on the surface motivated by intellect and an anglicised affinity with Newman. It seems to be the death blow for his class: the dripping of his baptismal waters 'must have seemed a final pale bloodletting to any ghosts of the Kirkwoods hovering in the air around' (*CE*, 291). William's subsequent marriage to nurse Kennedy may prompt the thought that he acted more shrewdly than perhaps he knew. For all its charm, William's behaviour can be seen as conforming to a remorselessly deterministic historical pattern. In Thomson's *Woodbrook* the 'real' Kirkwoods' house was eventually bought out in the 1940s by the Maxwell brothers, who felt that it had been taken from their family in the seventeenth century: it was 'theirs all along', 'before Cromwell put the Kirkwoods on this land' (*W*, 303). This is presented by the Maxwells, if not by Thomson, as an act of ancestral reparation for ancient injustice. That McGahern effects a transformation in which the fictional Kirkwood keeps the Big House is thus significant. The Kennedy–Kirkwood intermarriage will keep the Anglo-Irish name alive; a robin and a sparrow will feed together under the roof of the haunted house only because one of them changed species, as it were. Postcolonial hybridity is not presented as an emancipatory possibility: Lucy, brought up a Catholic but possessed of the 'clipped, commanding accents' (*CE*, 281) or Protestant bark of her beloved adoptive father, 'a Kirkwood to the bone' (*CE*, 289), is neither mistress nor subaltern. She no longer has the hinterland of a secure socio-cultural identity.

'The Conversion of William Kirkwood' ends with a fudged historical enactment of repossession and dispossession. Although it is true that, as David Malcolm has written, 'the Kirkwoods are presented with great sympathy' and 'seen as decent, honest, cultured and well mannered, if somewhat feckless and incompetent', this serves to make William's inadvertent abandonment of Annie May and Lucy all the more cruel.[32] The knowingness of the story is in showing how William will finally bring suffering *despite* his apparent powerlessness, suggesting that the retrospective account of the extinct Anglo-Irish class bears that perhaps unconscious trace of violent Irish history to come. The trajectory of the story is such that the 'ex-centric' William is converted and thus incorporated into the body politic of independent Ireland. Although this indicates the end of Anglo-Irish hegemony, the openness of the ending suggests that such appropriation still entails the recurrent process of 'driving out', of undead history.

McGahern's Kirkwood stories are concerned with the historical inter-penetration of residual and emergent orders, and formally constructed around the cyclical principle that a historical closing continues into an opening, and vice versa. In his script for the television play, *The Rockingham Shoot*, McGahern refers to 'the ordinary life of a new order [beginning] outside the walls' so that 'the old order [is] carried into the beginning of the new order'.[33] This does not suggest an unquestioning nostalgia for a terminated historical period, nor an implicit idealisation of Ascendancy culture. Rather, it reveals how history persists. The stories are not period reconstructions or 'genre pictures', as their aesthetic mode might first suggest. They eventually linger with the victims of the new socio-political accommodation, encouraging the reader to infer the ways in which history continuously determines the fate of its subjects.

'Nothing is ever over in Ireland'

McGahern's fiction is often drawn to how the foundational Law of the Father has been supplanted in the post-revolutionary state. The embitterment of the republican idealist is manifest in domestic tyranny and oedipal animus. The early fiction set in Leitrim or Roscommon is thus often associated with the claustral hearth of the barracks or the small farm. It is understandable, then, that McGahern's empathic imagination was drawn to that more spacious and unworldly domain of the Protestant 'other'. At the same time we must acknowledge that there is little attempt to represent the King-Harmons of the Rockingham estate, even in *The Rockingham Shoot*, in which they are the target of the schoolteacher's ire but not active protagonists. In 'Oldfashioned', too, the King-Harmons are mentioned but remain offstage: it is reported that the shell of their Nash house is dynamited. McGahern does not attempt to go inside this Big House, nor to ventriloquise the upper-class occupants of 'our own little Britain [which is] with us yet behind the demesne wall'.[34]

McGahern is not personally suffering from or sublimating the culturally moribund condition of Anglo-Irish culture. Comparisons between his stories of the residual Protestants and the canon of Anglo-Irish literature are thus bound to have limits. The Protestant Ireland McGahern looks back upon and transfigures is beyond even the post-mortem state of Bowen's ruined mills or that of Yeats' unexpiated spirits who haunt the ruined house of *Purgatory*. This is no mortmain grip of the Ascendancy: Gothic figures of morbidity, in which supernatural possession stands for the avenging return of the territorial dispossessed, are no longer sustainable. There is little self-conscious symbolisation of the Kirkwood house, which is not burnt out and does not crack like Poe's House of Usher. The loss of scale and grandeur is assumed: instead there is an acknowledgement of miniaturisation, depletion and 'ex-centricity'. The Kirkwoods are not like those Anglo-Irish characters who proudly deny their decline, who encircle themselves, resisting assimilation. They and the returning Sinclairs are domesticated and defanged: oddly residual, residually odd.

But in other ways the Protestant house of independent Ireland that McGahern represents extrapolates persisting tropes. For all its apparent serenity, the Protestant enclave cannot be a nurturing place for the young but must stand for impermanence and discontinuity. The Sinclairs' son is dead and Johnny cannot be adopted as their surrogate; the de facto Kirkwood, Lucy, will be stranded, rather like Bowen's orphaned children. In Seán O'Faoláin's 'Midsummer Night Madness', the philandering and dissolute Henn of Henn Hall, whose rolled 'r's are the last trace of his ancestral Anglo-Norman 'blazonry', is ousted from his Big House by the republicans. The old man finally leaves for Paris with his pregnant 'tinker' wife, Gypsy. The paternity of Gypsy's child is ambiguous: does it belong to Stevey, the IRA man, or to Henn himself? Anglo-Irish lineage is satirically cast as an absurd dynastic aspiration: Henn wishes to keep the name alive, the narrator comments, 'as if he were a Hapsburg or a Bourbon!'[35] In one of Yeats' iterations of ancestral anxiety, the Old Man of *Purgatory* kills both his father and son because of his fear of miscegenation and caste contamination. The mother, who owned 'This scenery and this countryside, / Kennel and stable, horse and hound', represents an archetypal Ascendancy Ireland. But she married a drunken groom, one who 'was not her kind'. The son is stabbed because he would 'Beget and pass pollution on'.[36] The questions McGahern raises, relating to the mixing of robins and sparrows, to appropriation and expropriation, possession and dispossession, are consistent with this preoccupation with the end of Anglo-Irish 'begetting'.

Elizabeth Bowen made the McGahern-like comment: 'Nothing is ever over in Ireland.'[37] This perhaps ascribes to Ireland a quirky exceptionalism which does not take into account that the historical present – Irish, British or otherwise – is never over, but remains open. The extent to which McGahern's texts 'know' this is finally undecidable. These stories are shadowed by a history of violence which has been repressed but threatens to haunt the present: this is a latency or occlusion which is consistent with McGahern's covert literary practice. We can say that they manifest an awareness of historical persistence while establishing that the present is not a subject of direct scrutiny. It is perhaps in the cryptic, implicitly self-reflexive ending of 'Oldfashioned' that McGahern is closest to diagnosing the retrospective form of these historical fictions, of looking at and away from 'only what is in front of him'.

Chapter 3

—

Love and Desire in John McGahern's Fiction: Searching for 'All Sorts of Impossible Things'

—

Sylvie Mikowski

In the early years of his 'career', McGahern was hailed as a realist writer, one who was able to offer an accurate description of what Ireland was like in the 1950s and 1960s, to the point that he was sometimes accused of parochialism.[1] There was also a good number of reviews to be found in Irish journals, such as the one by John Cronin entitled '*The Dark* Is Not Light Enough',[2] who found that this naturalism produced what Joyce, while defending his right to offer 'his fellow-citizens a good look at themselves in his nicely-polished mirror' called 'an odour of ashpits and offal'.[3] Even though *The Barracks* was awarded some of the most important Irish literary awards and *Amongst Women* received a very warm critical reception in 1990, the scandal caused by the banning of *The Dark* in 1965, the unease following the rewriting of *The Leavetaking* (1984) and the puzzling themes and images of *The Pornographer* (1979) all contributed to delaying McGahern's elevation to the position of iconic national writer until the publication of the aforementioned *Amongst Women*, the redeeming *That They May Face the Rising* Sun (2002) and the moving and beautifully crafted *Memoir* (2005).

Michael J. Toolan, for instance, wrote in 1981: '[…] the pornographer is ignoble and deplorable, a character neither interestingly or challengingly presented. I believe *The Pornographer* constitutes a misapplication of McGahern's literary talent.'[4] At the very least, therefore, it can be said that McGahern's early work was not universally acclaimed. The writer seems to have been well aware of the mixed feelings he aroused in his readers' minds, as can be inferred from a passage from the short story 'Oldfashioned', in which he draws the portrait of a young man who has become a film-maker, a sort of fictional *alter ego* of the writer himself, as evidenced by the way his career is described:

[…] later he made a series of documentary films about the darker aspects of Irish life. As they were controversial, they won him a sort of fame; some thought they were serious, well made, and compulsive viewing, bringing things to light that were in bad need of light; but others maintained that they were humourless, morbid, and restricted to a narrow view that was more revealing of private obsessions than any truths about life or Irish life in general.[5]

Those 'darker aspects of Irish life […] in bad need of light' can be interpreted as an allusion to the narrow-mindedness and repressive atmosphere prevailing in rural Ireland of the 1950s and '60s, or to the hopelessness of young lives facing nothing but the brutality of authoritarian fathers and the bleakness of small-town Catholic conformism, so well captured in McGahern's own depictions. However, this kind of social critique would not have been sufficient to justify the harshness of the censorship that fell on McGahern or the tepid reception which some of his work received: in this writer's opinion, the banning of McGahern's early work and his banishment from Ireland was imputable to the crudity and straightforwardness with which he tackled sex and sexuality in his writings. No other Irish writer of the period, except, but to a lesser extent, Edna O'Brien, who suffered a similar fate, dared to write about sex with the same bluntness and frankness as McGahern did, including, as we now know, some of its most obscure aspects, such as sexual abuse, particularly child abuse, which was rampant in Ireland when he was growing up, and even at the time when he was writing. An example of 'the things that were in bad need of light' is thus provided by *The Dark*, in which McGahern graphically describes how young Mahoney is abused by his father and almost suffers an uncomfortably similar fate at the hands of his cousin, a priest who is supposed to help him make a decision about his religious vocation. In the same novel, Mahoney's sister Joan is sexually harassed by the shopkeeper she has been sent to work for.

But McGahern's preoccupation with sex was not limited to simply denouncing criminal or pathological patterns of behaviour or to presenting a social critique of repression and sexual control in Ireland, even if that is a part of his work which deserves admiration for its courage, clearsightedness and subversive power. McGahern's emphasis on sexuality also entails a wider interrogation regarding the role of sexuality in human life, and in the first

LOVE AND DESIRE IN JOHN McGAHERN'S FICTION · 47

place the possibility or impossibility of relationships between men and women at large. There are of course many ways of defining McGahern's stories and novels – as *Bildungsromane*, as an aesthetic search for the perfect poetic expression, as existential quests, as realistic explorations of a given society, as attempts at recovering a traumatic past – but they can also be viewed as studies in the relationships between men and women, either through sexual encounters or through married life, in which the Irish context counts for very little in the end. As a matter of fact, McGahern's body of work can be divided between those stories told from the male perspective; those using the point of view of a woman, foremost among which stands *The Barracks*; and those embracing both men and women, the better to observe and depict their confrontation.

For what McGahern relentlessly exposes about sex, love and marriage is the unbridgeable distance which separates genders, the inevitable disillusion which accompanies sex and love, the repetition of the same mistake, misunderstanding or 'slip-up', so that the relationship between men and women appears throughout his work as an unappeasable longing for 'all sorts of impossible things'. Even McGahern's last novel, *That They May Face the Rising Sun*, often regarded as a celebration of harmony and serenity and evoking, according to Denis Sampson, 'a love that grows with time, that binds neighbours and friends into a tolerant and accepting community, an ideal community, in fact, in which each person is given sympathetic attention',[6] revolves to a large extent around the possibility or impossibility for men and women to fulfil each other's longings, as the seemingly uneventful chronicle of life around the lake nevertheless records a succession of marriages, separations, break-ups and failed love stories or gives examples of obstinate celibacy. The peacefulness of the natural environment, so forcefully evoked by McGahern's poetic prose in this last novel, doesn't hide the violence of sexual predators such as John Quinn, or the tragic fact that Johnny, the character who is buried with his head to the west so that he may face the rising sun, left for England after shooting his two beloved dogs to follow Anne Mulvey, who was, in Mary's and Jamesie's words, only 'using him'.[7] But it is in such novels as *The Barracks*, *The Leavetaking*, *Amongst Women* and all the stories featuring the recurring character of Rose as the stepmother, that alienation between the sexes within marriage is foregrounded as a major theme that is skilfully conveyed by the inevitable chasm between men and women, an element which McGahern drew from his own life, but which he forcefully used as the objective correlative of what Jacques Lacan called the 'impossible sexual relationship'.[8] The French psychoanalyst would also argue that between men and women, '*ça ne marche pas*' (it doesn't work), claiming, '*il y a un mur*' (there is a wall) – playing on the French words *amour* (love) and *un mur* (a wall).[9]

In *The Barracks*, for instance, space is strictly gendered and split, as the writer lays stress on the 'barracks room' where the policemen spend their days, and sometimes their nights, and the rest of the house, which is left to the care of Elizabeth, a space she shares with the children and sometimes the other policemen's wives, until she has to withdraw into the bedroom, where she dies. The separation takes on a dramatic intensity in *The Leavetaking* where the protagonist as a child is shunted between his father's and mother's houses, which he is forced to leave when she is on the point of death. In those novels, McGahern describes marriage as a sort of imprisonment where, to paraphrase Jean-Paul Sartre, '*l'enfer, c'est les autres*' (hell is other people). Regarding what some of the critics have highlighted regarding McGahern's intellectual and aesthetic kinship with Beckett, we can pinpoint that living together as a couple is also what is partially at stake in *Endgame*, where much of Hamm and Clov's suffering is due to their forced companionship: 'If I could kill him I would die happy', says Clov,[10] while both characters interrogate the nature of the bond which keeps them together:

> 'You don't love me.'
> 'No.'
> 'You loved me once.'
> 'Once!'[11]

Likewise, Elizabeth and Reegan resent the enforced intimacy that marriage involves, as evidenced in the following description of Sergeant Reegan:

> He sat facing the fire again, beginning to feel how intimate he'd been with them since he came into the house tonight, his mind still hot after the clash with Quirke, and he wanted to be separate and alone again. The pain and frustration that the shame of intimacy brings started to nag him to desperation.[12]

Elizabeth feels just as cut off from her husband: 'She'd achieved no intimacy with Reegan' (*B*, 49), 'silence lay between them like a knife' (*B*, 111). The couple does experience some degree of sexual intimacy, but it remains no more than a passing moment of stealthy instinctual release, a defence against the anxieties which assuage them separately, Elizabeth about her illness, Reegan about his frustrations at work: 'They'd try to fall apart without noticing much wrench, and lie in the animal warmth and loving kindness of each other against the silence of the room with its door open to the phone or anyone knocking, the wild noises of the midwinter night outside' (*B*, 181).

In *Amongst Women*, McGahern provides another example of a marriage where pain, inflicted and endured, underlies and defines the relationship between husband and wife, where love is replaced by need. Rose and Moran's courtship is described in terms of a carefully planned pursuit on the part of Rose: 'He neither went towards her nor withdrew and she saw that it could not go on like that',[13] whereas Moran is all too ready to accept and take advantage of the sacrifice she makes of herself: 'He had reason to suspect that she had saved money and his life could glow again in the concentration of her attention', disclosing how Moran views marriage as a means of fulfilling his own needs rather than as an opening out to another person. The rest of the novel highlights the feeling of entrapment at the heart of their relationship, entirely based on a dialectics of domination and submission, a pattern repeated in the stories 'Wheels' and 'Gold Watch', which feature the same character of a tyrannical, angry, ageing father and his wife named Rose.

But marriage is only the social form of the inevitable failure of relationships between men and women as viewed by McGahern. In many of his stories and novels, the writer returns to the character of a young male protagonist in search of sexual satisfaction and who most of the time fails to obtain it or to transform it into a more durable relationship. The brevity of the short story form allows McGahern to emphasise the casualness of his protagonists' chance sexual encounters, as if the choice of an adequate partner did not really matter. In 'My Love, My Umbrella', a few remarks exchanged between the narrator and a woman he meets 'in front of the Scotch House', 'the afternoon of a Sunday', as 'the band was playing', are enough to make the narrator 'anxious for her body' (*CS*, 65). In 'Along the Edges' we are told that the characters 'met just after broken love affairs, and had drifted *casually* into going out together two or three evenings every week. They went to cinemas or dancehalls or restaurants, to the races at Leopardstown or the Park, making no demands on one another, sharing only one another's pleasures, making love together as on this night in his student's room (*CS*, 188, my emphasis). We find the same kind of scenario in 'Gold Watch': 'It was in Grafton Street we met, *aimlessly* strolling in one of the lazy lovely Saturday mornings in Spring' (*CS*, 210, my emphasis). The narrator of *The Leavetaking* for his part tries his luck in the city dancehalls, where he comes across one of those 'tall, dark-haired' girls who keep reappearing in McGahern's stories.[14] The Pornographer of course is also a frequent visitor to those same dancehalls where his path meets that of Josephine, whose name is hardly ever mentioned in the course of the novel, suggesting her lack of real importance as a partner, and whom he brings back to the same kind of room as those featuring in other stories, where the same 'light from a chianti bottle'[15] burns just like in *The Leavetaking* and the story 'Along the Edges'.[16] These chance encounters regularly lead to an impasse, as the narrator or protagonist balances between the illusion of love and the sense of freedom afforded by a break-up. In *The Leavetaking*, the narrator feels honour-bound to propose to the first girl he ever went out with: 'Maybe in three or four years we could be married' (*L*, 90); likewise, the narrator in 'My Love, My Umbrella' tentatively asks his partner: '*would* you think we *should ever* get married' (*CS*, 70, my emphasis). In both cases, the very syntax of the sentence expresses the young man's doubts about the relevance and suitability of the proposal. The protagonist in 'My Love, My Umbrella' immediately accounts for his request by what he calls 'longings and fears rather than any meanings' (*CS*, 70). Those very words 'longings and fears' draw our attention to the self-deception at play in the encounter. In fact, the narrator's request may not be meaningfully and consciously addressed to the actual woman standing in front of him, but perhaps more to a secret, inarticulate part of himself, in other words, to his unconscious.

Lacan would call the episode a manifestation of the young man's desire, which according to his theory, based upon the symbolic phallic function, is impossible to bring to a satisfying end. The subject of desire, according to Lacan, is 'barred', that is to say alienated from its natural needs, and doomed never to reach a satisfying conclusion. According to Adrian Johnston, in his entry on Jacques Lacan in the *Stanford Encyclopedia of Philosophy*,[17] an essential characteristic of desire is its restlessness, its ongoing agitated searching and futile striving. No object it gets its hands on is ever quite 'It'. Moreover, drawing on Freud's theories of drives, and especially the 'death-drive', first laid out in *Beyond the Pleasure Principle*, Lacan introduced the concept of *jouissance* or enjoyment, also lying 'beyond the pleasure principle'. Freud thought that all drives might be said to be death-drives, meaning that each and every drive works contrary to the pursuit of the pleasurable as balance, gratification or satisfaction. Freud accounted for the existence of the death-drive by the 'repetition compulsion', that is to say the unconscious, spontaneous compulsive repeating of that which is painful or traumatic. Lacan's concept of *jouissance* likewise refers to an overriding tendency to repeat experiences or events. What's more, the acquisition of language, by making the human a speaking subject, makes him lose access to the immediate, undiluted enjoyment or *jouissance* in its raw, unmitigated intensities, which can return only in the form of what might be labelled 'limit experience', namely, encounters with that which is annihilating, overwhelming, traumatic, or unbearable.

McGahern's protagonists exemplify the role of the death-drive insofar as they are prone to associate sex and death; in 'My Love, my Umbrella', a story closely studied by both Richard Robinson and Pascal Bataillard,[18] McGahern tellingly mingles sex, death and compulsive repetition in the same sentence: 'They say the continuance of sexuality is due to the penis having no memory, and mine *each evening* spilt its seed into the mud and *decomposing leaves* as if it was always for the first time' (*CS*, 68, my emphasis). Repetition has long since been described as one of McGahern's main stylistic and thematic features, whether it involves the recurrence of the same types of characters, settings, sometimes the almost entire word for word repetition of passages or texts, or the habits which make up much of the characters' daily lives. The phrase 'the penis having no memory' may also be read as related to what Lacan calls the negation of the phallic function in that the male organ is bound to meet a limit, '*le fait que le désir mâle rencontre sa propre chute*' (the fact that male desire is faced with its own collapse),[19] as also illustrated in this sentence from *The Pornographer*, describing the narrator's sensations during sexual intercourse:

> The *moment* is always the same and new, the instinct so strong it cancels memory. To lie still in the moment, in the very heart of the flesh, the place of beginning and end, to snatch it out of time, to move still in all stillness of flesh, to taste that trembling moment again, to hold it, to know *it*, *and* to *let it go*, the small bird that you held, its heart hammering in the cup of the hands, flown into the air (*P*, 57, my emphasis).

What is striking here is the idea of the transience, vulnerability, and irremediable loss attached to the sexual act, together with the incapacity to name the experience in any other way than as a 'moment', an 'it', which reminds us of the absolute alterity of what Lacan calls the Other, or what we cannot know of *jouissance*, that which lies beyond the pleasure principle.

The impossibility of fulfilling their desire leads McGahern's male characters to indulge in an intense fantasmatic activity. According to Lacan, fantasy is a basic scenario filling out the empty space of a fundamental impossibility, a screen masking the void opened up by the reality that '[t]here is no sexual relationship'. That is why, he argues, fantasy is, in the last resort, always a fantasy of the sexual relationship, a staging of it. Young Mahoney in *The Dark*, for example, spends more time fantasising his life than actually living it, as is evidenced by the masturbatory episodes, which played a central role in the banning of the book: 'One day she would come to me, a dream of flesh in woman, in frothing flimsiness of face, cold silk against my hands.'[20] In *The Leavetaking*, the violent emotions aroused by the narrative of the all too real traumatic death of the protagonist's mother – what's more, based on the writer's actual memories – clash with the fuzzy, unconvincing, lifeless rendering of Patrick's encounter with Isobel in Part II. Isobel, despite McGahern's efforts at rewriting this flawed second part, remains a creature of mere words, a flat, underdeveloped character, precisely like those vague, featureless, undetermined objects which appear in dreams and fantasies. McGahern's staging of Patrick and Isobel's romance is almost as stereotyped and artificial as the bad pornographic scenarios elaborated by Young Mahoney in *The Dark* or by the narrator of *The Pornographer*. Besides, the ending of *The Leavetaking* suggests the uncertainty hovering about the future of the relationship, reinforcing its fantastic aspect, as McGahern repeats such hypothetic formulae as 'Ah, love, let us be true to one another', or 'I *would* pray for the boat of our sleep to reach its morning' (*L*, 170–1, my emphasis). The role of fantasy in a young man's psychic life is almost the entire subject of *The Pornographer*, in which the artificial nature of the pornographic material written by the protagonist is duplicated by the unconvincing narrative of his allegedly 'real' relationship with Josephine, who has no more consistency as a character than Isobel in *The Leavetaking*. As in the previous novel, too, the mechanical aspect of this relationship, mostly based on sexual pleasure, clashes with the emotionally charged evocation of the protagonist's visits to his dying aunt. As a matter of fact, and as already noted, the sexual fantasies these protagonists indulge in are always contrasted with the traumatic loss of their mother or with an obsession with death.

Lacan tells us in this regard that sexuality is how mortality is transmitted, in the sense that the giving of life also entails the giving of death, the sexual act thus always being an act of subtraction. Nowhere is this notion more vividly conveyed by McGahern than in the episode of *The Leavetaking* where the narrator recalls how his father's visits to his mother caused the relapse of the disease which finally killed her: 'he felt that if he'd got her pregnant that neither the pleasure nor the darkness would pardon a birth and a death in one pang, the pang that now was so weak that it had never happened' (*L*, 65). The Pornographer walks through the hospital ward where his aunt is dying, thinking that 'it was like being in the middle of a maternity ward in the night, all those women waiting to give birth to their own death' (*P*, 175), and later reflects that 'the road away becomes the road back' (*P*, 203), a phrase which McGahern also places in the mind of dying Elizabeth in *The Barracks* (*B*, 158). This image of circularity between birth and death keeps reappearing in McGahern's writings, also formulated as 'In my end was my beginning' in *The Leavetaking* (*L*, 156), or through the quotation from Matthew Arnold, 'Begin and cease, and then again begin' (*L*, 169) in the same novel. All of these images point to the death-drive reaching out 'beyond the pleasure principle' and causing the compulsion of repetition, or the yearning for *jouissance* which remains unknown and unreachable.

Lacan's *jouissance* is what is lost forever and can return only in the guises of what might be labelled 'limit experiences', blind or self-destructive actions, such as the one Halliday in *The Barracks* seems to have been drawn to, driven by a quest for an absolute that only his death in a car crash – which was probably self-inflicted – could fulfil. Confronted by the prospect of her own death, Elizabeth is brought to remember Halliday as someone who 'changed her whole life' (*B*, 65), because he 'put her through the frightful mill of love' (*B*, 65). However, the nihilistic questions which led him to destruction – 'What the hell is all this living and dying about anyway, Elizabeth? That's what I'd like to be told' (*B*, 85) – are not her own, as she seems in touch with a different, yet unspeakable, kind of reality: 'She could live her life through in its mystery, without any purpose, except to watch and bear witness. She did not care. She was alive and being was her ridiculous glory as well as her pain' (*B*, 94).

Now this combination of 'mystery, glory and pain' seems to echo the parallel Lacan establishes between women and mystics as well as what he calls the 'other *jouissance*'. For Lacan, woman, unlike man, is not wholly submitted to the phallic function. In other words, she is 'not-whole' (*pas-toute*) and is open to 'another *jouissance*', which the unconscious can know nothing about, which cannot be expressed in any language. Lacan compares it to the experience of such mystics as St Teresa or St John of the Cross, who wrote, according to him, to tell about their experience, while knowing nothing about it, except that it set them on the path to what Lacan calls ex-sistence.[21]

According to Lacan, mystics yearn for an absolute which remains a void that cannot be covered by the signifier; likewise, all along the searing narrative of Elizabeth's confrontation with the absolute of death and a form of 'ex-sistence', she endlessly strives to put a name on what she experiences, as in the scene where she visits a church and stares at an inscription on a bench, literally unable to assign a meaning to the letters:

> But soon her mind was shifting, not able to stay long on any one thing, her eyes gazing now at the initials cut in the bench where she knelt, some of them covered with so much grime and soot that those who'd carved them there must be long dead, the single letters cut in the wood that lent themselves to so many interpretations having endured longer than the hands that carved them; and a little way from her right hand she noticed the white trade-plate:
>> 'Hearne & co.
>> Church Furnishers
>> Waterford' [...]
> Her mind was giving the same attention to this old bench as it had given to the mystery of the world and Christ. There were no answers. (*B*, 165)

Thus the interpretation of signs and the interpretation of the 'mystery of the world and Christ' are aligned in one sentence, translating Elizabeth's parallel inability to decipher the mystery of her own 'shifting mind' and validating Lacan's comparison between the unknowable, undecipherable, feminine *jouissance*, and the experience of mystics: 'Her life was under the unimaginable God or the equally unimaginable nothing' (*B*, 59). Elizabeth listens to the Rosary every night, feeling the beads in her fingers, where 'there was a relic of St Teresa of Avila enclosed in the carved crucifix' (*B*, 73). Now the statue of St Teresa by Bernini is precisely the starting point of Lacan's Seminar XX, entitled *Encore*, in which he discusses feminine *jouissance* and mystics, whose writings, he says, are 'the best you can read', thus linking the Other *jouissance* and poetic language.

Contrary to McGahern's male protagonists, who mask the impossibility of fulfilling their desire by elaborating stereotyped fantasies, verging on caricature in the case of *The Pornographer*, Elizabeth Reegan comes closest to the figure of the poet. As a matter of fact, she is in touch with an unreachable, unknowable reality, which McGahern nevertheless strives to express through a series of epiphanies, such as the feeling experienced by Elizabeth on Christmas Day: 'And the day so quickly sank once the meal was over, there had been so much excitement and preparation rising to surges of *ecstasy* that they could not pace it properly to its end' (*B*, 183, my emphasis), or when she attends the Easter ceremonies: '[...] and always the *ecstasy* of individual memories breaking like a blood-vessel, elevated out of the accidental moment of their happening, and reflected eternally in the mirror of this way' (*B*, 195). Or again when she is overwhelmed by a crowd of memories and she tries to write them down on paper to send to a friend: 'And one fantastic afternoon at the end of January she went, *ecstatic* with remembrance, to the sideboard and got a pen and ink and paper to write to a friend of those days, a nurse with her in The London Hospital' (*B*, 187). Elizabeth then tries to find the proper words to express her feelings, but she keeps erasing what she has written, fearful that her friend might only see in her words 'sheer inarticulacy with a faint touch of *craziness*' (*B*, 187, my emphasis), a scene which clearly marks her out as a poet figure, but also combines qualities of inarticulacy and craziness often associated with the mystics, as they attempt to speak about a *jouissance* which remains unspeakable. In her disarray, Elizabeth does find a kind of solace and appeasement in moments when she gets in touch with a kind of 'love' which is both undefinable and unknowable, but that she is nevertheless able to experience:

> ... she'd be consumed at last into *whatever meaning* her life had. Here she had *none*, none but to be, which in acceptance must be surely to *love*. There'd be *no searching for meaning*, she must surely grow into meaning as she grew to love, there was that or nothing and she couldn't lose. She could make no statement other than that here, she had no right, she was only waiting and *she could not say or know more*. (*B*, 211, my emphasis)

In writing those lines, and through the character of Elizabeth, McGahern as a writer and a poet faced up to the call of the 'other *jouissance*', unreachable, unspeakable, but which he tried nevertheless to describe because, like his poet-like female protagonist, he may have felt in touch with an absolute lying beyond the pleasure principle. This was suggested in his essay 'The Image' when he claimed to be straining towards 'the one image that will never come'. In this phrase, the 'one' is evocative of singularity, wholesomeness, uniqueness, completeness, from which the split subject produced by the entrance into the symbolic order and language – the fact of being born – is forever separated, and that looms beyond the pleasure principle, and keeps our desire endlessly searching for the proper object. Julia Kristeva, working on Lacan's premise of the split speaking subject, tried to define poetic language as precisely that which resists the entrance into the symbolic or phallic order. She posited that 'there is [within poetic language] a *heterogeneousness* to meaning and signification [...] which operates through, despite, and in excess of signification and produces [...] "musical" but also nonsense effects'.[22] The word 'semiotic', which she used, means, according to the Greek etymology, 'a distinctive mark, trace, index, the premonitory sign, the proof, engraved mark, imprint – in short, a distinctiveness admitting of an uncertain and indeterminable articulation because it does not yet refer [...] to a signified object'.[23] Kristeva further argued that to the cleavage, discovered by Ferdinand de Saussure, between the signifier and the signified should be added another cleavage between the semiotic and the symbolic, between poetic language – associated with the maternal – and rational language – associated with the paternal. Any signifying practice, Kristeva claims, associates both forms of language; but in poetic language, she adds, the semiotic 'tends to gain the upper hand at the expense of the [...] predicative constraints of the ego's judging consciousness'.[24]

That definition of poetic language is helpful in analysing McGahern's type of writing, which combines indeterminacy of identities, disconnectedness in narration, discontinuity in story-time, looseness of plot structure and the absence of any clear meaning, all of which can be related to Kristeva's definition of the semiotic activity as an element 'introducing wandering or fuzziness into language and *a fortiori* into poetic language'.[25] His novels and stories are full of short, juxtaposed sentences, through which the writer seems to try and recover fragments of impressions and memories rather than provide the reader with any in-depth analysis of the narrator's feelings, as was the case down to his last book, *Memoir*:

My mother's bicycle was lifted on to the lorry with my small bicycle. The iron beds were left last. The joints had rusted in the dampness and the sections would not come apart. Bicycle oil and brute strength were tried. Neither worked. A hammer was found. They started to beat the sections apart.[26]

We can find no plot as such in McGahern's novels, the flow of narrative instead being more or less based upon the unfolding of the characters' lives, and often, as is the case in *The Barracks* or *That They May Face the Rising Sun*, on the cycle of the seasons, to the point that the books can be read more like chronicles than actual novels. Moreover, with each new novel McGahern tended to play more and more with anachronies, or a disregard for the logical chronology of events. A certain indeterminacy characterises his writings. The first cause of this indeterminacy is the play on personal pronouns meant to designate the enunciators of the utterances, as analysed by Stanley van der Ziel in relation to *The Dark*,[27] creating an instability of the narrating agency which mirrors the protagonist's floating, still undefined identity, as is repeatedly suggested by the protagonist's calling himself 'a drifter'. The 'you' narrator doesn't seem to allow himself to claim himself as an autonomous subject able to say 'I'; in this regard, McGahern's stylistic choice can be said to match what Kristeva calls 'the unsettled and questionable subject of poetic language'.

What's more, Kristeva's view of semiotic language as being attached to the maternal brings us back to McGahern's split world between men and women and to Elizabeth Reegan as the central figure of the artist in the writer's oeuvre. On the one hand, the character of Elizabeth is believed to have been based on McGahern's own mother Susan, insofar as she lives a secluded life in a remote village married to an uncouth, self-centred policeman – rendered all the more difficult because of her literary sensibility and culture – and then dies prematurely of cancer. On the other hand, the reading of *Memoir* teaches us that Susan McGahern was very different from the character of Elizabeth, if only because she was very religious and wished her son to become a priest, whereas McGahern shaped Elizabeth's anguished agnosticism to match his own. That identification allows us to suggest that Elizabeth encapsulates both a projection of the writer's own preoccupations and a re-creation of the beloved maternal figure. The superimposition of the maternal – what has been lost forever – with the figure of the artist might be the way McGahern finally managed to transcend the unbridgeable gap between male and female as described above, insofar as poetic language, according to Kristeva's theory of the semiotic – which the French psychoanalyst and literary critic applied to studies of Stéphane Mallarmé, Antonin Artaud, Marcel Proust or Louis-Ferdinand Céline – identifies not precisely as feminine, but associates with the memory of the mother's body. McGahern defined writing as 'the instinctive movement of the vision as it comes to life', a means for him to return to that unconscious state which preceded our entrance into the symbolic order, to recover the rhythms, the sounds, and other impressions attached to that time which preceded 'this bewilderment between our beginning and our end' (*P*, 13). For McGahern, art was an attempt to repeat, to recover, to remember, what was taken from us forever; art was 'an attempt to create a world in which we can live'.[28]

Chapter 4

—

Evening in Cootehall: Reading John McGahern's Late Style

—

Eamonn Wall

Writing in *Outstaring Nature's Eye* in 1993, the first book-length study of his work, Denis Sampson noted that 'John McGahern's fiction has had a large and loyal audience for thirty years, yet the critical reputation of Ireland's most important contemporary novelist remains enigmatic'.[1] Today, more than a decade after his death, McGahern's work continues to enjoy both a loyal and growing readership. The quality of the prose he has left assures us that his legacy is resistant to changes in taste and fashion while his subject matter, rooted in the local and the universal, in tradition and in revising and resisting tradition, in the many-sidedness of the human condition, continues to hold our attention and influence how we read fiction and view our world: 'Like other regional writers, he made it his aim to go deeper into the soil of personal experience so that it is distilled by poetic reception until it assumes mythic patterns.'[2] To identify McGahern as a regional writer is not to make a pejorative judgement on his work; on the contrary, it is to place it beside the fictions created by other regional writers such as Willa Cather and Alice Munro, both renowned authors who have created mythic worlds from within limited geographical spaces. We are fortunate that in the more than two decades since Denis Sampson published his study, many other scholars have dedicated their talents to exploring John McGahern's work and it is no longer possible to believe that his critical reputation remains enigmatic. His later work in particular, with its intense focus on society in its moments of transformation, engages with themes and concerns that continue to be deeply felt and contentious. Edward W. Said has noted of Constantine Cavafy's verse that 'the poem reveals and consecrates the moment before history closes around it and it is lost to us forever', and this is equally the case with McGahern's work, the later fiction in particular.[3]

A few summers ago, I passed a few hours in Cootehall, County Roscommon, and not for the first time. My brother and his family live nearby and over the years, having been a long-time admirer of McGahern's work, I've taken advantage of opportunities to visit places associated with his novels, stories and non-fiction, seeking to absorb some more of his place lore and to cross-reference walked space against its imaginative equivalent. It was as a result of reading McGahern that I first became aware of Cootehall, Ardcarne, Oakport and other locations of his work. Had I not read *The Barracks*, *Amongst Women* and *That They May Face the Rising Sun*, I would have had neither the impetus nor the inclination to explore these settings. In like spirit years ago while living in Nebraska, I had made a literary pilgrimage to Red Cloud, Willa Cather's hometown and the location of the Willa Cather Foundation and Visitor Center where, in addition to books written by and about Cather, one can purchase Cather coasters, buttons and mugs.[4] Wandering through Cootehall, peering through the windows of the old barracks, sitting under a tree to look out across the water was a rare privilege on a lovely warm evening. Even though I was in a place that is central to McGahern's life and work, I was also very much aware that, beyond the setting, I was outside of things. I did not know anybody – even the names I was able to recall had been retrieved from McGahern's fictions: Reegan, Moran, Guard Casey, Kirkwood, Lavin and a host of others. Furthermore, I was an outlier on the John McGahern tourist trail, an idea that might have amused or horrified the retiring and private author. At present, unlike the splendid space created in Cather's honour in Red Cloud, there is no McGahern Centre in Cootehall though plans are afoot and fundraising has begun for the creation of a John McGahern Reading Room that will be the centrepiece of the refurbished barracks.[5] Another group has proposed building a County Leitrim Interpretative Centre in honour of John McGahern in Mohill, already the site of the John McGahern Library, housed at the up-market Lough Rynn Castle Hotel.[6] Also significant is the growing body of scholarship that has been inspired by McGahern's fiction and which, I would argue, is of greater importance than brick and mortar memorials. From Denis Sampson's first study to Stanley van der Ziel's and Richard Robinson's recent output, through the work of Eamon Maher, Frank Shovlin and Dermot McCarthy, we can count a growing number of monographs on the subject of McGahern's writing. In addition, the many articles and reviews of his work published by a distinguished international cast of authors from Seamus Deane, Seamus Heaney, Declan Kiberd and

John Banville, to John Updike, Jonathan Raban and Belinda McKeon, allow us to understand more deeply the complexity of his work and the originality of his vision. An astonishing addition to the complex blending of people, time and place in McGahern's fiction is Pat Collins' 2005 documentary *John McGahern: a private world*, that serves, in part, as a companion piece to *Memoir*, but also as an absorbing backward look at the life of the artist.[7]

Great changes have altered Cootehall's shape in the decade since McGahern's death as a result of the frenzied construction of new homes in the village during the Celtic Tiger period. Interviewed by Shashank Bengali, Dymphna O'Regan, a former classmate of McGahern's who now runs one of the village's two pubs, noted that 'it's a good thing that he's not here anymore to see it because he would just be absolutely horrified at what has happened'.[8] After the 2008 economic collapse, a large development in the village languished as a 'ghost estate'. Geographer Rob Kitchin told Bengali that 'if McGahern could see some of those fields now, he'd be spinning in his grave'.[9] When one imagines contemporary Cootehall, one cannot avoid Eóin Flannery's term for the literature related to such places: 'the poetics of ruination'.[10] Of course, ruination is a guiding theme of McGahern's early novels *The Barracks* and *The Dark*, though in these fictions the focus is on body and spirit rather than on the environment. Cootehall, in common with other locations that we associate with literary figures, has been partially overlaid by modernisation, with the result that it is no longer the same village that McGahern knew, or that he wrote about. Of course, the world that McGahern presented reached for believability rather than veracity. As he noted, 'Among its many obligations fiction always has to be believable. Life does not have to suffer such constraints, and much of what takes place is believable only because it happens. The god of life is accident. Fiction has to be true to a central idea or vision of life.'[11] The Cootehall of McGahern's youth is overlaid with the mature author's fictional representation of it. In 'Sailing to Byzantium', Yeats fixed the author and art in an 'artifice of eternity'.[12] Though his work endures, McGahern's more temporal landscape fades as a consequence of its dilution by development. Yeats', on the other hand, is fastened to immortal art and is resistant to development. But as Sampson declares of the author, 'The Leitrim–Roscommon world he has invented is the anchor of his imagination, to which he always returns, because, as he has said, it is real. "One inherits one's place, just as one inherits one's accent, one's language. What's interesting after that is that one belongs to humankind."'[13] As admirers of McGahern's work, we enjoy on visits to Cootehall, Mohill, Carrick-on-Shannon and other places our brief moments of habitation in the spaces where McGahern's imagination took root. At the same time, these visits are enjoyed at a remove from a world reinvented for fiction, and they occur in another temporal space. The Cootehall of McGahern's fiction is the imaginative terrain the author has invented from the raw space of life experience and there is no need for the two to be made tightly congruent. As readers visiting Cootehall, who quickly become aware of how places are altered both by the passage of time and by the hands of developers, we accept the disjunction between the village of McGahern's work and its present state because we cannot do otherwise. At the same time, trusting McGahern's integrity, lured by the grace of his prose, and guided by his narrative gifts, we accept his deep representation and his fictional truth of time and place.

If violent ruination is a feature of McGahern's early fiction, inexorable change and transformation, for better or worse, is a guiding concern of his later work. As outsiders or visitors, we are not privileged to enjoy extended contact with local people; therefore, McGahern's finely drawn characters, because they are so believable, are easily substituted. One night, Moran in 'High Ground' passes Ryan's Bar and hears the voices of after-hours drinkers engaged in conversation:

> I walked quickly, swinging the bucket. The whole village seemed dead under a benign moon, but as I passed along the church wall I heard voices. They came from Ryan's Bar. It was shut, the blinds down, but then I noticed cracks of yellow light along the edges of the big blue blind. They were drinking after hours. I paused to see if I could recognise any of the voices, but before I had time Charlie Ryan hissed, 'Will you keep your voices down, will yous? At the rate you're going you'll soon have the Sergeant out of his bed,' and the voices quietened to a whisper. Afraid of being noticed in the silence, I passed on to get the bucket of spring water from the well, but the voices were in full song again by the time I returned. I let the bucket softly down in the dust and stood in the shadow of the church wall to listen. I recognised the Master's slurred voice at once, and then voices of some of the men who worked the sawmill in the wood.[14]

Like Moran, I walked through Cootehall and listened in. The story's protagonist, a young native who has returned home from university, is, like me, something of an outsider as a result of his academic success. Senator Reegan, a local politician, hopes to recruit Moran to take over the master's position as the principal of the local school, an effort that horrifies him. Like Moran, readers stand outside the pub to catch the drift of conversation inside to better understand the larger narrative it belongs to. McGahern too listened in and crafted fiction from fragments of speech overheard and from observations of lives briefly witnessed, seeking to give it life before history enclosed it. Though readers, myself included, will be drawn to those places where McGahern lived and worked, we should resist too close an alignment between biography and art, as is underlined by van der Ziel, who nevertheless accepts that many events described in McGahern's fiction rely on memories of lived experience. However, such a reading of his fiction 'finally tells us very little about the way in which those raw experiences were transformed into great and universal works of art'.[15] An irony posed by *Memoir* and *John McGahern: a private world* is how intertwined lived experience and imagined art are in his work and how subtle and nuanced the various displacements are. At the same time, what George Seferis noted of Cavafy, another author whose work is rooted in lived experience – 'outside his poetry Cavafy does not exist' – can be equally applied to McGahern.[16] Nevertheless, and to complicate matters, one is constantly reminded while visiting Cootehall, Aughawillan and other places in this part of Ireland of being in locations that McGahern thought about, wrote about, and lived in; in short, one is in what could be described as 'McGahern Country'.

My particular focus in this essay is on McGahern's later work, from *High Ground* onward, and my wish is to examine it in relation to what others have observed on the subject of late style, Edward W. Said and Katie Roiphe in particular. Said is interested in exploring late style while Roiphe, working within a narrower framework, engages with final style. Said has defined late style as follows: 'Each of us can readily supply evidence of how it is that late works crown a lifetime of aesthetic endeavor. Rembrandt and Matisse, Bach and Wagner. But what of artistic lateness not as harmony and resolution, but as intransigence, difficulty and unresolved contradiction?'[17] Roiphe's study, in its form a bringing together of narrative and traditional scholarship, blends autobiography with an interest in 'writers and artists who are especially sensitive or attuned to death … who can put the confrontation with mortality into words – and in one case images – in a way that most of us can't or won't'.[18] In relation to McGahern's work, Denis Sampson points out that it is 'an organic whole' that through the decades grew in sophistication, refinement and effect.[19] The organic nature of McGahern's fiction, its subtle though powerful process of development, is guided by how he read the work of others, as is clear in the essays collected in *Love of the World*, as well as by the practice of composition. Sampson's view is supported by van der Ziel's recent *John McGahern and the Imagination of Tradition* and by Eamon Maher's astute reading of McGahern's later work in *John McGahern: from the local to the universal*. As Maher reminds us, McGahern's late and final phases are also 'the swansong of a disappearing civilisation, of the rural Ireland in which he grew up, where he now lives and which provides the backdrop to his best fiction'.[20] In an interview with Maher, McGahern, elegantly and by use of wise understatement, captures something of an older human's sense of time and place when he states that 'we are part of nature, like the animals and the trees, and we are all part of that passing world we learn to love and to leave'.[21] In contrast, a quote that Roiphe culled from Sherwin Nuland's *How We Die* indicates how modern death can be sanitised: 'Modern dying takes place in the modern hospital, where it can be hidden, cleansed of its organic blight, and finally packaged for modern burial. We can now deny the power of not only death but of nature itself.'[22] In his conversation with Eamon Maher, as well as in that great late short story 'The Country Funeral', the final piece of *Creatures of the Earth: new and selected stories*, and in the tender and evocative treatment of the preparation of Johnny's body for burial in *That They May Face the Rising Sun*, we witness McGahern's firm embrace of death as an event belonging to nature. The formal shape of *That They May Face the Rising Sun* is natural and organic in how it is guided by the shifting of seasons and by the movements of humans. As McGahern's time on earth narrows, his embrace of it expands. The closer he comes to being absorbed into the earth physically, the more all that is natural and organic underlines his aesthetic. A balance between the artist, his art and the world is achieved.

In his explorations of late style, Said is less interested in tracing specific literary and musical works that crown lifetimes of achievement than those that resist closure and resolution, in part because in his own life – as a Palestinian exile who was ill while writing his own late work – such national and political desires were unachievable. Among the authors and works that Said favours are Theodor Adorno, from whom he borrows the 'late style' term; Lampedusa's *The Leopard* and Visconti's film version of that novel; Euripides; and Constantine Cavafy. If McGahern has a late style, an argument can be made that it begins with the publication of 'Gold Watch' in *The New Yorker* in April 1980 – it is collected in the American edition of *Getting Through* and in the Faber edition of *High Ground*, a work revealing the ingenuity, depth and quiet passion of his last phase. It was also in 1980 that McGahern declined Brian Friel's invitation to be part of the Field Day enterprise and which heralded a change in his work. This is how Stanley van der Ziel explains it: 'In his fifties, McGahern became increasingly attracted to the gentler neoclassical values of other eighteenth-century authors such as Austen, Goldsmith, Locke and Hume. Over the decades that followed, he found himself drawn to forms of pastoral nostalgia that had been previously unavailable to this work.'[23] He declined an opportunity to play a part in a new literary and cultural adventure in favour of retiring more deeply from the distraction of public life to rework his fiction, while at the same time remaining alert to what transpired in the public sphere. From rural Leitrim, McGahern explored ordinary and heroic lives in the manner of Cavafy's 'Byzantine Noble, in Exile, Versifying':

But since I've been exiled here (curse that spiteful
Irene Ducas) and am frightfully bored,
it's not at all unseemly if I divert myself
by crafting verses of six or seven lines –
divert myself with mythological tales
of Hermes, and Apollo, and Dionysus,
or the heroes of Thessaly and the Peloponnese;
or with composing strict iambic lines
such as – if I do say so – the litterateurs
of Constantinople don't know how to write.[24]

Though Denis Sampson points out that McGahern's style is organic, he also observes 'a coherence of preoccupation and style' from *High Ground* onwards.[25] An alternative late style, or what Roiphe might call a writer's last or final phrase, comprises *That They May Face the Rising Sun* (2002) and the final four stories gathered in *Creatures of the Earth: new and selected stories* (2006), works that reveal a growing ecological awareness on McGahern's part. If we isolate *Memoir* as a work of McGahern's final phase, Roiphe's work can be a useful guide. The writers she has chosen to focus on, all writing towards the end of their lives – Freud, Updike, Sendak, Sontag, Thomas and Salter – are authors who, in their work, 'are especially sensitive or attuned to death, who have worked through the problem of death in their art, in their letters, in their love affairs, in their dreams'.[26] From *The Barracks* onwards, death is an obsessive presence in McGahern's fiction. Though none of these theories will authoritatively decode McGahern's later work, they do offer us new ways of contextualising it and find some deep echoes in how Stanley van der Ziel reads his work from the final phase of his career, *Memoir* in particular. For van der Ziel, McGahern's final phase is underlined by an intense attention to the minutiae of everyday life that allows the quotidian to reveal something of the essence of the great mystery that is life itself.[27] Van der Ziel, writing a decade after McGahern's death, is aided both by having the whole of McGahern's oeuvre at his disposal, and by the passage of time. *Memoir* was written from a life point similar to that of the final works of the authors that Roiphe explores. As far as Said's ideas of 'intransigence, difficulty and unresolved contradiction' as aspects of late style are concerned, one will hardly find a greater example of this than Moran in *Amongst Women*, though here, in contrast with what Said has noted, these matters concern the character rather than the author, though they are also of concern to the author. The Moran of this novel is an embodiment of national and personal irresolution and contradiction. If anything, old age has sharpened rather than blunted his edges:

> 'Don't you remember the day it is? Monaghan Day! The day when McQuaid always used to come from the fair in Mohill and we had to make the big tea.'
> 'What's that got to do with anything?' Just as he resented gifts he resented any dredging up of the past. He demanded that the continuing present he felt his life to be should not be shadowed or challenged.[28]

To Moran, slights absorbed in young adulthood morph into destructive life-guiding truths.

Having been shunted to one side after serving honourably in the War of Independence, he carries with him a hatred of the new order that emerged to rule Ireland in the wake or the Anglo-Irish Treaty. In old age, Moran prefers the possibilities inherent in the living present to more abstract and unrealistic ideas of closure that promise only the silence of death. Yeats and McGahern, who pushed their work in new directions late in their careers, resisted closure, as it promised stagnation – a form of literary death – rather than innovation. At this point, it should be noted that Said's idea of late style is not universally embraced, as Ben Hutchinson has pointed out: 'Yet the most important single undertaking of the disciple of lateness studies as it has emerged over the past ten years has been to debunk this universalizing myth of late style – to show, indeed, that there is no such thing, only innumerable late styles, a plurality of creative and critical constructs.'[29] Said's and Roiphe's versions of this process, separate though related, are among two possibilities present among others. Perhaps Eamon Maher would provide an alternative evaluation, seeing McGahern's career beginning with 'a minor classic, *The Barracks*', and proceeding through various phases to *Amongst Women* and *That They May Face the Rising Sun*, the works of McGahern's maturity.[30] All McGahern scholars have noted a studied and organic development through the decades.

Said's hero, Theodor W. Adorno, and McGahern share much. By living in Leitrim at a remove from first-hand interpersonal literary activity McGahern resisted the *zeitgeist* that Adorno loathed, one that changed in his lifetime from the pub-centred version that is satirised in 'Bank Holiday' and 'Parachutes', to a more multimedia-driven version of the present. Both *Amongst Women* and *That They May Face the Rising Sun* are crafted in like manner to what Said observes of Lampedusa's *The Leopard*: 'Its major technical innovation is that the narrative is composed discontinuously, as a series of relatively discreet but highly wrought fragments or episodes, each organized around a date and in some instances an event ….'[31] Late style, as Said views it, involves the author in a debate with form, not just traditional form but also with the author's own developed ideas of formal order. McGahern's attitude to this idea is complex: the form of the late work does change to something more organic while, at the same time, 'tact, manners, and reason', other kinds of form as Stanley van der Ziel reminds us, become more vital to his artistic purpose.[32] What Said notes of Euripides' late work can also be applied to McGahern's in how early and late period work might be read: 'Partly because of his relative lateness, Euripides uses his plays to repeat, reinterpret, return to, and revise his somewhat familiar material' – a dynamic that underlines *Memoir*.[33] The material of *Memoir* will be familiar to readers of *The Barracks* though it is very different in style, genre and voice to the earlier work as it was composed at a later stage in the author's development. What is invisible perhaps is how literary this material is, how events from the past become blended with what the author has read, as van der Ziel shows.[34] Of course, McGahern's own appreciation of the Goldsmith poem will have developed and changed through his own lifetime from young schoolboy to mature author. Said views

Euripides as 'a poet of sadism', a term that might be applied to McGahern's portrait of Moran in *Amongst Women*.[35] In *The Bacchae*, 'Dionysus … is perfectly prepared to go on playing with, harassing, and finally destroying the mortals who have slighted (but not seriously wronged) him',[36] in much the same manner as Moran is driven to physically assault his sons, Luke and Michael, and emotionally and psychologically violate Rose, his second wife, in *Amongst Women*:

> Rose poured him his tea. The table was covered with a spotless cloth. As he ate and drank she found herself chattering away to him out of nervousness, a stream of things that went through her head, the small happenings of the day. She talked out of confusions: fear, insecurity, love. Her instinct told her she should not be talking but she could not stop. He made several brusque, impatient movements at the table but still she could not stop. Then he turned round the chair in a fit of hatred. The children were listening though they kept their eyes intently fixed on their school books.
>
> 'Did you ever listen carefully to yourself, Rose?' he said. 'If you listened a bit more carefully to yourself I think you might talk a lot less.'[37]

For Moran, to inflict pain is to be powerfully alive and to warrant attention. Perhaps he does not intend to be a sadist or does not even enjoy inflicting pain, but sadistic violence is for sure a way for him, and for many other of McGahern's male characters, to assert masculinity and control. Moran and others, shunted to one side after independence by the leaders of the new state they had helped found, and wounded in this process, will exert tight and rigid control over the little family republics they lead. McGahern reminds us that rage and disappointment – that become values to men like Moran – are ill-suited to fostering family harmony. In *Amongst Women*, Moran concludes that the new state has been failed by its leadership; likewise, his own work as a family leader fails to the extent that none of his children have settled near Great Meadow, the family home. Violence allows Moran to control his family though his work is undone by the passage of time, which takes his children away from him and out into the world. Rose, who had been out in the world, and bargained with herself to return, remains with Moran.

All commentators agree on the importance that certain writers have played – Flaubert and Joyce among others – in influencing McGahern and helping him develop his craft. It is clear that age in no way hindered this development, as he seemed as eager to learn in maturity to the same extent as the young author Denis Sampson has traced. Let me illustrate how I understand this by means of an anecdote. In 1990 I had an opportunity to interview Brian Moore, an author whose work I had admired since my teens. After spending a couple of hours in his presence and enjoying the experience greatly, I typed my notes and compared what he had said to me to what he had revealed to others who had interviewed him down through the decades. In hindsight, I understood the degree to which Moore's remarks to me had been rehearsed over many years and I began to read his late novels in the same way – as works written from inside a comfort zone. McGahern, on the other hand, continued to develop, to move outside of that warm space he was familiar with. It is true that McGahern reprised material over his career as an author; however, from *The Barracks* to *Memoir* one notes reinvention rather than repetition. An important late influence is Alistair MacLeod in whose work McGahern saw, I believe, a world much like his own, as Declan Kiberd has identified:

> Precisely because his reviews were occasional, there is an elegiac quality, a sense of sadness in shutting not just the book but a window on a world which may never be seen again …. The long lingering titles favoured by MacLeod – 'As Birds Bring Forth the Sun', 'The Closing Down of Summer' – seem to be echoed in that given by McGahern to his last work of pure fiction *That They May Face the Rising Sun*. It is based, like MacLeod's laments for the ebbing rituals of the Maritimes in Canada, on the notion that a tradition may live on in the very lament for its passing, and that the account of the dying of a code will invariably become the central narrative of the world which takes its place.[38]

Both McGahern and MacLeod, to borrow Eamon Maher's comment on McGahern's work, 'build up a picture of a civilisation that will soon have disappeared'.[39] The grandmother, for example, in MacLeod's 'The Road to Rankin's Point' is the last of her family to work this remote piece of land in Cape Breton, Nova Scotia. Likewise, in 'Gold Watch' and *Amongst Women*, the young have left the rural west for better-paying jobs and deeper social lives in Dublin and England. Though the worlds of these men and women are disappearing, what has been lost has been encoded into what will replace them at the intersection of history and memory, as Kiberd points out. Also, from MacLeod, McGahern has developed a sharper ecological consciousness that allows him in his late stories and in *That They May Face the Rising Sun* to view the world less anthropologically: non-human life garners new respect. Here is McGahern writing in praise of MacLeod's work:

> MacLeod's careful work never appears to stray outside what quickens it, and his uniqueness is present in every weighted sentence and the smallest of gestures. He writes about people and a way of life on Cape Breton, Nova Scotia, that has continued relatively unchanged for several generations, since the first settlers went there from Scotland at the time of the Clearances. They work as fishermen, miners, smallholders, loggers, lighthouse keepers, migrant workers. They live in a dramatically beautiful setting provided mostly by nature and hostile to much human endeavor. Animals too have their own place within this proud and fragile interdependence and are part of a fierce and unsentimental tribal affection. The poetic, the religious and the superstitious instincts are always close. As we come to know this world, it is poised on the edge of extinction, like the bald eagles MacLeod writes about so well.[40]

That They May Face the Rising Sun makes much of the troika McGahern locates in MacLeod's short stories: 'the poetic, the religious and the superstitious'. I do not intend to denigrate Brian Moore's achievement – I value his work more than ever – but to note that it stalled rather than developed in his own late phase, unlike McGahern's, which continued to grow. Moore used many settings in his late work while McGahern remained rooted mostly in a single locality where formal manoeuvre was not easy, though he did achieve it. Perhaps, McGahern is like the Yaghans Bruce Chatwin describes in *In Patagonia*, who 'were born wanderers though they rarely wandered far'.[41] Yeats and McGahern enjoy important late phases while Moore does not; at the same time, Ralph Ellison enjoys no late phase, but who complains because we have *Invisible Man* to savour? Brian Moore, from *The Lonely Passion of Judith Hearne* to *Black Robe*, has left us with many classic works. Katie Roiphe records an observation that James Salter makes in *Burning the Days*, his memoir, that 'life passes into pages if it passes into anything', a pithy phrase that registers profoundly with what McGahern recorded in his prose, in the interplay of memoir and fiction that underlines his work in various genres, and in how he absorbed the work of others, recording their influence in fiction and essays.[42]

Illness does not deter writers from their work. Susan Sontag noted that writers can get 'terrific energies from facing them in an active and conscious way', and that for her, 'writing is a way of paying as much attention as possible'.[43] Stanley van der Ziel finds a similar impulse in McGahern's work: 'One of the perennial obsessions of McGahern's writing was with meticulously recording the small things which many people only begin to notice when they are close to death. He may only finally have come to articulate this truth clearly and concisely in ... *Memoir*.'[44] In *Amongst Women*, Moran articulates this as follows: 'He had never realised when he was in the midst of confident life what an amazing glory he was part of.'[45] Van der Ziel finds a heightened sense of attentiveness present in *Memoir*, McGahern's last work.[46]

To date, because it is still somewhat in its infancy, McGahern criticism is often entwined in what the author has noted in interviews and written in essays and reviews. How he answered Denis Sampson's and Eamon Maher's questions, for example, has led scholars to probe the roles played by Austen, Joyce, Proust and others in the formation of McGahern's aesthetic. The gathering of his essays into *Love of the World* by Stanley van der Ziel brings McGahern's thoughts on writers and writing into sharp focus, with such pieces as 'The Image', 'The Solitary Reader' and 'An tOileánach/The Islandman' being frequently cited as revelatory. From the work already undertaken, we are developing a clear idea of what McGahern sought as a writer, the matters he prioritised as being important, and how he saw himself within literary tradition.

Though I do not wish to overemphasise the sources that underline my own commentary, I do believe that what Said offers in *On Late Style: music and literature against the grain* and what Roiphe presents in *The Violet Hour: great writers at the end* provide us with some new ways of seeing McGahern's work, particularly those novels and stories crafted later in his career – notwithstanding that McGahern is such a singular literary artist that neither Said's nor Roiphe's theories may match his work in quite the same way that they do the work of others. Said has noted of Palestinians that 'we are the people of message and signals, of allusions and indirect expression',[47] a people who engage with the world in ways reminiscent of those favoured at Great Meadow and by, as Eamon Maher has so nicely phrased it, 'The Lake People' of *That They May Face the Rising Sun*.[48] Said's exploration of Lampedusa's *The Leopard* opens up the temptation to consider the prince and Moran of *Amongst Women* as twins. One finds too in his discussion of Cavafy, the great poet of a disappearing Greek

Alexandria, an outlook that registers with McGahern's: '… in Cavafy, then, the future does not occur, or if it does, it has in a sense already happened. Better the internalized narrow world of limited expectations than that of grandiose projects constantly betrayed or traduced.'[49] In *Amongst Women* such a mode of thinking, though more convoluted because it involves Moran, guides his decision to discourage Sheila from studying medicine in university in favour of a safe position as a civil servant in the Department of Finance, a 'narrow world of limited expectations'.[50] At the same time, important differences can be traced between the communities presented by both writers. The Greek community of Alexandria, like the Turkish community of Salonika, has been largely erased. The Irish communities traced so lovingly by McGahern in *High Ground*, *Amongst Women* and *That They May Face the Rising Sun* have been replaced and renewed rather than erased. McGahern, in his often searing portraits of hard and brutal characters, makes it clear that some aspects of life in postcolonial Ireland are best seen through the rear-view mirror of a car moving at high speed. In these works we observe that a particular era is passing, or as Declan Kiberd phrases it in relation to *Amongst Women*, that the novel is 'the essential chronicle of a whole phase of our nation's life'.[51] The phase ends while the nation continues. In present time, our visits to these corners of Ireland that appear in McGahern's work reveal to us, as we pass through, much in the way of industry, family life, writing – things of the human spirit – that serve as reminders that communities, often under stress, continue to grow and thrive just as McGahern's did during his time. Unlike the reality that MacLeod reveals in 'The Road to Rankin's Point', when the narrator grieves that 'for the first time in centuries since the Scottish emigrations there is no human life at the end of this dark road', Irish communities survive.[52] The organic process is not interrupted, and it guides both communities and its writers. And writing continues to emerge and develop – think of Kevin Barry's work that covers some of the same physical landscape as McGahern's.

McGahern wrote of his world. Like Miłosz, I think that at some level he saw the audience for his work dealing with past and present would probably be found sometime in the future. Of the authors that Roiphe writes about, John Updike, who wrote admiringly of McGahern's work, is his closest twin, with Moran and Angstrom of the Rabbit novels being two sides of the one coin, perhaps.

As we enlarge the context in which we discuss McGahern's work, the measure of his achievement only increases as it becomes more relevant and complex. Both McGahern and Said were exiles – the former from the space that disappeared when his mother died and the latter from his Palestinian homeland – and both authors wrote their final books while living under threat of grave illness. Said notes that late style 'has the power to render disenchantment and pleasure without resolving the contradiction between them. What holds them is tension, as equal forces straining in opposite directions, is the artist's mature subjectivity, stripped of hubris and pomposity, unashamed either of its fallibility or the modest assurance it has gained as a result of age and exile', a fitting way of capturing the spirit and achievement of McGahern's late work.[53] Of course, examining McGahern's work alongside the authors that Said and Roiphe include in their studies helps us understand his work in new ways, and enlarges its context beyond Ireland and into the larger Anglophone world and even further. Even though the physical locations of McGahern's world are somewhat narrow, they find imaginative equivalents in such places as Updike's New England and Cavafy's Alexandria and, as a result, in both modern and contemporary writing. What is of concern in Cootehall, Carrick-on-Shannon and Mohill is particular to its specific time and place while being simultaneously relevant to worlds distant from it. McGahern's late work in particular succeeds so well because at no time does its author lose sight of the tensions and complexities that underline ordinary life and make fiction engaging. Always, as a literary artist McGahern seeks to develop and improve by challenging himself. Like Yeats, he resists static maturity by rejecting its comforts and wisdom in favour of exploring uncertainty and the unknown. In his late work, things are not resolved. As long as McGahern's work remains available, it will be read and admired. As a result, readers like me will set out in search of Cootehall and those others places that serve as locations of his work. Like Willa Cather's Red Cloud, McGahern's village is off the beaten track – the former given definition by prairie and the latter by water. Both are places, to my mind, of great beauty and endowed with their individual harmonies: between past and present, natural and built environments, and light and dark. McGahern's work brings Cootehall, and other places we can refer to as belonging to McGahern Country, into rich and complex literary reality.

Chapter 5

—

A Child is Being Beaten:
Anatomy of Reaction to *The Dark*

—

Niamh Campbell

The text is (should be) that uninhibited person who shows his behind to the *political father.*[1]

To begin, a thought experiment. The 'antisocial thesis' in queer theory, a countercultural call to challenge the pastoralism of assimilatory politics, may be seen as one of several theoretical positions which seek to read culture, not merely for evidence of dissident sexualities, but also for a kind of semantic vacuity which emerges from the construction of queer motivations as 'failure' – or perhaps of failure as queer – where the arbitrations of value involved in this are normative, hierarchised and implicitly capitalist. It finds its major genesis in Lee Edelman's *No Future* (2004), a work which takes aim at the politically dominant logic of heteronormativity by rejecting the cultural figure of the child as a sign 'for the universal value attributed to political futurity'.[2] 'Reproductive futurism, ideologically registered by the child as a figure for political as well as biological futurity, also purifies this figure – 'the Child' – such that it mediates a form of sacralisation which Edelman interprets as 'a fantasy of recapturing [the] lost imaginary unity' underpinning the symbolic order. *Dis-identification* from this means making a wilful concession to the construction of queerness as a series of figures 'bodying forth, within the logic of narrative, the dissolution of that very logic'. The thought experiment I propose is a hypothetical application of the antisocial thesis to Irish culture. The ultimate aim of this line of enquiry is to interrogate, reframe, and queer established and current readings of a significant modern novel of child abuse – John McGahern's *The Dark* (1965).

Almost at once, the playful grotesqueness of Edelman's anti-politics becomes simply grotesque, since the idea of militating against the privileged right to futurity nominally awarded to children in a state with a recent, popularly notorious, history of institutionally incarcerating and abusing children is objectionable in a way his original idea does not mean to be. We might say in its defence that Edelman is talking about a *symbol*; but then again, so are we. His best-known example – little orphan Annie – might be supplemented by the child actor in promotional posters for Alan Parker's adaptation of *Angela's Ashes* (1999): this would be comparable to supplementing the plucky logic of the self-made American citizen with the sentimentalising of brutalised children at work in certain examples of 'misery literature'. In a way, this complements Edelman's broader contention that a symbolic investment in reproductive futurism does not serve the interests of real children, but rather seeks to subject everyone to an idealised developmental destiny. The 'child of our identifications' is not a real historical child but an emblem, available for mobilisation in favour of a particular interpretative neutralisation of biopolitical violence within the context of the state.

The child of our identifications is also a eugenicist figure – white, able-bodied, and heterosexual. As such, its American context is at odds with an important aspect of reproductive culture in post-independence Ireland: the fact that a ban on contraception obliged many women to undergo multiple pregnancies, subtending an ethnicised association with over-population. McGahern's remarks on this are illustrative:

> At this time, because of the power of the Church and the Church's teaching, many married without any sexual knowledge or knowledge of the person they were marrying. The men generally married for sex …. The result was usually the arrival of a large number of children in rapid succession. There were families in which the children were cherished, but many more where they were resented as unwanted mouths that had to be fed, the unpleasant and unavoidable results of desire …. The ideal of society was the celibate priest. The single state was thus elevated. The love of God was greater than the love of man or woman; the sexual was seen as, [sic] sin-infected and unclean.[3]

The association drawn between children and abjected sexuality is reinforced by the writer's recollection of the practice of 'churching', or the ritual re-admittance of women who had recently given birth into the congregation, as 'cleansed'. The practice, symbolically speaking, amalgamates the figure of the child, the woman, and the sexually abject – associations which, I would further argue, effect a gesture of homogenisation, whereby there is little distinction between sexual interaction between adults and the sexual exploitation of children.

McGahern's second novel *The Dark*, which Denis Sampson describes as 'an existential study of [an adolescent] consciousness in an indeterminate state', is also a work which discloses details of domestic and sexual abuse in a family cell.[4] Commentators have not dwelt on the banning in detail; as Val Nolan argues, in an article which competently bucks this trend, it has largely been presented as 'a *fait accompli* [with] little emphasis placed on understanding the events surrounding the affair despite its centrality to McGahern's life, work, and reception'.[5] One hazard of this is the novel's revision as a 'watershed' moment in modern Irish history, a moment of revelation contending with an often hidden facet of Irish life, which is not borne out by the evidence Nolan collects. His survey of official and unofficial reaction, journalistic commentary and anecdotal response indicates that McGahern's detractors and defenders were never explicit on the point of domestic or sexual abuse, with outrage centring instead on the writer's dismissal from his job as a schoolteacher – which does not necessarily mean that readers *did not* pick up on the, potentially epochal or representative, depictions of intergenerational predation in *The Dark*. It does, however, suggest a lack of adequate language to account for these depictions *as* representative, and this qualification should be kept in mind when turning to a more recent piece of commentary by Fintan O'Toole. Writing in 2006, O'Toole praises *The Dark* for performing a prescient feat of pedagogy by osmosis. It is worth quoting at length to map the logic of its interpretation:

> By accurately describing the human interiors of Ireland, McGahern helped to alter Ireland's sense of reality. The starkest example of this is the issue of child sex abuse. When it hit the headlines in the 1990s, it was spoken of as a stunning and awful revelation, a secret that hardly anyone knew. Yet it is there in black and white in *The Dark*, thirty years before. The book opens with the young protagonist, Mahoney, being forced to strip naked and bend over a chair to be beaten by his father, who derives a sexual pleasure from the act. Shortly afterwards, the boy is sexually abused by his father. Later, he stays in a priest's house and the priest comes into the room at night. The description is eerily like something that would be spoken aloud in *States of Fear* or the Ferns Inquiry. Such awful privacies were unspoken and, in the case of *The Dark*, unspeakable. Officialdom

had no place for them, and though most Irish people knew about them, they did not want to really know them. But McGahern's calm persistence, his unrelenting integrity, drove them into our collective heads. The very conservativeness of the surface, the avoidance of shrillness or stridency, made the act of insinuation all the more explosive.[6]

O'Toole's discursive framing of abuse (a 'narrative' of progression from atavism to enlightenment) is blinkered in its address. None of the 'collective heads' involved belong to bodies that are, or have been, abused. A novel of thwarted ambition becomes a herald of triumphalist normativity: its terminus is testament, when 'awful privacies' are catalogued and accorded status in public discourse. This absorption of extra-official insinuation into an officialdom shaped by humanist hand-wringing does not abolish, or even question, the existence of officialdom, nor undermine its arbitration of the knowable. Instead, the process by which 'most Irish people' initially insulated themselves against an 'awful' understanding is inverted: 'collective heads' – the body(less) politic – are thus quarantined against association with a culture of endemic abuse by dint of its otherness. *Conservativeness of surface* becomes the stuff of stealth instead of evidence for the banality of evil, and all that is other in *The Dark* risks being politically neutralised.

It is helpful to compare this to another discursive attempt to recruit *The Dark* to a politics of aftermath. Peter Guy's 2010 article 'Reading John McGahern in Light of the Murphy Report' has the peculiar virtue of not reading John McGahern in light of the Murphy Report, but rather of seeking to exonerate the church, both by mobilising McGahern's pronouncements on the psychosocial values of religion, and by interpreting the author's experience of abuse in the home as proof of a problem not confined to members of the clergy. Thus, McGahern's suggestion that '[p]eople do not live in decades or histories' but rather in 'moments, hours, days' forecloses on 'retrospective judgment'; his construction of mid-century religious life as obsessed with sexual morality to the 'almost complete exclusion of the spiritual' is taken as writ, and his personal experience of abuse at the hands of his father is cited as proof of the existence of this practice among 'the laypeople'. Retrospective judgment is, in fact, employed by this critic to revise recent history, recasting mid-century Ireland as a world of 'traditional' communities in which 'the utter irrevocability of death [is] all the more bearable' for the rituals of Christianity, and the 'mercantile class', presumably within fumbling distance of a greasy till, strikes a 'bargain' with the clergy to perpetuate a repressive status quo. The sole authority on all of this is John McGahern: in lieu of any primary historical source, Guy offers us an image of the writer as a public intellectual 'perceptive of the exigent nature of clerical life', as well as such rhetorical turgidities as the fact that 'the *episteme* dictates the nature of an offence' or '[in] the new dispensations [sic], all that was good is tarred indiscriminately with the bad'. He also works to hail the reader as one whose relational obligations are not to the abused:

> What was acceptable among the closed ranks of the hierarchy (both civil and clerical) in the 1960s is today regarded as a gross violation of trust. It is all that and more, but retrospective analysis is a dangerous preoccupation, because child abuse, as it is defined today, is 'the mistreatment of a child … including physical violence, neglect, sexual assault or emotional cruelty'. Can anybody guess how many people would be dragged before the courts today if we applied retrospective judgment, using the aforementioned criterion [sic], on those who mistreated a child in the period after the inception of the state?[7]

Reader, it may even extend to you.

Guy's invocation of mathematical sublimity here demands critique. We are being invited, if implicitly, to entertain the notion that the crime of 'child abuse' might be 'dangerously' extended to include people we relate to, identify with, and resemble – a movement which, far from revising our approach to normative behaviour in Irish society, instead makes of 'abuse' a null category and constructs those who would call for it to be recognised as hysterical. We should respond with anger for obvious reasons, but also because McGahern is being invoked as an authority on this position, which makes evident the darker implications of a naively humanist approach that adopts the language of liberal inclusivity in the interests of a dominant group. In a similar, if less pernicious, way, the 'shrillness [and] stridency' O'Toole credits McGahern with avoiding suggests the promiscuous surplus of definitions latent in Guy's conception of child abuse as a legislative category; by comparison, the persistent integrity by which 'collective heads' are enlightened suggests a linear movement from darkness and obscurity to the transparency of a symbolic regime which now not only recognises abuse as a crime, but also enjoins a degree of interpretative consensus in the form of official, state-sanctioned accounts, apologies and tributes. Of these, the official 'government apology' proposed in the Ryan Report for inclusion on a public monument to victims of abuse in institutions – the monument, entitled *Journey Into Light*, has since been vetoed, although its title captures the persistence of a linear narrative or 'journey' to atonement in step with the state's developmental destiny – registers this discursive emphasis on transparency, even as it, like O'Toole's commentary, quarantines normative citizenship against implication in abuse. 'On behalf of the state and of all the citizens of the state, the Government wishes to make a sincere and long overdue apology to the victims of childhood abuse, for our collective failure to intervene, to detect their pain, to come to their rescue': a sentiment which both suspends the citizen-status of the abused and, moreover, of abusers, and refrains from actually apologising for abuse itself.[8] That a nominal celebration of vigilance entirely complements forms of social organisation metonymised by the panopticon is curiously overlooked. We might say there was no lack of *vigilance* in Magdalene laundries, borstals and industrial schools.

Journey Into Light represents an extension of O'Toole's retelling of *The Dark*, and complements Guy's revisionism. Each example works in the interests of one of two dominant groups – the clergy and the body politic, or normative citizenry, respectively – neither of which is constructed to contain in its ranks those who have been targets of biopolitical and intimate violence. This is not to say such groups are explicitly excluded, but rather that the terms of address employed by Guy and O'Toole do not, implicitly, refer to them, reproducing the impulse to quarantine at work in the government apology. Bracketing his attempt to exonerate abusers by dissolving the category of abuse for one moment, it is worth saying that Guy's argument that the church has been scapegoated is not without truth. Since he is committed to insisting on the 'exigency' of clerical authority, however, he is unable to appreciate the structural injustices built into this, and every, hierarchical institution, and to acknowledge what the sociologist Marie Keenan has described as 'organised irresponsibility' – a reflexive emphasis on solipsism, self-policing, and an abstract or intellectualised approach to moral conduct in clerical training, with the result that Keenan's interviewees and analysands, all convicted abusers, were 'unable to make good moral judgments in situations that required self-reflection, personal awareness, and the ability to put themselves in the shoes of others'.[9] 'Lay', as Guy would have it, attempts to reduce institutional abuse to a clerical aberration are not, therefore, without truth either, since what is in evidence here is the exigencies of Catholic organisational culture – exigencies reproduced outside of this context, in the form of sovereign, secular bureaucracy, which intersects with clerical organisation in the carceral institution.

Inhabitants of these institutions in post-independence Ireland were not full members of the state at the time of their incarceration, but examples of what Giorgio Agamben has called 'bare life' – a state of embodied existence which has been overcoded by political economy to the point that it no longer simply exists *for itself*, but is disposed in some instrumental way towards the state without the privileges of citizenship. When biological life is not antecedent or adjacent but rather *central* to political life – such as in the conversion of material bodies to docile bodies in the service of capitalism– it is no longer possible for the body to inhabit the condition which Agamben, after Aristotle, delineates as *zoë* (the 'simple fact of living'). The body can only now be processed as *bios* ('the form or way of living proper to an individual or group'), and as such any exclusion from the body politic does not restore pure life but recreates the body as an altered or lesser life.[10] Among the most compelling implications of this are both the centrality of organisational strategies to the policing of biopolitical 'stock', and the subsequent production of bodies which possess neither autonomy nor the right to protection from the state. This means that the social sub-category of bare life supplies a stock of bodies it is acceptable to abuse, or rather, in relation to which abuse is not recognised as abuse. The impulse to quarantine I have identified here should be considered alongside this.

'The Use of Reason'

When the protagonist of Colm Tóibín's 'The Use of Reason' (2007), a career criminal, recalls his adolescence at an industrial school named 'Lanfad' (a thinly veiled Letterfrack) he also remembers a singular and epiphanic instance of violence that echoes the voyeuristic composition of the opening scene of *The Dark*. Two boys who have attempted to escape are forced to lay 'facedown on an old table with their trousers around their ankles', as a Christian Brother beats them 'across the buttocks … with a strap'. The protagonist witnesses this because he has climbed into a window from outside:

Suddenly, as he watched this scene, he noticed something else. There was an old light box at the back of the games room. It was used to store junk. Now there were two brothers standing in it, and the door was open so they had a clear view of the two boys being punished. He could see them from the window – Brother Lawrence and Brother Murphy – realising that the two brothers administering the punishment must have been aware of their presence too but perhaps could not see what they were doing.[11]

We hardly need to be told that the brothers in the light box are masturbating. Their eyes are 'fixed on the scene in front of them – the boys being punished, crying out every time they were hit with the strap', and, in this condition, they do not look like 'men in charge', but like 'old dogs panting'. Just as the image remains with the protagonist 'as if he had taken a photograph', it is presented to the reader as a suspended and hermeneutically saturated tableau – apprehended visually because there is no explication, just composition – which must be interpreted iconographically.

Appearing two years after the Ferns Report, 'The Use of Reason' draws on a large store of public information regarding abuse; at the same time, the knowledge this bestows is partial. Before and after the horizon of official history is introduced, the sole vector or author of the scene is the protagonist, who stands in another 'light box' channelling perspectival omniscience and taking in events without being seen. Such is the habitual privilege of the reading audience, who also observes unobserved, and makes a claim to total knowledge based on context and signification. There is no reciprocity, only volume, and a series of variously covetous and controlled gazes: the audience 'gazes' with the protagonist who gazes at the brothers in the light box who gaze at the punishment. This line of logic links the window, the light box, and the primary locus of action, which is the bodies – or rather, the buttocks – of the boys, in an apparatus of capture conditioned by what Michel Foucault has described as 'the grid created by a glance, an examination, a language'.[12] Because the image is like a 'photograph', however, it encompasses both the eideticism of the glance and the attention of the gaze, and the combined effect of these is authority – the reading subject knows what is happening, in the sense of being able to locate this scene historically and affirm its verisimilitude, without being explicitly told. In different but intersecting ways, both of these revelations pertain largely, if not exclusively, to power relations, and pivot on the simulated or affective visual *transparency* offered, if not fetishised, by the scene. Nothing can happen without the window or the luminous force of both 'gazing' and plain language; emphasis is placed on comprehension rather than empathy. This is neither shocking nor inappropriate, but rather in accordance with the logic of bodily torture.

In *The Body in Pain*, Elaine Scarry, drawing on testimonies and reports of political torture, theorises the calculated or punitive pain inflicted in persecution or punishment as a means of objectifying or externalising power, or 'the conversion of absolute pain into the fiction of absolute power', transforming the cutaneous surfaces of the body – its movements and expressions – into the signifying screen or *tabula* for the 'language' of power and submission.[13] From a political and a performative point of view this process crucially translates involuntary bodily movement, in conjunction with the deliberate or mechanical motions required to inflict pain, into a code that is stable and legible, 'made possible by the obsessive mediation of agency': the body as cipher for the 'incontestable' binary of dominant and submissive or, moreover, of *subject and object*.[14] The tortured body's status as an object is effectively mounted *on* it, as a sign, such that visible or palpable reactions to stimuli are instantly processed by an abstract system which both requires and tyrannises the object of its expression. Scarry spatialises this:

> It is the intense pain that destroys a person's self and world, a destruction experienced spatially as either the contraction of the universe down to the immediate vicinity of the body or as the body swelling to fill the entire universe. Intense pain is also language-destroying: as the content of one's world disintegrates, so the content of one's language disintegrates; as the self disintegrates, so that which would express and project the self is robbed of its source and subject.[15]

In 'The Use of Reason', the bodies of the boys who are beaten are treated of briefly, and it is significant that theirs is the only gaze not, apparently, levelled at anything; neither require development as characters because they serve as representatives for the wider body of boys incarcerated at the school. In spite of this, their bodily presence or bodily objectivity – their bodies *as objects* and not subjects, since we have no access to their consciousness and are not directed, 'visually', toward their faces – functions as the central point of application and attention in the scene.

Posture, indispensable to sadomasochism as much as to choreography or figurative art, 'unites only one action and its bodily point of application', and sustains a tension between gesture and surface; we are given the boys' posture explicitly, they are 'facedown', such that focus is narrowed to their exposed buttocks.[16] Corporal punishment is not always, or even usually, confined to this particular permutation; as anecdote and allegation would have it, hands, backs, ribs and even feet also feature as the loci of assault, while McGahern's 'The Recruiting Officer' vividly reconstructs 'the whistle and thud' of electric wire used to beat a schoolboy on the legs.[17] There are numerous ways in which bodies might be ritually mortified but the quality of articulacy attendant upon the beating detailed here is a condition of its figural starkness: a prostrate posture communicates subservience and suggests feminisation by dint of its receptive sexual function.[18] The buttocks, a site of reception for the simulated thrusting of the beating itself, performed with a phallic 'strap', confirms this association, which is unlikely to be lost on the reader. As these bodies are bent in reception, what they receive are not only blows from the strap but the perspectival lines of several gazes; that of the masturbating brothers, and that of the protagonist. Force is diluted in strength as it travels, and the ordered aggression of the beating is processed as a surrogate penetration or phantasmatic intimacy by the brothers in the light box, to be processed (gridded) anew as a more diffuse or abstract composition by the protagonist and the reading subject. Violence, then, is a condition of form *and* content in this scene: a violence of 'the field of spectatorship' – which is also 'the field of civilisation', because the field of signification – *and* of the cutaneous field, of both the buttocks and the posture which exposes it in this way.[19] This posture is, in turn, contextualised by and contingent on the room in which it occurs, as the room is a frame, the light box is a frame, the window is a frame, the page is a frame, and the final or primal framing device that facilitates all of it is the body itself – just as nothing can be 'seen' without the window, there can be no meaning without the 'screen' of flesh onto which pain-as-power is inscribed.

What creates a screen or tabula? Or, to put this differently, what is the difference between a vacuum and a screen or frame or tabula, or grid, where both of these forms of spatialisation are essentially identified by their emptiness, and hence receptivity? The answer, in Foucault's meditation on *Las Meninas*, is light, the 'common locus' of pictorial representation.[20] In *The Dark*, the symbolic conspicuousness of light (of enlightenment, of electrification, of the 'heavenly mansion' of Yeats' 'The Choice', from which its title is taken) is charged with meaning; in Tóibín's short story, nothing could happen without the light box, and this particular detail emphasises readerly involvement or 'gazing' as a form of 'light' or enlightenment. A conspicuously visible grid or composition enjoins an opacity which contradicts the claims to knowledge and comprehension associated with a scopic regime – although, of course, to approach it in this way is to make a *critical choice* to do so, and to resist exhaustive schemes or formulae for interpreting a painting, or a vision of aggressively mediated pain, or a textual scene. The beholder, arrested before the visual or textual scene, must engage with this opacity, and is thus potentially open to the possibility that 'the affective force of [such] moments might be deployed to propel ethical generosity'.[21] In the case of Tóibín, such a reading practice would mean attending to the semantic obstruction presented by the 'screen' of flesh mobilised, here, to inscribe mastery. It would mean, in a way, deconstructing or dis-identifying with what Laura U. Marks describes as phenomenological 'Thirdness': a means of taking direction or interpreting an image or sign under *instruction*, in this case, 'as' a representative depiction of Irish child abuse; a disclosure, an image of visual 'truth'. Such dis-identification involves reading the scene, instead, as artificial, representative or *citational*: as a problematically standardised *sign for a signified* which is absent because it is perceived to be 'past' or historical, because the subjectivity of victims is often occluded, and because its *signs* (official reports, official apologies, popular consensus) form part of a discourse which seeks to manage affective response in a way conducive to political economy. In a very significant way, this hinges on testament and confession.

The Dark
'Say what you said because I know.'

The first demand of *The Dark* registers its core thematic and structural tenet of confession; what Foucault, appropriately here, has described as the 'dark twin' of torture, and interpreted as a means of articulating a relation to mastery:

> Confession frees, but power reduces one to silence; truth does not belong to the order of power, but shares an original affinity with freedom: traditional themes in philosophy … would have to overturn by showing that truth is not by nature free – nor error servile – but that its production is thoroughly imbued with relations of power. The confession is an example of this.[22]

Foucault's point here subtends the interest in transparency and revelation which has characterised certain 'narratives' of abuse in Irish culture – the production, that is, of truth through testament and confession. This, as I have shown, underwrites an arc of development which must be exclusive, and which works to preserve normative citizenship against implication in it. To critique it, we can begin with the putative 'truth' which results from the ostensibly omnipotent *urvater*, Old Mahoney's, demand for confession in this scene, the scrambled or obscured word 'F-U-C-K': a word made strange by censorship and converted, as Anne Goarzin suggests, into a kind of object-trigger, extending its associations with displaced violence onto 'the heavy leather strap he used for sharpening his razor', which twitches uncannily like 'an animal's tail', and is used to threaten a son who has uttered a phallic word with surrogate castration ('I'll cut that arse off you') and surrogate penetration ('Into that chair with you. On your mouth and nose. I'll give your arse something it won't forget in a hurry').[23] These gestures are counterfeit gestures, or fantasies; when O'Toole, above, describes the protagonist as being 'beaten' by his father, this detail is technically incorrect – the belt 'never comes', or rather collides with the leather seat on which Young Mahoney lies prostrate, exploding like 'a rifle crack' on the armrest, redoubling the military associations accruing to the father ('March, march, march') while proposing a field of prosthetic flesh in the form of the chair and the belt, both made of leather.[24] This scene is also *sodomitical*: it excessively illustrates a sexual posture, or illustrates it *as excessive*, an effect borne out by at least one critical response:

> A number of fairly specific forces constrain the characters [of *The Dark*]. Perhaps chief among these is the dead mother of the family. Her absence facilitates a grinding and remorseless emphasis on the petty viciousness, the frustrations and lovelessness in the relations between a man bereft of sexual love, and his children, bereft of maternal love.[25]

The suggestion that the absence of a 'good woman' to interpose, as a kind of sexual shock absorber, between a man and his children is the 'chief' explanation for abuse is both objectionable and inadvertently revelatory. That Michael Toolin, the critic quoted, does not intend to say this but says it anyway means that it may be thought of as a slip or a tic; which is to say as a symptom, disclosing something of the brutality of the family cell as it radiates outwards from the father figure, the arbiter of phallic plenitude, in a gesture which is, like narrative, linearised – beginning with the sexual subject and terminating in a sexual object that exists *for* the subject, and is passive. It is true that Old Mahoney relates to his son, on at least one occasion in *The Dark*, as a surrogate wife, sharing a bed with him and attempting to engage in a fantasy of sentimental omnipotence ('There's no need to be afraid or cry. Your father loves you') which obscenely idealises his attachment to the role of 'father' and the power that comes with this. Old Mahoney must be written off as aberrant by Toolin because his excessive investment in this normative role betrays an adjacent fantasy that is barely concealed by the received discourse of platitudes and truisms he inhabits; at the same time, his insistence on this speech pattern, which is alternately vicious and sentimental, obliges the reader to interpret his actions against the grain of his self-constructed subject position and engage with it *as* a fantasy. As such, when Old Mahoney underscores the ideological edifice of the family by presenting its inevitability as a thing of common sense, claiming that '[e]ven Up Above there was trouble. There's differences everywhere […] Everyone loses their temper and says things and does things but as long as you know there's love there it doesn't matter', we are aware of both the banality of this proclamation and its radical incommensurability with what is actually taking place between father and son.[26]

Sigmund Freud's 'A Child Is Being Beaten' is a study of sexual fantasy which allegorises this particular fantasy image. It is hard to fathom the beating of children as a popular fantasy now, and there is a sense in which Freud's patients, who attach 'feelings of pleasure' to their identikit 'phantasy', are responding to a form of paternal authority in its earliest domestic articulation – siblings and schoolmates being beaten 'on the bare buttocks' by figures who all, for Freud, metonymise the ur-father. Female analysands, always already proximate to masochism, are beaten by their father, whereas male analysands may fantasise about being beaten by their mother, but even this is devolved symbolically by Freud to place the *pater familias* in the position of authority. This beating, moreover, stands in for or constitutes a primitive version of genital love:

[The] original form of the unconscious male phantasy was not the pro-visional one that we have hitherto given: 'I am being beaten by my father,' but rather: '*I am loved by my father*.' The phantasy has been transformed by the processes with which we are now familiar into the conscious phantasy:

'*I am being beaten by my mother.*' The boy's beating is therefore passive from the very beginning, and is derived from a feminine attitude towards his father [...][27]

The consequence of this is irradiated by both subsequent revelations of child abuse as a phenomenon and the legacy of claims that Freud suppressed evidence of inter-generational abuse by naturalising the family romance: '*The beating-phantasy has its origin in an incestuous attachment to the father*' (italics in original). The anchoring of quotidian masochism in the narrative of heteronormativity also has the effect of endorsing a vision of sexual congress which, in its amplified symbolic form, is essentially violent, consisting in the application of an action (spanking/thrusting) to the flesh – a gesture which, theoretically, negates or dissimulates gender. This is not to say that being penetrated is defined, by Freud and by the broader ideology of gender difference, as anything other than constitutively feminine, but rather to emphasise the ambivalence which is glimpsed in this depiction of masochism. Analysands' focus on 'bare buttocks' may also be nuanced, since this is the site of the anal 'cut' which Edelman considers a symbolic appendage related, but not identical, to the wound of castration: a 'penetrable hole' that presents a threat to heteronormativity by declaring the penetrability of the male subject as well as the female.[28] Precisely what makes this threatening is its association with the figure of the penetrable woman which must symbolise passivity, both as a social actor and through bodily hexis, or 'political mythology realized, *em-bodied*, turned into a permanent disposition'.[29]

I have said that censorship is signalled or anticipated at the beginning of *The Dark*, in the de-familiarisation of 'fuck' as 'F-U-C-K'. Since this word 'just came out' – 'The filth that's in your head came out, you mean' – it is very much a symptom – or an accidental, wayward, and involuntary expression – of the unconscious meeting a symbolic terminus in obscenity; as such, it is, for the protagonist Young Mahoney, de-cathected, or disconnected from the unconscious through the process of its (deformed) symbolic articulation. The symptom is that which cannot be translated and, as both a *linguistic* symptom and a sinthome (an especially idiotic, which is to say meaninglessly material, symptom), 'fuck' or 'F-U-C-K' in this instance is entirely without a communicational trajectory. Any meaning or any cathexis we may invest it with is excessive or supplementary, which is to say *fantastical*, and this fantastic function relates directly, I would contend, to the scene's sublimated, inverted or alternative implication – namely, that instead of depicting the threat of a beating and the execution of a 'measured passion' translating to cruelly stoical punishment, instead of showing the father's self-restraint and displacing his libidinal drive by emphasising psychological torture rather than physical torture ('the same hysterical struggle, and he hadn't been hit yet, it was unreal'), the father would simply beat the son and we would be 'witnessing', as it were, a prosaic example of domestic squalor. That the beating doesn't come but remains imaginary does not diminish the horror of the scene or the son's self-evident terror of his father, but it does lodge this non-scenario firmly in the realm of fantasy, where the clean lines of ideology are stretched and distended by *jouissance*, producing effects that both register the pleasures of ideological identification and threaten to expose ideology as ridiculous or opaque. Thus the immovable, impenetrable and untranslatable tic of 'fuck' becomes the dull medial substance of several immanent interpretative investments. Its meaninglessness is the non-logic of a scene constructed, at the objectively symbolic level of ideology, as following from a transgression – from the son's utterance of the word 'fuck' – but not actually elaborating on or substantiating that transgression ('I didn't say anything'). On the surface, Old Mahoney is punishing his son because the latter has uttered a taboo word; beneath this surface, at the level of 'our dirty fantasmatic imagination', he is actually punishing 'the filth that's in your head', which is to say *all taboo*; all that must remain below the level of language, and which surfaces only inadvertently.[30] Mahoney's narrative of paternal duty seizes, with surreptitious bad faith, on the ideological imperative to govern one's family in the context of a society which radiates outwards from this nucleus, its most primary structural unit. It also echoes, in a more conscious way, Freud's palimpsestic overlaying of the 'child beating' fantasy with the script of the family romance, a gesture which suppresses or negates the implication that child-beating is, in and of itself, a source of arousal for adults.

It might also be said that, in embracing his paternal authority to such a grotesque degree, Old Mahoney 'dissects' and lays bare the darker truth of the *Urvater*, and its descendant patriarchal order – not consciously or heroically, but a way that is accidental, a hazard of over-emphasis, and left, ultimately, for the reader to 'dissect'. By the end of *The Dark*, this beaten child has grown to a man who asserts, while lying in bed with the father who has, in the past, exploited him sexually, that 'I wouldn't have been brought up any other way or by any other father', a conclusion which irritated critics and continues to be objected to.[31] John Cronin's '"The Dark" is not Light Enough' is an article from 1969 which, in common with other early responses to *The Dark*, interprets the novel as 'not successful' in its attempt to further detail the 'dark conditions of [a] fictional universe' executed 'perfectly' by *The Barracks*.[32] McGahern's failure is, moreover, a failure of form. For Cronin, the 'stygian universe' Young Mahoney inhabits is too unrelenting, and not illuminated by sustaining flashbacks or middle-aged wisdom, as in *The Barracks*, and as such lacks perspective; unlike James Joyce's *A Portrait of the Artist as a Young Man*, which makes of Stephen Dedalus a pessimistic but successful human subject because '[Joyce] employs a high-flown rhetoric which both carries the youthful arrogance and simultaneously undercuts it'.[33] In the 'high-flown' rhetoric Cronin praises in Joyce, we find a particular regard for pedagogical heritage as a point of access for the protagonist who comes to socialised authority via induction but not indoctrination: McGahern's protagonist, by contrast, is violently indoctrinated to the 'stygian universe'. His early acceptance of defeat, and of 'calmness even in the face of the turmoil of your own passing', is indeed unearned and premature. It is significant, however, that Cronin does not find the stygian universe structure to be anomalous where it occurs in *The Barracks*, for the principal reason that, in this work, it is more persuasively scaffolded and graduated; the difference in *The Dark* is that Young Mahoney's anti-triumph refutes such measured and thus defensible pessimism, becoming instead penetrated or filled by it passively, finding victory in this receptive and essentially feminine gesture.

We might say that Young Mahoney's surrender is precisely what the 'stygian universe' demands of him, and the fact that Cronin goes so far as to interrogate McGahern himself on this point indicates, perhaps, the degree of urgency or instability this poses to the 'real world' of Irish society – especially since the *bildungsroman*, and the *Portrait*, are associated with a kind of nationalised apprenticeship, whereby the youth learns to inhabit a role in public culture. For Joyce/Stephen, this translates as a form of exile which is also a 'creation' of a literary supplement for the race and the place, while, for the McGahern constructed by Cronin, it goes no further than a rueful dismissal of the 'pie in the sky' at a question-and-answer session in Belfast. Of course this is 'confused and unsatisfactory': it has reproduced the bleak but aesthetically and emotionally substantiated cosmos of *The Barracks* to a *sinthome*, in the sense of over-identifying with its ideology so intently that Young Mahoney becomes an avatar of it. If we take the liberty of conflating the 'stygian universe' with the cultural climate of post-independence Ireland, its lack of resolution also becomes politically pertinent. An underdeveloped comparison with *The Catcher in the Rye* provides a last possibility for insight; where Holden Caulfield's language is so 'larded with kid-phrases' it remains, to a degree, unable to absorb the full severity of the world he encounters, ensuring a sense of readerly distance, Young Mahoney's voice and textual presence is so per-meated with the oppressive existential tenure of his world that it becomes, in itself, opaque.[34] This results in the sudden change of heart, as Young Mahoney leaves university, which has been criticised by Cronin and others as lacking a credible motivation. It is, instead, unclear or 'unsuccessful' – 'stubbornly inhospitable' – and as such forecloses on any satisfying consensus regarding the intentional programme of *The Dark*.[35]

It is this sense of opacity, stasis, suspension and deferral which, like the blow from the leather belt which 'never comes' in Young Mahoney's nightmarish opening scene, I hope to identify here as fundamentally queer. It is an effect which thwarts conventional narrative momentum in favour of what might be rather orthodoxly described as a *perversion*, in the sense of blocking or redirecting the typically progressive energies of narrative, heteronormative reproduction, and personal growth. At its first appearance *The Dark* creates a different kind of blockage, attracting literal censorship; in the record of its banning as retold by Cronin, a particular ellipsis recurs, whereby the most explosive content of the book itself is not explicitly named by its defenders or detractors. In the aftermath of the Ryan, Murphy and Ferns Reports, as well as numerous publications, studies, enquiries and television documentaries disclosing several interlinked histories of institutional and familial abuse in Ireland, the courageous frankness of *The Dark* can be reinterpreted – in Fintan O'Toole's analysis above, the book is effectively credited with a degree of narrative coherency and political progressivism which is not, in fact, materially accurate. *The Dark* is still, I would argue, an opaque, unnerving and problematic book which deliberately short-circuits the usual satisfactions attendant upon the *bildungsroman*, a format usually used to recalibrate and celebrate normal social development and integration. The anti-climactic closing scene echoes the opening scene, then, in more ways than one, both by locating father and son in bed once again but also in failing, conspicuously, to deliver on the terms of those narrative templates which are ambivalently hovering over the start and end of *The Dark* – *bildungsroman*, family romance, abuse survival narrative, torture-and-confession text – but in failing to conclusively reproduce any of these, McGahern's novel actually lives out the promise of its queerly charged opening scene instead. The ambivalence indicated by this may be taken as an ethical gesture inviting us to approach it, and to approach our recent history more generally, differently, recognising – among other things – our own implication as readers, observers, social actors and citizens.

Images of Place and the Role of Memory

Chapter 6

—

Ecology, Time and Scale in *That They May Face the Rising Sun* and *Memoir*

—

Eóin Flannery

C oming in the wake of a spate of earlier Irish autobiographical narratives across the 1990s, *Memoir* was immediately viewed as having an intimate link with the startling fictions that preceded its appearance towards the end of the author's life.[1] For many readers and critics, McGahern's earlier fictional works, particularly *The Barracks* (1963) and *The Dark* (1965), with their exposure of physically and sexually violent patriarchal domestic regimes, as well as their respective treatments of Irish Catholicism and the legacies and the limits of Irish national independence, were assumed to take significant impetus from the author's biography. In another respect, part of the appeal of McGahern's fictional writings, and of his life-writing, then, quite apart from the stylistic mastery exhibited therein, was the sense that not only were these lives and narratives derived from the author's own memorial landscape, but that they were fragments of a national or communal suite of memories. And each of these aforementioned ways of reading or understanding *Memoir*, and *That They May Face the Rising Sun*, are unselfconsciously tethered to particular spatial, temporal and/or imaginative scales. Both of these narratives intersect in terms of their respective portraits of human and non-human ecological relations, but they can also be read productively through the analytical resources of ecocriticism. The intention here is not to delimit an ecocritical reading of McGahern's work to the confines of a 'localist' school of thought; rather it is to expose the necessary concatenated scalar proportions – temporal and spatial – in which the acts of memorial and fictional representation take place.

In drawing *Memoir* to a close, McGahern outlines the background to his return to the landscape of his formative years. After residing briefly at Cleggan with his wife Madeline, they decide to re-settle, not specifically in County

Leitrim, but that is the outcome. In these final pages, McGahern reprises the notions of loss and recovery, cyclicality, and the apparent economy of interdependence between human and non-human ecology. Abstracting from the catalogue of historical local detail that comprises the narrative, the author offers two complementary reflections on his journey back home and, metacritically, on the form and content of his autobiographical storying. First of all, he states: 'The people and the language and landscape where I had grown up were like my breathing: it would take years to gain that knowledge in a new place.'[2] His point chimes with earlier sections that highlight the intensity of local dwelling observed by McGahern. There is a well-earned, resilient and deeply founded sense of local identification generated over time, which cannot be accrued with haste, transience, or without full commitment to the landscape and language of the local environment. And such a reading accords with that of the prominent ecocritic Lawrence Buell, in the sense that McGahern's narrative is marked by a 'place-sense', which 'is a kind of palimpsest of serial place-experiences'.[3] McGahern's return to these climes is both physically real and symbolic – it is suggestive of the extent to which formative environmental conditions are elemental to the marrow of individual dispositions, and it also indicates the mutually constitutive relation that obtains between past and present. In this register, he writes: 'This is the story of my upbringing, the people who brought me up, my parents and those around them, in their time and landscape. My own separate life, in so far as any life is separate, I detailed to show how the journey out of that landscape became the return to those lands and small fields and hedges and lakes under the Iron mountains' (*M*, 260–1). Within the conceptual and *scalar* frames of *one* form of ecocriticism, McGahern's *Memoir*, then, begins and ends with deeply affective professions of personal and memorial rootedness in this landscape, and partakes of the ethics of dwelling and 'everyday nature' that are informative of much contemporary ecological writing.[4] From this perspective McGahern's oeuvre is legible in terms of cultural forms, which, in Michael Cronin's terms, 'deepen and complexify a sense of place in order to ensure not only its flourishing in the present but its viability into the future'.[5] As we shall argue, this is a legitimate but not the only scalar perspective from which to broach McGahern's work; equally, when one does address the 'locality' of McGahern's *Memoir*, and *That They May Face the Rising Sun*, it is imperative to eschew facile sentimentalisations of these peoples and locales.

The question of scale as it relates to human epistemologies and ontologies is one of the central concerns of critical interventions across the field of ecocriticism. Scalar proportions have become key modes of reading and writing human engagements with the planet and its histories – human and non-human. And matters of environmental scale have been thrown into sharp relief by the emergence of what geologists refer to as 'the Anthropocene'. The Anthropocene is generally acknowledged as the innovation of atmospheric scientists Paul J. Crutzen and Eugene F. Stoermer, appearing in their co-authored essay 'The Anthropocene' in 2000.[6] This coinage is a reflection of the quantifiable impact of mankind on the ecological functioning of the planet's atmosphere, and it is traced back to the period that witnessed the commencement of the Industrial Revolution. Motivated by the tangible acceleration of anthropogenic degradation of the non-human world, and by their accumulated scientific evidence of the irreparable scars inflicted on the global environment by humanity, Crutzen and Stoermer diagnosed that humanity has, in fact, ascended to the role of geological agent. Such a point compels us to think of our history as part of natural history, not just political, economic, artistic, and so on. In other words, religious and philosophical questions on man's relation to nature, which assumed its dominance, have, through increased industrialisation and its attendant corruption of natural resources and pollutant run-offs, become a devastating ecological reality.

Poetry has typically been the genre that has been given primary significance within mainstream ecocritical literary studies, and it has been a critical commonplace to question the effectiveness of prose narratives in representing the core concerns of ecocritical analysis. Adam Trexler has produced the first and most complete study of the novel genre in the context of global climate change. Trexler's study *Anthropocene Fictions* commences by furnishing a cursory critical genealogy, as well as an intellectual back-story of the concept of the Anthropocene, but also poses a series of telling questions that link the scientific sphere with that of culture, or a corrective co-identification of the scientific with the broadly cultural.[7] Included within Trexler's catalogue of questions are:

Setting aside questions of fact, how has the immense discourse of climate change shaped culture over the last forty years? What tropes are necessary to comprehend climate change or to articulate the possible futures faced by humanity? How can a global process, spanning millennia, be made comprehensible to human imagination, with its limited sense of place and time? What longer, historical forms aid this imagination, and what are the implications and limits of their use? [...] And finally, how does climate change alter the forms and potentialities of art and cultural narrative?[8]

The early inquiries listed above are fairly standard in ecocritical circles, as the ontological and epistemological urgencies to which global climate change is causal force critics to re-consider the shapes, possibilities and responsibilities of all forms of human narration as acts of power on non-humanity. Further importing the Anthropocene into literary and cultural studies, Timothy Clark encourages scholars to take into account necessary 'derangements of scale' in undertaking effective ecocritical readings of literary texts. Clark's specific point relates to the incommensurability between individual environmental actions and consciousness, and the actual scale of ongoing and future climate change. Clark argues that: 'Climate change disrupts the scale at which one must think, skews categories of internal and external and resists inherited closed economies of accounting or explanations.'[9] He adds: '[s]cale effects in particular defy sensuous representation or any plot confined, say, to human-to-human dramas and intentions, demanding new, innovative modes of writing that have yet convincingly to emerge'.[10] Clark, then, devotes attention to the ways in which neglect of scale effects manifest within literary and cultural criticism; he asks: 'How would it be to read and reread the same text through a series of increasingly broad spatial and temporal scales, one after the other, paying particular attention to the strain this puts on given critical assumptions and currently dominant modes of reading?'[11] Thus introducing a plurality of scales to a critical or creative work operates both within the text (in terms of context and figuration), but also disturbs the acts of writing and representation themselves (creative and critical) at a meta-level. 'Deranging' literary criticism, then, becomes a species of 'deranging' liberal politics, in one respect; the self-alienating 'scalar' reading strategy employed by Clark disavows individualistic, character-driven or plot-driven analyses as the only legitimate form of literary engagement.

Clark's much anticipated *Ecocriticism on the Edge: the Anthropocene as a threshold concept* is one of a number of publications within the field to unpack the Anthropocene in terms of orthodox models of literary and cultural criticism. In some respects, Clark's intervention is a further assault on orthodox historicism witnessed in earlier ecocritical publications. And Clark underscores the profound philosophical implications of the advent of the Anthropocene; in his estimation the idea 'blurs and even scrambles some crucial categories by which people have made sense of the world and their lives. It puts in crisis the lines between culture and nature, fact and value, and between human and the geological or meteorological'.[12] The lines between natural and human histories, previously understood as insoluble, have been drained of such integrity, and thus the boundaries of human subjectivity are rendered insecure. Clark's work has been seminal to the contouring of Anthropocene ecocriticism, particularly his attention to the re-calibrated scalar proportions of literary and cultural criticism on foot of humanity's role as planetary geological agent. The Anthropocene may have reached some level of definitional clarity from a geo-scientific perspective, but what the Anthropocene means for the human imaginary and for the future of humanity is far from certain. Part of the disruptive charge of the Anthropocene is precisely such volatility, and, of course, as we have mentioned, the sheer scales on which humanity's future is placed under threat.

Yet, the disruptive force of the Anthropocene is nested within everything we do in the present, as well as linking us directly to humanity's history since the Industrial Revolution. The 'norms' we in the Global North have established, inherited and continue to live by are, counterintuitively, poisonous agents, extensions of our own desires that offer nothing assured other than the destruction of the biosphere. But it is when Clark broaches the issues that attend scale, and of the implications for humanity and for literary and cultural criticism, that he touches upon familiar ground, as well as rising to his most astute in terms of the future trajectories for ecocriticism. As he details: '[s]cale effects in particular defy sensuous representation or any plot confined, say, to human-to-human dramas and intentions, demanding new, innovative modes of writing that have yet convincingly to emerge'.[13] It has been noted that one of the ways to gloss Clark's broader project is as a critique of historicism, or, in exact ecocritical parlance, historical anthropocentrism. The latter is adjudged, as is widely established, as the perpetrator of global climate change, but for Clark an assault on historicism goes beyond merely identifying the guilty party of global climate change.

The question of scale makes the local, the immediate and the microsocial consequential; just as capitalism 'empowers' the individual consumer, the Anthropocene enlists us all as geological agents. But, of course, what the consequences might be in the imminent future or within longer-term timeframes can too often only be guessed at or 'imagined'. In a sense, as geological agents we know that humanity's imprints are spoiling the planet, but, for many, these are invisible and remote imprints and effects – large in scale, certainly, but distant in spatial and temporal terms, and therefore hard to grasp and to act upon. The challenge, then, is to re-tune our imaginative, conceptual and empathetic scale frames; we are no longer simply 'human', we have ascended to a different scalar order in terms of our climatic impacts, and must as a result face the heightened scalar implications and costs of our newly found geological agency. Such newly emerged geological agency re-enforces the notion that any viable ecocritical praxis will remain terminally limited if it does not and cannot embrace a necessary interdisciplinarity. In other words, the sheer scale of the issues means that attenuated cultural readings and critical exegeses within ecocritical cultural studies are, in a sense, playing with one hand behind their backs. But what is just as important is that cultural agents who partake of ecocritical practice need to be flexible and deranging in their future methodologies. And this is an angle I will tentatively take on the received resolute locality of aspects of McGahern's work, in particular *That They May Face the Rising Sun* and *Memoir*.

The agency endowed to non-human nature by McGahern, and, secondly, his temperamental humility and wonder at these intimate ecological phenomena and organisms, are readily apparent from the outset of *Memoir*. The opening line of the book might state boldly that 'The soil in Leitrim is poor' (*M*, 1), but there is a dynamic abundance and durability to the ecology of that locale. Amid the copious hedgerows of 'whitethorn, ash blackthorn, alder, sally, rowan, wild cherry, green oak, sycamore', non-human ecology flourishes: '[…] these hedgerows are full of mice and insects and small birds, and sparrowhawks can be seen hunting all through the day' (*M*, 1). Elsewhere, the imprints of a living ecology are evident in the 'beaten pass the otter takes between lakes […] and in quiet places on the edge of the lakes are the little lawns speckled with fish bones and blue crayfish shells where the otter feeds and trains her young' (*M*, 1). The page-long portrait of non-human nature does not give way to human presence until the very end of the first page. McGahern establishes the vitality and the viability of the natural domain as a determining preface to his personal familial narrative. His bond with such natural surroundings in all of its micro-detail becomes increasingly familiar to the reader, however, as we progress through *Memoir*, and the privacies of his emotional memories of his deceased mother are revealed. In another vein, it is easy to see how such a portrait might be sympathetic to an ecocritical mind-set that values familiarity and responsibility towards one's immediate physical environment. Such ecological consciousness is equally palpable in the opening gestures of *That They May Face the Rising Sun*, a fictional narrative that touches upon similar germane issues as *Memoir*. The earlier novel begins with a poised and balanced still-life: 'The morning was clear. There was no wind on the lake. There was a great stillness. When the bells rang out for Mass, the strokes trembling on the water, they had the entire world to themselves'.[14] The descriptive economy of McGahern's opening lines here registers the unsentimentalised relationship between author and landscape, and between many of the novel's characters and their immediate environs. Though lacking the grip of sentimentality, the human and non-human ecologies around the lake are intimately linked in terms of temporal and spatial scales. *That They May Face the Rising Sun*, thus, touches upon many of the ecocritical thematics also present in the later *Memoir*. McGahern's texts, then, focus on issues pertaining to local identity; speed, temporality and cyclicality; human and non-human ecological relations; and the proximity of industrial time and so-called 'natural' time, and they impress the variety of diachronic and synchronic scales in which humanity is implicated.

Denis Sampson underscores the interdependence of place, memory and imagination in McGahern's work. Sampson's introductory comments in *Outstaring Nature's Eye* emphasise the extent to which McGahern 'wrote with [...] [the] authority of the places in which imagination was rooted'.[15] And part of this rootedness appears in the author's mapping of the defining temporal coordinates of that landscape and of the communities that subsisted therein. Thus cycles of time and seasonal repetition are key thematic and symbolic indices across *Memoir*. As Sampson later notes: 'The rituals of planting and reaping, of haymaking and potato-picking, and the dependence on rain and sun represent an elemental way of life'.[16] Decoded with a place-based ecological sensibility, this is a milieu that demands physical engagement with the natural world – all life in this environment is mutually enabling and mutually destructive, and the cycles of reproduction are husbanded through laborious and repetitive bodily exertions. For McGahern, cyclicality is a matter of seasonal time, of artistic form and also of the inescapability of origins. Furthermore, in *Memoir* the yields of agricultural labour are not garnered with industrial efficiency, as the patterns of seasonal harvesting return us to a culture that is removed from the tyranny of accelerated productivity.

Changing seasonal activities and weather conditions act as memorial spurs in *Memoir* – blossoming, reaping and immersion in the abundance of nature temper a narrative that is often fixated on the violence of the father–son relationship. With the New Year turning, and 1943 beginning, 'primroses and violets started appearing on the bank above Brady's pool on our way to school. A field for oats was ploughed and sowed and harrowed and rolled. Part of another field was turned into ridges for potatoes' (*M*, 76). The botanical profusion outlines the route to school for the young McGahern, and the author poeticises his memory with the use of an internal rhyme in the first sentence of this extract. The daily repetition of the school day is garnished with the seasonal beauty of a variety of flowers, which is expressed in lyrical mode by the autobiographer.

But McGahern also references the seasonal responsibilities of the new calendar year, as he sketches the four-part process of planting oats, in addition to turning the soil for a crop of potatoes. The laborious, the beautiful and the routine are remembered here by McGahern in a passage that entwines the personal and the ecological in cyclical time and seasonal duties for the subsistence of life. However, in tune with our complication of the scalar pluralities of McGahern's work, the apparent and insistent 'default scale of human terrestriality' might be read as problematic or suspect in the context of global climate change.[17] Is this another instance – Keats' 'Ode to Autumn' is another – where the reductive temporal frames of the human and artistic scale render the 'natural' cycles of life and time merely instrumental to their progress? In other words, the natural becomes a backdrop despite the apparent celebration – what we have is a tyranny of anthropocentric scalar consciousness, one which refuses the displacement or derangement of scale. Furthermore, we might posit that the narrative's adherence to cycles of seasonal time as structural devices for remembrance and meaning actually disavows the overwhelming scales on which human life unfolds. Insisting on the integrity of the local seasonal routine facilitates the concentration of textual meaning and agency at the level of the human – a point that ecocriticism informed by Anthropocenic scale effects sharply contests.

One of the most affective passages exploring the roots and textures of locality and homeliness, as well as the notion of nature, or non-human ecology, as a temporal marker of human action and human life in *That They May Face the Rising Sun* concerns Jamesie's wife, Mary. Over the course of this reflective section of the novel, a physical description of place gradually gives way to an emotionally charged recollective account of Mary's memories of her father and his idiosyncratic habits. Mapped from the geographical locus of the narrative, McGahern offers a lyrical portrait of memory and 'ruination':

> Below the Ruttledges' stood the entrance to the house where Mary had grown up on the edge of the lake, its stone walls and outhouses hidden in the tall trees. In the middle of the living room an ash tree had taken root where they had played cards and said the Rosary in the evenings before raking the ashes over the red coals; but it was still easy to see what a charming, beautiful place the living house had been, a stone's throw from the water. The blue of the pieces of broken delph in the shallows of the lake out from the piers even spoke of prosperity and ease. Cherry and apple and pear trees grew wild about the house, and here and there the fresh green of the gooseberry shone out of a wilderness of crawling blackthorn. Hundreds of daffodils and white narcissi still greeted each spring by the lake with beauty, though there was no one near at hand to notice. (*RS*, 92–3)

The passage opens with emphatic human presence, in the form of the Ruttledge house in the present. This standing house shadows the remnants of a former homestead, and in the passage above moves from such presence to a human absence at its close. McGahern takes the reader from this accommodation within nature to a sense of displacement, even irrelevance. Over the course of the passage, also, McGahern interblends different forms of temporality; again the opening, human-centred portions of the piece affirm the imprints of domestication on the landscape, and these are associated with the patterns and mind-sets of linear time. This is a time of progress and futurity, but one that is firmly implanted within human temporal scales. The edificial assertion of Mary's erstwhile home is both metaphor and metonym; its decline and disrepair is an apt metaphoric sign for the ease and inevitability of human temporal limits. Equally, the house itself is metonymic of the broader gradual but insistent spatial contestations and accommodations between humanity and non-humanity. Indeed, the shards of 'delph' poignantly strewn in the lake might equally be legible as further metonymic remains of sundered human settlement. The house is a spatial figuration for the precarious, transient foothold of humanity within what might be termed the global ecosphere.

The linear time of humanity is, then, entwined with the cyclical time of the organic non-human life that abounds on the verges of the lake – a cyclical time that humanity intersects with, but that outstrips and outlasts the current, and past, human presences on and proximate to the shoreline. In an image that is part of a recurring sequence of images and references, McGahern blurs distinctions between interiority and exteriority with the siting of the ash tree within what once functioned as the interior space of Mary's childhood home. It is an image that suggests 'ruination' from one perspective; the security and the integrity of the structure, together with its threnody of memories, are infiltrated and lain waste by the intrusive presence of the tree. Yet, the image also reveals the transient artificiality of domestic spaces per se; McGahern's image, in another respect, hints at the absurdity of such human habitations yet does not disavow the intensity of affective feeling that they generate and accumulate. The rituals of domestic leisure and subsistence are replayed in the penumbra of the current 'occupant' of the home, and the ash tree's reclamation of spatial prominence is also a reminder of the relative scalar limits of human temporal inhabitation here and elsewhere. Within the narrative, Mary's memories are played out within the frames and scales of human *narrative* time; in other words, they are accessed and recalled as narrative fragments of memory. But equally, here, and in *Memoir*, McGahern calls attention to the relationship between human narrative time and other, more vast, temporal scalar proportions.

The treatment of Mary's former home, and of the memories housed within that space, are immediately preceded by an account of the routines of the agricultural life of the Ruttledges. Catalogued as part of this labour are weed-pulling, as well as the thinning of carrots, lettuce, onions, beets and parsnips. Tellingly the passage introduces this flurry of husbandry with another suggestive temporal reference: 'The days disappeared in attendance on small tasks' (*RS*, 92). The tasks themselves are small-scale, yet it is the way in which McGahern highlights their centrality as keys to the structuring of time, of human time, that seems germane to our larger argument. The linear narrative time of human chronology is conditioned and moulded here by the demands of cyclical time. Yet this is not to suggest any form of mutual alienation or conflict in this specific instance; elsewhere in both *Memoir* and *That They May Face the Rising Sun*, however, we can note moments of friction between competing temporal trajectories. The catalysing effects of such agricultural demands are not fetishised in McGahern's text, but there is a sense of tangible mutualism between the human and non-human in this micro-climate by the lake. And this impression is furthered by the aforementioned ways in which McGahern paints the relationship between interiority and exteriority at various junctures.

The passage cited above continues: 'These evenings they ate late. In the soft light the room seemed to grow green and enormous as it reached out to the fields and the crowns of the trees, the green banks and the meadow and trees to enter the room with the whole fullness and weight of summer' (RS, 92). Though delivered in an alternative register, this evocative description of the Ruttledge house once again appears to suggest the merging of the external with the internal; it points to a sensual and material continuity between the two respective spatial contexts. But, of course, such lambent descriptions can also be deciphered as resonant figurative representations of an acutely sensitised ecological consciousness. Leavened by the presence of agricultural disease, labour and death across the narrative, poetic moments such as this do not lapse into vapid sentimentalism; rather they are hard-won moments savouring the sensuous and proximate plenty of non-human ecological phenomena. There is always an accommodation between the human and non-human in McGahern's texts, and there is a recognition of the relativity and variety of times and of timescales, both within human communities and societies, and across the species barriers between humanity and non-humanity.

Yet time is also seen as an oppressive abstraction, and as an unwelcome distraction, at points in *That They May Face the Rising Sun*. One of the features of the novel is the nature of local sociability and the rituals and habits attendant to such circles of sociability. In one of many scenes featuring Jamesie and Ruttledge in conversation, time is portrayed as an external intrusive force, with its mechanised manifestation summarily dismissed by Jamesie. As part of a vaguely comic exchange, McGahern gestures to a degree of incompatibility between the sustaining and affective conversational codes of the neighbours, and the linear urgency of mechanised 'clock-time'. The interior domestic scene is set with a prompt allusion to such time: 'All through the evening the pendulum clocks struck. There were seven or eight in the house, most of them on the walls of the upper room. The clocks struck the hours and half-hours irregularly, one or other of them chiming every few minutes' (RS, 103). The clocks, symbolic of structure and coherence, as well as anthropocentric codifications of temporality, are also heirlooms and connections to past generations within Jamesie's family. However, in this instance, they are little more than barriers to the free flow of conversation; Jamesie's appetite for local gossip is frustrated by the external dictates of these rigid temporal mechanisms. As Ruttledge moves to leave, and to bring the evening to a finish, Jamesie inquires: 'What hurry's on you?' […] 'Isn't the evening long? It's ages since ye were over' (*RS*, 103). To which he quickly adds: 'Who cares about time? We know the time well enough.' […] 'Do you have any more news now before you go?' (*RS*, 104).

The same clocks reappear later in the novel, and later in the year, when Ruttledge is once more in Jamesie's house watching the All-Ireland final. And again, there is a tension between the affective atmosphere in the house occasioned by the shared experience of the sporting events and the calm regularity of the chiming clocks. In McGahern's terms, the warm conviviality of the occasion is tempered by the time-pieces: 'The irregular striking of the clocks from every quarter of the house throughout the match served as a cool corrective to the excited commentary' (*RS*, 191). These are not isolated protests against the conformities of 'clock time' in McGahern's work, nor are they, perhaps, the most urgent or emotive rebuke against such temporal organisation. However, they are fractions of a broader patterning within this novel, and in *Memoir*, in which competing and overlapping temporal regimes or dispositions are in evidence. The clocks, facets of the industrialisation of time and space alluded to at various junctures in McGahern's works, reinforce the relevance of 'scalar' ecocritical reading as they are potent, and ubiquitous, devices through which humanity strives to exert its will and its forms on a volatile external environment. Indeed, the clock, in these instances, represents an alternative ethic of living, which itself recalls the broader 'moralisations' of time, efficiency and punctuality that abound in the globalised, capitalist North.

As we have seen, McGahern does not retreat into any species of cloying sentimentality in either *Memoir* or *That They May Face the Rising Sun*, yet neither are these related narratives evacuated of affect, particularly that generated by proximate, interdependent local living. But again, this is not to argue that McGahern's localities can be conclusively hived off from the imprints of either the national or global scales or contexts. The ecological consciousness palpable in McGahern's narratives, then, is not conditioned by a form of crude or insular fetishisation of place or of the purity of rural living. Instead, and in this case in comic form, McGahern is keenly attuned to the practicalities of rural environments, and to the necessary 'hierarchies' characteristic of such environments. Two resolutely local men, Patrick Ryan and Johnny, Jamesie's brother, have a brief exchange during one of Johnny's annual visits home from England, out of earshot of Ruttledge. In this conversation Patrick Ryan provides an insight into the priorities of farming, and these are neither idealised nor sentimentalised:

> You know yourself that you have to be born into land. That brother of yours kept them afloat in the beginning. Everything round the place are treated like royals. There's a black cat in there with white paws that'd nearly get up on its hind legs and order breakfast. You'd not get thanked now if you got caught hitting it a dart of a kick on the quiet. The cattle come up to the back of the house and boo in like a trade union if the grass isn't up to standard. [...] There's an old Shorthorn they milk for the house that would nearly sit in an armchair and put specs on to read the *Observer*. (*RS*, 80)

This exchange couples a biting wit with an emphatic acceptance of the practical relations that obtain in this agricultural context; and there is no sense in which rural local patterns of living are valorised as exemplary from ecological or ecocritical standpoints. The baldness of the opening statement by Patrick Ryan is not a lapse into a cossetted form of local exceptionalism, but constitutes a laboriously accrued comprehension of the aforementioned lived practicalities. This might seem remote from an ecocritical politics, but, on the contrary, it eschews exogenous idealisations of what are more often modes of living that must negotiate the demands of everyday labour and precarity, together with the economic, political and environmental insinuations of national and global scales.

Yet the shadows of destructive change, on larger scales, to these geographies are gestured to early on in *Memoir*, and are punctuating presences at various junctures across the narrative. At the end of the first page, McGahern reflects that 'the very poorness of the soil saved the field when old hedges and great trees were levelled throughout Europe for factory farming' (*M*, 1). His beloved childhood playgrounds, then, avoided rationalisation through their lack of utility and productivity. Clearly not cast in a polemical idiom, McGahern's remarks, nevertheless, resonate with an ecocritical argument that resists the calculus of accelerated modernisation, and that targets multi-scalar interpretations of such historical narratives. The time and place of these changes may be displaced within McGahern's memorial narrative, but within the kind of 'deranged' scalar exegesis forwarded by Clark, they are not merely incidental. As Martin Ryle comments: 'History is making the ordinary fields of Leitrim into emblematic presences. They remind the writer and reader not of the lost intensity of youth (as in Wordsworth) but of the continent-wide effects of the progress which has yet to reach this margin'.[18] In the same paragraph, Ryle proceeds in his ecocritical reading of McGahern's opening memorialisation of his native fields, and also links it to *That They May Face the Rising Sun*: 'Throughout Europe for some time now, the multiple crisis of "the environment" has been moving the question of remembered, surviving, and threatened pleasures, in places at the edge of modernisation, to the centre of metropolitan consciousness. McGahern's last two books, through and beyond their scrupulous naturalism, give a compelling sense of remembered and still surviving landscape that embodies the cultural dream-memory of pastoral'.[19] Its evocation makes these last works as readable and as significant in a wider international context as in the local and national setting that all McGahern's fiction commemorates. Yet, Ryle's reading does not go far enough in its situation of the vast environmental hinterland of McGahern's writing.

Invoking adjacent scales and the same socio-economic processes as Ryle's argument, one of the abiding themes of the latter half of *Memoir* and of *That They May Face the Rising Sun* is emigration – a phenomenon defined by geographical mobility and temporal distance. McGahern's family are deeply impacted by emigration to England, and the author is sensitive to the emotional wounds of separation that provide an effective wedge into a consideration of his broad ecological vision and its relationship with the politics of speed and time. McGahern writes: 'People did not live in Ireland then. They lived in small intense communities which often varied greatly in spirit and character over the course of even a few miles', and for Irish emigrants, 'Part of the pain [...] was that the small communities they had left were more real [...] than the places where their lives were happening' (*M*, 210). And within the confines of these communities, McGahern continues a few paragraphs further along: '[...] the local and the individual were more powerful than any national identity, and much of what was postulated was given no more than lip service' (*M*, 211). At one level, both of these abstract points accent the intense locality of communal and individual dwelling in Ireland at the time. Despite professions of national fealty, bonds are resolutely rooted in the immediacy of daily life. The emigrant's displacement, their inability to adapt their habits and processes of selfhood and living are based on the inextricability of locality and memory. Having physically exited their formational community, the emigrant cannot easily substitute it with a foreign 'imagined community'. Yet, if we take Clark's point that the Anthropocene demands new reading strategies founded on disruptive scalar effects, then the local ripple effects of emigration must be read in terms of Irish national history, but also as fractional of the global progresses of anthropocentric liberal capitalism. Read at this scale, McGahern's familial, communal or local instances of emigration are certainly depersonalised, as is the immediacy of loss and trauma. But this scale necessarily renders the human at the centre of the economically compelled emigration narrative just another 'thing' within the degrading global ecosphere.

The struggle between distance and time is woven into McGahern's recollective narrative in *Memoir* through references to the gradual encroachment of railway transportation in his home county. The stirrings of Irish transportational modernisation register in his childhood landscape, again in relation to his life with his mother. In fact, there are strong echoes of the recalled experiences on the same Arigna railway recorded in *That They May Face the Rising Sun* in the form of Ruttledge's recollections of his childhood (*RS*, 240). In *Memoir*, McGahern's portraits of the railway's inefficiency are couched in farcical comedic guise. Due to the rationing of fuel during the Second World War, 'the trains had to run on the low-grade Arigna coal, and sometimes it would have been faster to walk the four miles of sleepers from Aughawillan to Ballinamore than to take the train. I think it was seen more as a social outing, when such outings were rare, than a means of transport' (*M*, 71). Contrary to the locomotive dynamism of efficient railway transport, the common perception of this addition to Irish rural infrastructure was of a means of gathering for the local population. The promise of increased speed, the conquest of distance, in ecological terms, is of secondary value in this context. In the last sentence McGahern captures the tension between leisure, even indolence, and the productive utilisation of time. Countering the industrial logic and scale of the lumbering trains, he sketches a disposition more attached to unhurried social interaction.

Impressing the acceptance of the limits of technological advancement, in comedic fashion, McGahern describes good-humoured toleration of the train's labours: 'On the steep incline, we often had to climb from the train and walk to the top of the hill while the empty carriages slipped back down the track and waited for the engine to get up steam and make another run at the hill. There was never any complaint' (*M*, 71). In this instance the contours of the landscape itself impede the steady progress of the train and, again, there is a reversion to the basic mode of pedestrian travel. The episode represents, in parvo, McGahern's concern for the disappearance of a particular way of living in Ireland. His ecological eye, in this and other ways, is set upon a community and a lifestyle that is not dependent upon speed and ruthless efficiency. There is consonance between a committed mode of 'dwelling' in the present and through memory, and a sceptical detachment from networks of modern, accelerated living. But equally, this farcical rendering of rural transportation, particularly that motored by 'low-grade Arigna coal', cannot be severed from the kinds of scalar readings we have conducted thus far. That the regular and predictable inefficiency of the train is of primary narrative significance for McGahern, together with the local communality of the experience, does not invalidate our reading. Though firmly rooted in the past, what McGahern's narrative reveals latently here is an 'emergent human and planetary reality'; just as the scale effects of the Anthropocene are emergent, so too are the narratives traces within *Memoir*. The dominant farcical micro-scale is re-read, then, within the frames of an emergent critical consciousness of pollution, narratives of economic efficiency and global climate change. In other words, under the lens of the macro-scale it asks questions about the emergent costs of such local communal comedy.

We will conclude with a related episode, one that has clear ecocritical relevance. Bound up with the development of the railway system is the coal-mining industry at Arigna, referenced above, and it is telling later in *Memoir* how the miners are perceived by the young McGahern. Having taken the train, this time alone to visit his father in Cootehall, he meets with a group of miners on the road from Drumshanbo to Cootehall: 'I met miners on bicycles coming home from their work in the pits, wearing hats with the miner's lamp, their faces and hands black, their clothes black. What was strange and frightening were the eyes shining out of the black faces under the hats' (*M*, 103). Though a minor event in his longer narrative arc relaying his slow progress to Cootehall, the miners' presence is suggestive of the conditions of modernisation insinuating themselves into the resolutely rural settings of the author's childhood and adolescence. The miners are an incongruous, even sinister, sight for the young boy, but their apparent spectral appearance is, in fact, more premonition than haunting. And while the presence of iron ore mining at Arigna goes back centuries, as far back as the medieval period, we might well read this industrial presence in McGahern's locality as metonymic of impending and future patterns of industrialisation and modernisation that impact upon the ecological integrity of such localities, in the Irish context and elsewhere. Almost immediately after his encounter with the miners, McGahern takes the final turn for Cootehall. On this road, 'There was little traffic, a few carts, people walking, one or two bicycles, a few cattle on the long acre' (*M*, 104) – again astride his bicycle, McGahern is in familiar territory at this point: silence, relative solitude and a distinct lack of compulsion. He decides to rest and he gazes 'upriver at the piles of huge rocks along the banks that had been blasted when the river was deepened and widened for the Shannon Hydroelectric Scheme' (*M*, 104). Mining and the industrial preparation for the hydroelectric plant at Ardnacrusha downriver exert ferocious violence on the landscape in the pursuit of innovation. But at the same time both Ardnacrusha, and later Arigna, are symbolic of the ways in which international, global political and economic forces influence the lives and the landscapes in distant local contexts. Indeed McGahern captures this sense of the interaction of the local and the global in his memory of the Shannon Hydroelectric Scheme: 'I had heard of French engineers who had worked on the Scheme, many of them good musicians. Some had married local girls who went to live with them in France when the work was finished' (*M*, 104). It is clear that McGahern is not unapologetically dismissing such traces of modernisation, but what we can divine is his deft sensitivity to these steady but emergent alterations to the ecology of the Irish rural landscape, and to the consequences for the life cycles and patterns of living for the residents of these geographies.

As we have seen, the local and the global do converge within *That They May Face the Rising Sun* and *Memoir* – at times consciously and in tensions, but as we have also demonstrated, at others, and from an ecocritical perspective, the global is tangible only as an emergent presence as we decode, and potentially 'derange', the narrative within the more protracted temporal scales and spatial scales of the Anthropocene. And that, in many respects, is the kernel of Clark's text; we have become over-reliant on critical reading strategies that do little to unsettle a humanist or anthropocentric consensus. In Clark's terms: 'The retrospective light of the Anthropocene casts into new relief developments that many regard as human advances, including social changes such as the rise of the liberal values of individualism, and personal freedom, for these cannot now be disengaged from such environmentally degrading impacts as increased consumption, individual property rights, growing markets and expanded resource use'.[20] In our terms, then, importing the Anthropocene into critical literary studies does not disavow the force of the local, rather our readings must now recognise the necessary and long-term imbrication of local and global or micro-scale and macro-scale in our interdisciplinary exegeses of literary and cultural texts and artefacts, particularly those that have been consistently championed as exemplars of one scale or the other. Equally, as Clark impresses, as both geological epoch and as conceptual resource, the Anthropocene places the consensual adherence to the scales of historicism under profound stress. Readings of McGahern's oeuvre often veer between, or aggregate, formalist analyses that foreground his stylistic affiliations with Irish and European predecessors, and historicising critiques of his body of work as a resource with which to gauge the moral temperature of the nation across a particular period of time. Yet, following Clark's lead, neither approach transcends the anthropocentric historicism underpinning the consensual cultural politics of liberal humanist criticism. As we have outlined, one of the signal advances offered by ecocritical methodologies in the Anthropocene is the capacity to see through and beyond the necessary attachments of local rootedness to the ways in which we are implicated in the immense scalar proportions of deep historical time and global spatiality.

Chapter 7

—

'The purity of feeling […] [of] the remembered "I"': Remembrance, Atonement and Celebration in John McGahern's *The Leavetaking*

—

Claudia Luppino

In loving memory of Hugh Garvey

*T**he Leavetaking* (1974; 1984)[1] belongs to the most experimental phase of John McGahern's career, a phase during which he attempted to find adequate stylistic means to convey his poetic vision. This search sometimes resulted in clumsy sentence structures, not fully convincing characters and uncertain internal divisions. And yet this struggle at the level of language and syntax reflected and translated a philosophical and aesthetic quest for meaning and purpose in life.[2] The works of this period are often overlooked by critics, or dismissed as flawed and transitional. McGahern himself was aware of the difficulties he encountered, and conscious of the limits of what he attempted, but he also saw this experimental moment as a necessary step to attain a serene style and an accomplished vision. His writing process was slow and meticulous, and numerous drafts were produced before his novels and short stories were finally published, in a strenuous search for accuracy and beauty. *The Leavetaking*, however, is unique, in that the substantial revisions that affected the narrative resulted in a second, revised edition, some ten years after the novel's first appearance.

The publication of *Memoir* in 2005,[3] shortly before McGahern's death, brought new attention to *The Leavetaking*, for the way in which it retrieved and recycled, as it were, language and imagery from that early novel. The section devoted to his mother's death when he was a young boy, in particular, is reproduced almost word for word. A plausible explanation for this is that writing down the story of that primal and irreversible loss, and the feelings that accompanied him then and in the years that followed, must certainly have been an exacting process, hence the recourse, in *Memoir*, to the same sentences he had painfully forged for *The Leavetaking*. As the numerous episodes, characters and phrases from other novels and short stories that reappear on the pages of his memoir confirm and highlight, interesting links and porous borders exist between the fictional universe and the real-life experience of this writer. *The Leavetaking*, however, features in *Memoir* more extensively and more explicitly than any other of his fictions, and in connection to that crucial watershed that the circumstances of Susan McGahern's premature death represented for her son as a person and as an artist. The entanglement of grief and guilt, of memory and imagination that *The Leavetaking* stages in embryo would soon emerge as the pattern underpinning McGahern's entire work, and as the quintessential kernel of his poetic vision.

This chapter reassesses the importance of *The Leavetaking* and casts a light on the different reasons why it deserves new critical attention. Paul Ricoeur's theories about memory and forgetting are deployed alongside those non-fictional writings in which McGahern expressed his conception of the role of art and described the mechanisms of his creative process, to show the prominent place and the crucial role of *The Leavetaking* in the panorama of his works and along the path of his aesthetic evolution.[4]

Mirroring the author's real-life experiences closely,[5] McGahern's third novel tells the story of Patrick Moran's last day as a teacher in a Dublin school, shortly after his marriage to an American divorcee named Isobel. Long flashbacks punctuate the chronicle of this last day and account for the protagonist's close relationship with his mother and for the circumstances and the impact of her death when he was only a child. In the 'Preface to the Second Edition' of the novel, McGahern explained that the two parts into which *The Leavetaking* is divided are 'deliberately different in style' (*L2*, 5), in fact the more poetic and intense the first one, the more journalistic and detached the second, in the attempt 'to reflect the purity of feeling with which all the remembered "I" comes to us, the banal and the precious alike; and yet how that more than "I" – the beloved, the "otherest", the most trusted moments of that life – stumbles continually away from us as poor reportage' (*L2*, 5).

What he had attempted was the result of a distinctive way of working as an artist. As early as 1968, McGahern outlined his aesthetic principles in a short text titled 'The Image'. In what was to emerge as his fundamental artistic manifesto, he described the artist's journey as 'long and complicated', because

> image after image flows involuntarily [...] and still we are not at peace, rejecting, altering, shaping, straining towards the one image that will never come, the lost image that gave our lives expression [...].[6]

In a Proustian quest for 'the lost image', McGahern was a demanding artist, who reworked his material continuously (hence not the most prolific of writers), or as Eamon Maher has put it, one who 'chisel[led] away at his work in an attempt to get his words right' through 'a style that is deceptively simple and clear'.[7] In this context, the rewriting of *The Leavetaking* is typical and symptomatic of that process of condensation, of narrowing down, of reduction to the essential, that characterises McGahern's work as a whole, with its relatively small number of characters, places, names, themes and situations.

When *The Leavetaking* first appeared in 1974, McGahern was at the centre of what critics have referred to as 'the middle period' of his writing career. The works that date back to those years (*The Leavetaking*, *Getting Through* and *The Pornographer*)[8] are characterised by a high degree of formal experimentation and mark the transition from the gloomy atmosphere and the young protagonists of his early narratives to the more optimistic views, the mature characters and the serene style of his later and more unanimously acclaimed fiction. While the explicitly experimental style of the works of this middle period 'may have seemed unclear' or 'clumsy' to readers and reviewers,[9] they proved a fruitful and necessary moment of stylistic transition.

In the case of *The Leavetaking*, the appearance of a French translation in 1983 offered the author the opportunity to reflect on that narrative again.[10] He realised that he 'had been too close to the "Idea"', and that 'the work lacked that distance, that inner formality or calm, that all writing, no matter what it is attempting, must possess'.[11] While Part One was left untouched in the second edition, Part Two was extensively reworked.[12] The most obvious change was a substantial shortening, with the elimination of the more reflective and philosophical paragraphs, and the veering of the focus towards language and the idea that we perceive ourselves and others in radically different ways. Significantly, a few paragraphs were also added, which echoed the Preface and ultimately reinforced the writer's wish to clarify his artistic views through this novel. The following, 'new' extract illustrates this agenda well:

> When I thought of how poorly I had grasped the images of Isobel's early life, how I had to translate them into my own and how clear my own were [...], it grew clear that different images must be as vivid in her own mind. [...] The whole dear world of the beloved comes to us with the banality of news reports, while our own banalities come to us with the interest of poetry. It did not seem right. The contrary should be true, but it would be as impossible to reverse as to get trees to lean towards the sea. (*L2*, 143)

The relevance of the rewriting of *The Leavetaking* transcends that particular novel and acquires its full significance when seen as a decisive stepping stone in the writer's own path of aesthetic evolution. Again, this is something McGahern was keenly aware of, to the point of admitting that he 'would actually have stopped as a writer' if he had not 'broken out of [his] own moulds' in *The Leavetaking*.[13] The analysis of the various non-fictional texts that punctuate McGahern's writing career shows the striking consistency with which this writer outlined his aesthetics throughout the decades, ranging from 'The Image' (1968; 1991), through the Preface to the second edition of *The Leavetaking* (1984) and several interviews, and all the way up to the Preface to *Creatures of the Earth* (2006), with the same few but paramount principles reaffirmed with clarity and conviction. Artistic creation, for McGahern, started from personal memories or, in his own words, from those images that reside in a 'still and private universe which each of us possess but which others cannot see'.[14] As the memorable refrain of *The Leavetaking*, of 'memory becoming imagination', very effectively summarises, the imagination supports memory by filling its gaps and by fixing its inconsistencies. A preoccupation for formal perfection, finally, demands that memories be reworked in order to function in a work of art: a narrative structure, therefore, is imposed to give them shape and meaning and to organise them as a chain of causes and effects. McGahern saw how, unless they 'were reinvented, re-imagined and somehow dislocated from their origins', his stories 'never seemed to work. The imagination demands that life be told slant because of its need of distance.'[15] Art thus conceived provides the human being with a shield, which hides and protects, but also empowers: art is 'an attempt to create a world in which we can live [...] a world of the imagination over which we can reign, [...] [a] Medusa's mirror, which allows us to celebrate even the totally intolerable'.[16]

Consistently with the centrality of memory in the creative process, McGahern's fiction relies heavily on autobiographical materials, a crucial bond that a number of interviews, and ultimately *Memoir*, have confirmed and in some cases revealed. This can be somehow puzzling, given McGahern's outspoken antipathy for self-expression in art: he conceded that a writer can and must only write of what he knows well, when he declared: 'I suppose [my fiction] is [autobiographical], in that it comes from a certain limited experience of life.'[17] But simultaneously he also stated that 'autobiographical writing is mostly bad'.[18] The subtle intertextual play that binds and blends fact and fiction in his writings, however, is undeniable, and the investigation of such *liaisons dangereuses* represents a challenging and most interesting task for the critic.

In a broader context, autobiographical narratives can be regarded as an expression of that retrospective tendency of much contemporary Irish fiction which critical studies have extensively commented upon. Autobiography, in fact, and despite its critical neglect and marginal literary status (it is no coincidence that Liam Harte has characterised it as the 'Cinderella genre'[19]), represents a significant area of Irish writing. While composing their self-portraits, writers explore their own past and that of their country, connecting private and collective experiences. The result is a compelling amalgam of memories, historical events and imagined details. Such a blurring of fact and fiction challenges the very notion of authenticity that one would expect as implicit in this type of narrative. Like any other account of the past, however, an autobiography is not a mere mirror-like portrait, it implies a selection and a commentary, as well as a complex process of reconstruction and reconsideration. A narrative structure is necessary to see life as meaningful and coherent and to appreciate the continuity between past and present.[20] The process of composing an autobiography thus requires a working-through of past traumas and, ultimately, a disarming of the past and the imaginative liberation of the self.[21]

Adding further nuances and layers of complexity to autobiography proper, autobiographical fiction is by definition not as strictly subject to the constraints of being true to the facts, hence it can select and omit, and incorporate imaginary events and details much more freely. Its positive value resides precisely in allowing the author to disengage from the duty – and the embarrassment – to be true to 'what really happened' and to offer instead a more or less embellished version of his/her story. In this sense, autobiographical fiction provides a platform to re-imagine one's past and one's self. Such a reading of autobiographical narratives as 'masked' autobiographies[22] points to what Philippe Lejeune has theorised as the 'autobiographical space', namely, to that hybrid dimension where both autobiography and autobiographical fiction belong, but which cannot be reduced to either, their relation being not one of competition (in terms of accuracy, complexity, truth), but one of kinship and complementarity.[23]

The crucial role that memory played for John McGahern, both as the starting point of artistic creation and as the structural and thematic kernel of most of his novels and short stories, encourages and renders apposite the application of Paul Ricoeur's theories about the uses and abuses of memory to the critical analysis of the Leitrim writer's works. In *Memory, History, Forgetting* (2004), Ricoeur explores the ways in which memory, in all its forms and functions, works and fails, is exercised or manipulated. He illustrates the kinship of memory and imagination, for the ways in which they both work through images, and he warns against the risk of confusing memory and imagination and the ultimate unreliability of memory. And yet, the French philosopher insists, memory is of crucial importance in our perception of reality and the construction of our identity, because, he explains, 'we have nothing better than memory to guarantee that something has taken place'.[24] As we saw, McGahern's creative process starts from an intimate repertoire of images and memories, which are forged into sentences and given coherence through the imagination, and thus turned into something 'believable' and 'true to a central idea or vision of life'.[25] The 'truth' that McGahern is interested in is that of his poetic vision: not the mere account of facts, then, but the composition of a coherent and accurate picture and the movement towards (if not the achievement of) something that transcends the materiality and the absurdity of everyday existence. For the characters that populate his narratives, memory is the fundamental instrument through which they perceive and filter the world around them and construct their sense of themselves, trying to find a balance and a harmony between past and present and with other human beings.

Another part of Ricoeur's analysis of memory which proves particularly relevant to understanding McGahern's aesthetics is his identification of different types or levels of so-called 'abused memory'. Drawing extensively on Freud's essays 'Remembering, Repeating, and Working Through' (1914) and 'Mourning and Melancholia' (1917),[26] Ricoeur explains that what he calls 'pathological memory' is a type of 'blocked memory' which results from the 'compulsion to repeat' a traumatic past event: the patient believes that s/he is remembering that event, but in fact s/he is imprisoned in that past dimension, unable to work through the trauma or to move on in the present and in a healthy relationship with other people. The death of his mother when he was a young boy was a seminal event for McGahern (and for so many of his characters), and the insistent return of his novels and short stories to those circumstances and to their related emotions and long-term effects can be seen as a compulsive repetition of a primal and primary loss. Through endless small variations, McGahern's fictional personae struggle to work through that same childhood trauma and to disengage their adult selves from the fragility and the sense of guilt that that trauma determined. In *The Leavetaking* (and in real life, as *Memoir* shows), a few days before the protagonist's mother died of cancer her husband sent a lorry to collect their children and furniture and to transfer them to his own lodgings, leaving the woman to die alone with only a nurse, a priest and her sister by her side. In the infernal noise of the hammering apart of the rusted bed frames, the young boy was called upstairs to his mother's room:

> 'I came to say goodbye, mother,' the priest had a hand on my shoulder as I bent to kiss her, and as lips touched everything was burned away except that I had to leave at once. If I stayed one moment longer I was lost. Panic was growing: to put arms about the leg of the bed so that they'd not be able to drag me away, to stay by that bed forever.
> 'Goodbye, mother.'
> I had to turn and walk, get out of that room. (*L2*, 71)

The painful parting from his beloved mother, mixed with the excitement and the distraction of the lorry waiting outside, translated in a hasty goodbye. With the hindsight of adult recollection, the massive impact that her death and that final leavetaking had on him is clear:

> A shadow was to fall forever on the self of my life from the morning of that room, shape it as the salt and wind shape the trees the tea lord had planted as shelter against the sea, for in the evenings they do not sway as other trees in the cooling wind, but stay stubbornly bent away from their scourge the sea, their high branches stripped of bark and whitened, and in the full leaf of summer they still wear that plumage of bones. (*L2*, 71)

The crucial importance of *The Leavetaking* lies precisely, I believe, in the way in which this novel stages the centrality of the mother figure and the circumstances of her death. The hasty goodbye to his dying mother would torment the protagonist of *The Leavetaking* for a long time, the acute remorse at having wasted that last hour he could have spent with her haunting him for long years afterwards: 'She must have felt that I too had abandoned her' (*L2*, 75). To make matters worse, that sense of guilt and betrayal would also be connected with the promise that he would become a priest and say mass for her. Her deep faith and the prospect of her first-born embracing a life of purity and prayer seemed to bring her some comfort during her long illness. But he would let her down, and the phrase 'One day I would say Mass for her' punctuates the narrative of *The Leavetaking* like a refrain and a constant reminder of that broken promise. The temptations of the flesh are too strong for Patrick, and he is unable to accept the 'death in life' of priesthood. As the opening paragraph of Part Two explains, the decision to become a teacher appeared like a second best, having been his mother's profession and being seen at the time as 'the second priesthood':

> One day I'd say Mass for her.
> I felt I had betrayed her in that upstairs room. Through the sacrifice of the Mass I would atone for the betrayal, but that in its turn became the sacrifice of the dream of another woman, became the death in life, the beginning only in the end. That way I would make good her dream. That way I would deny her death with my living death. That way I would keep faith. But I was not able to keep faith. The pull of nature was too strong [...]. Guilty and furtively I turned to a second best – I would teach. [...] The Training College itself was reassuringly like a seminary [...]. (*L2*, 85)

Becoming a teacher was, thus, a compensation for reneging on the promise to become a priest. But literature was soon discovered as a more satisfactory replacement vocation for that broken promise: becoming an artist is his way of 'atoning'. As Eamon Maher has beautifully put it, writing was 'his means of paying homage to his mother and of coming to terms with the psychological toll'[27] of her premature loss. In this light, it is not difficult to appreciate how *The Leavetaking* is, in the words of another commentator, 'an attempt to atone for a sense of wrong done, to admit guilt and receive forgiveness', as well as the expression of 'the need to recover the "lost beloved", to shape grief into a symbol of the "lost image"'.[28] The notion of atonement is crucial here, referring, as it does, to an intimate process of understanding, accepting and recovering. The idea of atoning evokes the utterly private dimension of expiation or reparation through suffering or sacrifice, a deeply religious (if not merely Catholic) approach to guilt and to the acceptance of a punishment to obtain forgiveness and to find harmony again, as the origin of the word, from the Middle English phrase 'at onement', in harmony, poignantly signals.

It is important to remember, nonetheless, that John McGahern insistently rejected the conception of art as self-expression or therapy. His is an art of memory and celebration: the writer retrieves the images that populate the most intimate chambers of his inner world and, through carefully chiselled words and the aid of his imagination, he gives them a shape and a rhythm that allows for beauty and truth to emerge. The stress, in other words, is more on the celebratory than the therapeutic power of art. Towards the beginning of that other experimental novel *The Pornographer*, the protagonist's preparatory rites before he sets out to work at his typewriter trigger the memory of his preparations to serve mass as an altar boy.[29] Such a desecrating association of the writer of pornography with the priest is of paramount importance, because it reveals how McGahern conceived of writing as a sacred and transforming activity performed through rituals and capable of transcending mundane reality and of revealing something higher, or deeper. This is where Ricoeur's analysis of forgetting, and of the related problematic of forgiving, guilt and reconciliation with the past, also appears useful and pertinent. For Ricoeur, forgetting is not an enemy or a weakness of memory but, rather, an important counterpart and an indispensable ally to balance and to negotiate memory's right measure.[30] McGahern's art of memory and celebration can be seen as the activity through which he gradually managed to 'forget' or, rather, to overcome the blocked memories of his childhood traumas and to let go of his senses of guilt. As an artist, he carried out a lay spiritual activity, so to speak, celebrating the beauty of life through the ceremonies and rituals of writing. I agree with Maher's idea that writing about his mother's death 'was a key element in [McGahern's] evolution as an artist, a type of catharsis or purging of the trauma it induced in the young boy and, subsequently, the man'.[31] While the boy in *The Leavetaking* says a final goodbye to his mother, he fails to do so in *Memoir*. Dermot McCarthy has convincingly argued that that discrepancy 'is further evidence that from the outset McGahern, consciously or unconsciously, used the writing of fiction to redress the incompleteness of life'.[32] Art allows us to create alternative scenarios, to readdress and to reshape real-life events and to forge them into something different. *The Leavetaking* performs precisely such a transcendent act of transformation of the personal and the mundane into the universal. In this sense, and through memory becoming imagination, the mother's premature death and the long years of grief and guilt that followed are overcome on the written page through the celebration of the world of beauty that she introduced him to and that she embodied. Grief, regret and guilt might be the dominating emotions of a vast section of *The Leavetaking*, but the undeniably hopeful and open feeling that marks the end of that novel – for how uncertain the future of the couple might be[33] – can surely be read as a first manifestation, in embryo, of the more optimistic and celebratory atmospheres characteristic of McGahern's later fiction.

In conclusion, this chapter has proposed a reassessment of the importance of *The Leavetaking* in the panorama of John McGahern's writings. Its value – and its flaws – as a formally experimental novel have perhaps caused the essential part that it played in the evolution of the writer's aesthetic views to be overlooked. Reading *The Leavetaking* alongside *Memoir*, in particular, allows an appreciation of three key elements of McGahern's fiction. Firstly, both the earlier, fictional work (*The Leavetaking*) and the later, non-fictional narrative (*Memoir*) rely extensively on personal memory but integrate it with other materials (imagined details in the novel, letters and other people's recollections in the memoir), weaving a complex and multi-layered textual fabric and a coherent and believable narrative. Secondly, the recourse to the same imagery and the same language in the most crucial and poignant sections of both works points to the blurring of fact and fiction, ultimately to the juxtaposition and intersection of autobiographical fiction (*The Leavetaking*) and fictionalised autobiography (*Memoir*). Finally, and perhaps most importantly, the presence not only of common contents, but also of a common vision, in a work dating back to the early '70s and one published over thirty years later demonstrates how the aesthetic and thematic kernels outlined at a very early stage of McGahern's writing career remained constant. The centrality of the mother figure, the appreciation of the beauty of nature, of the small acts of kindness and of the rituals and ceremonies of everyday life, and the conception of art as a deeply spiritual activity may only emerge as fully shaped and more effectively expressed in McGahern's mature fiction, whereas still in embryo in the novels and short stories of his youth, but a *fil rouge* is undeniably there and well visible. 'The purity of feeling of the remembered "I"', the phrase

McGahern used to refer to the different ways in which we perceive and represent the self and the other, encapsulates the power of art to cleanse reality from its inconsistencies, to infuse memories with imagined details, and thus to give shape and meaning, or as McGahern said, 'to create a world in which we can live' and 'to celebrate even the totally intolerable'.[34]

Chapter 8

—

'The Sky Above Us': John McGahern, 'The Image' and Paul Butler's Photographs of County Leitrim

—

Anne Goarzin

I t is no easy task deciding on a methodology that might do justice to the terse beauty of John McGahern's writings in the wake of more than a decade of plentiful critical commentary that has encompassed a myriad of readings incorporating structuralist approaches and intertextual influences, as well as eco-critical or societal readings, or Lacanian interpretations. McGahern scholarship is now embracing more recent New Materialist readings focusing on trauma or affect, as the articles in this collection show. Paul Butler's photographic projects entitled respectively *Still* (2013) and *The Deep Well of Want* (2016)[1] provide a refreshing incentive to go back to the image that is at the heart of McGahern's writing, through his visual interpretation of McGahern's Leitrim. They also offer a renewed opportunity to envisage the now familiar oeuvre through a less academic and more personal prism. Branding a new identity for Ireland was famously achieved in the modern era by the likes of W.B. Yeats and Paul Henry, as John Fanning has shown:

> Irish artists were conveniently at hand to fulfil this role, favouring the West of Ireland as the essence of the new nation. If W.B. Yeats was the copy-writer for the Irish nation brand then Paul Henry was the art director. His iconic painting *Connemara Landscape*, designed for the London Midland and Scottish Railway, marked a turning point. Using a range of muted colours he achieved an authentic result and his ability to 'express the universality of our relationship with the land' struck an immediate chord with Irish people all over the world who could immediately identify with the unique translucent lighting of the west of Ireland.[2]

However, one should be wary of labels as they often tend to forge an idealised, pre-digested Irish identity. I will contend that Paul Butler's photographs do more than stick with a registered literary trademark and that they open up onto a 'McGahern Country'[3] that may not be fixed, nor indicated by road signs, or guided with the help of internet apps, and which is still first and foremost located in the texts of the novels, the short stories, the essays, as well as in the readers' minds.

Looking at things from the perspective of academic ethnography (not to say archaeology), my own research makes me an 'early McGahernian' of the female kind, as well as of the French kind. It is likely that among the reasons why McGahern's literary works quickly rose to popularity as early as the late 1980s in France was the growing interest in Irish Studies within French universities, fostered by their developing international ramifications through well-established scholarly national organisations such as SOFEIR, and international ones such as IASIL or EFACIS.[4] It may be said that McGahern reached academic consecration when *The Barracks* made it to the *Agrégation* syllabus for the academic year 1995–6, and was studied by all the candidates taking this very competitive teaching exam nationwide. There were several collections of essays published as a result of this early academic fame,[5] as well as day-long conferences devoted to the writer's first novel. In addition, John McGahern came to deliver lectures at French universities and even made an appearance on Laure Adler's TV show *Le Cercle de Minuit* in 1996.[6] Simultaneously, the books began reaching a more general public as they were translated by George-Michel Sarotte for *La caserne*[7] and by Alain Delahaye, who is mentioned by McGahern in his preface to the second edition of *The Leavetaking/Journée d'adieu* as an influence behind its revision.[8] One can safely say that McGahern's books were more popular in France than in Ireland in the early 1990s and doctoral theses kept coming in a steady flow,[9] as well as book chapters and conference papers which often focused, with good reason, on the Irish context (censorship, the repressive influence of the Catholic Church) as well on the distinct use of literary images and stylistic devices, or recurring structures and invariants in the novels and short stories (as memory, or as repetition). Most of these academic essays were indebted to structuralism (even more than to post-structuralist theories of deconstruction), and over-all they fostered a firmly grounded systemic aesthetics, as Eve Meltzer describes it:

[...] the structuralist movement first launched its attack on humanist 'mythology'. Initially inspired by Ferdinand de Saussure's success in founding a 'science' of linguistics based on exclusive study of the governing system of language (*langue*) as opposed to its manifestation in particular languages (*langages*), the structuralists contrasted the objectivity and scientificity of the study of structures underlying social and cultural phenomena to the subjectivism of a 'humanist' emphasis on creativity, freedom and purpose.[10]

Meltzer acknowledges nevertheless that 'structuralist and poststructuralist discourses have provided many disciplines within the academy with a common language at least since the end of the 1960s, by which time, as Elizabeth W. Bruss writes, "the symptoms" of this theoretical imaginary, "heretofore fugitive and for the most part manageable, could no longer be ignored"'.[11] And while she speaks from the perspective of contemporary art history, her proposal to counter the 'spectacle of discourse' provided by structuralism and post-structuralism appears as a valid one for scholars of literature too. She offers to challenge what she has termed 'the impact of antihumanist thought that we more often than not think of the object as a mere effect of preexisting systems and conceive of identity categories as based on structural notions of difference'.[12] It might be rather liberating to conceive of 'the current exhaustion of structuralist/poststructuralist discourse' and to realise the limits of 'theory [that] can oscillate between serving as a critical tool and as an object of historical study'.[13] But Meltzer stresses this does not imply a complete and utter rejection of systems, as structuralism may not have been in vain after all: 'It is the structuralist "adventure" that we have to thank for bringing together such terms, concepts and modes as these: "system" and "structure", "information", scientistic reasoning and diagrammatic forms; an affection for the disaffected; the condition of belatedness; an extreme skepticism of the visible married with a sense of epistemic mastery over otherwise "invisible" structures [...].'[14]

These days the main reason for my reluctance to add my own voice to the chorus of bright and, fortunately, renewed critical readings of McGahern's novels, short stories or critical essays is that I feel that the constraints of the academic format and theory sometimes fail to convey accurately what Kathleen Stewart has called the 'live surface' of the texts.[15] Bound up by its tendency to privilege symbolic meanings and ideologies, we forsake the immateriality of meanings and we fail to attend to ordinary affects, Stewart writes, or 'to trace how the potency of forces lies in their immanence to things that are both flighty and hardwired, shifty and unsteady but palpable too'.[16] What results from this is that academic critical assessment often remains enclosed in its distinctive world of structures and models. Yet admitting to this also nods in recognition to a universal quandary which the creative artist is not spared, as McGahern notes about the elusiveness of the revelation of one's 'unique world' through the language of literature:

> The Muse, under whose whim we reign in return for a lifetime of availability, may grant us the absurd crown of style, the revelation in language of the unique world we possess as we struggle for what may be no more than a yard of lead piping we saw in terror or in laughter once.[17]

In *Ordinary Affects*, Stewart writes: 'Models of thinking that slide over the live surface of difference at work in the ordinary to bottom-line arguments about "bigger" structures and underlying causes obscure the ways in which a reeling present is composed out of heterogeneous and coherent singularities.'[18] Giving up on 'representational thinking and evaluative critique'[19] thus seems more in keeping with McGahern's view that *structures* may be envisioned as both reassuring and futile since in the end, they are mostly strictures, and 'all is outside':

> The superstitious, the poetic, the religious are all made safe within the social, given a tangible form. The darkness is pushed out. All things become interrelated. We learn sequence and precedence, grown anxious about our own position in the scheme, shutting out the larger anxiety of the darkness. There's nothing can be done about it. There's good form and bad form. All is outside.[20]

In other words, it is the 'fugitive symptoms' of the structuralist imaginary that I intend to examine but not to treat, nor solve using scientific/structuralist medication. Instead, I shall turn to Paul Butler's photographs of McGahern's Leitrim which he chooses to pair with chosen excerpts from the texts, thus suggesting possible combinations and substitutions. I argue that text and image do not function 'in themselves', as separate entities or as system or fixed framework: rather, the combination allows the viewer, and the reader, to 'fold' their own subjectivities into the study of the photographs and acknowledge a multiplicity of readings and materials. In this way, they offer 'ways of approaching the complex and uncertain objects that fascinate because they literally hit us or exert a pull on us'.[21]

The Photographs: Paul Butler's *The Deep Well of Want* and *Still*

Being given the opportunity of coming back to McGahern's writing 'from the outside', as it were, through the moving photographs of Paul Butler, provides a means to achieve a more idiosyncratic reading. I use the term 'moving' on purpose here because these are images that literally operate a movement between the text and the photographs, as well as having a capacity to affect and to be affected. This empirical method also seems to be more apposite to the visual dimension of McGahern's texts, in a way that was also faithful to the author's crucial statement: 'I write because I need to write. I write to see. Through words I see.'[22] Paul Butler's photographs thus point to the essence of McGahern's writing and invite us to reflect on it.

'The Image' as McGahern conceives of it derives from ordinariness. It emerges from confused impulses or sensations that fail to be accounted for by words – but in spite of its confusion and immateriality, it can be accounted for in a text that weaves vision and rhythm as well as 'instinct' and the 'complicated' nature of the interaction between all these terms:

> When I reflect on the image, two things from which it cannot be separated come: the rhythm and the vision. The vision, that still and private world which each of us possesses and which others cannot see, is brought to life in rhythm – rhythm being little more than the instinctive movements of the vision as it comes to life and begins its search for the image in a kind of grave, grave of the images of dead passions and their days [...]. It is here, in its search for the one image, that the long and complicated journey of art betrays the simple religious nature of the activity: and here, as well, it most sharply separates itself from formal religion.[23]

In spite of its apparent abstraction, this seemingly theoretical text in fact points to a *practice* and to how bodies and things interact in this searching movement. It speaks of how we notice the world around us, and how we find ways to write and to portray what Kathleen Stewart has described as the 'fractious, multiplicitous, and unpredictable [...] disparate scenes [...] a tangle of trajectories, connections, and disjuncture'[24] – which tends to overcome the fixity of the symbolic. And interestingly what (according to Stewart) emerges from this practice of our everyday lives are 'ordinary affects', that is 'the varied, surging capacities to affect and be affected that give everyday life the quality of a continual motion of relations, scenes, contingencies and emergences. They're things that happen.'[25] Similarly, Butler's photographs are objects that call for the viewer to move through things and scenes, and to determine visual, intellectual, blurry or clearer attachments with these elements of the landscape of County Leitrim.

It is through the emerging image, the child of vision and rhythm, that 'The darkness is pushed out', as McGahern has his narrator say in his most metatextual novel, *The Pornographer*, and it is what makes 'All things become interrelated'. Drawing on Gilles Deleuze for whom 'Theory *is* practice',[26] it appears that imagining new methods 'to deal with the fluidity, multiplicity and vagueness of reality'[27] is essential. Strikingly, McGahern's idea that 'all things become interrelated' is a match to Deleuze's key concept of '"assemblage" that seeks to account for multiplicity and change (or becoming) [...] [and] is the *crafting* of boundaries between what is present, what is manifestly absent, and what is Othered'.[28] The novels and short stories speak of the absence contained in presence as well as of the potential that this absence holds for the viewer – and Paul Butler's photographs provide a concrete visualisation of this.

What these dynamics of presence and absence produce is a slight change, an imperceptible move in relationships, in language, in situations or in beings. It is the ability of McGahern's writings to 'other' or to make the boundaries shift slightly between his world and the reader's that is also exemplified in Paul Butler's conjoined visual and textual approaches. His photographs, he explains, allow him to 'assemble' his own affection for the Leitrim landscape and people:

There was no end to this magic; the inspiration from McGahern's world was definitely influencing my view through the lens. I really enjoyed exploring the many derelict and abandoned cottages dotting the coun- tryside; they are a treasure trove of remnants from a fading world. It was amazing to step inside and find the curtains still framing the windows, or religious memorabilia fixed to the walls, or the old kitchen utensils left in place. I found myself, out of respect, recording these scenes, as if I was a photographic archaeologist, recording a scene for posterity.[29]

But the images also allow the viewer to inscribe his/her own affect into them, through the quotations from McGahern's texts which accompany the photographs, and to 'make a relation' by soaking in the narrative voice's perspective, or identifying with the character's, as in the image below. Here, Butler pairs the photograph with the possibility of something happening outside the frame:

Somewhere, outside this room that was an end, he knew that a young man, not unlike he had once been, stood on a granite step and listened to the doorbell ring, smiled as he heard a woman's footsteps come down the hallway, ran his fingers through his hair, and turned the bottle of white wine he held in his hands completely around as he prepared to enter a pleasant and uncomplicated evening, feeling himself immersed in time without end.[30]

From *Still*, 'The outside world. Cornageeha, Co. Leitrim'. © Paul Butler

Because it is also reminiscent of the 'dusty cretonne' of Eveline's window curtain in James Joyce's *Dubliners*, Paul Butler's photograph provides a renewed point of entry. He also suggests new relations between texts and images, pointing to unexpected details of the Leitrim environment, as in the photograph below.

From *Still*, 'The scullery window. Cornageeha, Co. Leitrim'. © Paul Butler

One might argue that the photographs simply document a dwindling rural life. Yet one could also say that McGahern's text as mediated by Paul Butler's photographic eye is what makes them exist more intensely as an 'assemblage'. Anecdotally, Paul Butler was kind enough to let me access the whole of his collection before he decided on which ones would go into the exhibition. Thus, in my attempt to come up with a more empirical approach to McGahern's text, I spent some time myself pairing the images with passages that stood out for me, knowing confusedly that it would take me somewhere. It turns out that this *exercice de style* led me to experiment with a 'textual' *punctum* different from the photographer's own – and in a rather fruitful way. Butler's references are all to works of fiction: they weave the image with excerpts from novels or short stories. On the other hand, my own 'story' for the following image was an excerpt from McGahern's collected essays *Love of the World*:

> One such small ruin stands on the shore of Laura Lake. The two thick, common piers, common to this area and on which the gates were hung, are no more than ten paces from the water, obscured by fuchsia bushes. The gates are gone, as are the roofs of the building within, but the stone walls are intact. Although a sturdy sycamore has taken root in the main living room, it is easy to see from the shapes that remain how delightful it must have been when it was a working farm.[31]

From *The Deep Well of Want*, 'A Holy Font. Near Ardagh, Co. Longford'. © Paul Butler

It might have been the presence of the lakes in McGahern's collected essays that prompted me to choose a text which, from its first sentence, encapsulates the implacable sense of inevitability and conveys the vision through the rhythmicality of the sibilants in 'such', 'small', 'stands' and 'shore'. 'One such small ruin stands on the shore of Laura Lake' – and yet, the isolation of the 'small ruin' and the rounded words of the self-contained liquid world of 'Laura Lake' also unexpectedly suggests the comforts of the solitary expanse of water.

Another instance of a different pairing occurred with the following image, which Paul Butler matched with an excerpt from *The Barracks*,[32] while I read it in a more theoretical way, as an image about the 'nuances' it takes to suggest (rather than represent) ordinariness.

Madness, like banality or boredom and murder, can be written; but when they are, the writing itself can never afford to be any of these things. For instance, prose has never been more alert to every shade of nuance than when writing about boredom, which is the opposite of the state it is attempting to reflect and bring to life.[33]

From *The Deep Well of Want*, 'Teresa & Perfume. Near Ballinalee, Co. Longford'.© Paul Butler

The photograph in this instance calls to me through a detail in the image from which I cannot escape. It may be unintended by the photographer and yet it offers a renewed access to McGahern's text. Roland Barthes, writing in *Camera Lucida*, called this the 'punctum': 'it is this element that rises from the scene, shoots out of it, and pierces me'.[34] It is 'the sting, speck, cut, little hole – and also a cast of the dice'[35] that disturbs the 'studium', which stands for the familiar interpretation of the photograph, one that does not require special acuity and relies on acquired knowledge.[36]

As Kathleen Stewart underscores: 'The first step in thinking about the force of things is the open question of what counts as an event, a movement, an impact, a reason to react.'[37] Hence to me, this photograph packs stories of intimate life and faith, of femininity and of domesticity. It might be a still life, but it is one that is alive. It captures these stories through focusing on the ironing board, a flask of perfume, religious imagery, the rust-coloured crucifix and metal crown of ivy of the mirror, the tiny boxes. Like many of Paul Butler's photographs, it frames ordinariness through windows, a mirror there, elsewhere a gate, or the edge of a mantelpiece, the decrepit walls of a room. But it also pays inordinate attention to details. So if we are to determine what counts as an event here, in the midst of the apparent ordinariness, one might say that it is the way in which we relate to the image: it is how we 'enter the middle, the between' in a creative way that makes the event. For in the middle is where life is at its most potent, as the anonymous figures who populate McGahern's anecdotes suggest:

'I suppose, now, there wouldn't be too much happening down in Leitrim?' the barman laughed.
'It's peaceable,' the man seemed to agree, 'but not too peaceable. Middlin' peaceable. What you want, like where we're from, across the river. Belcoo. Yes. Middlin' peaceable. The sky above us.'[38]

Thus the practice of creating photographic images that are both informed and inspired by McGahern's locations makes for more than a juxtaposition of two distinct mediums, as Paul Butler's pairing of image and excerpts from texts motions towards the potential that resides in the assemblage of these mediums, and in the force of one's personal perception. Indeed, rational, critical or aesthetic accounts might rule that if taken separately, these images of abandoned houses and lonely fields and lanes speak of backward-looking nostalgia, or that the accumulation of hodgepodge things – from heaps of plastic containers in the shape of Our Lady of Lourdes, to a kitchen range or a confessional – makes for a catalogue of kitsch objects that are only spared the charge of bad taste by the eeriness of an environment that seems half-lived in, half-deserted. But they would miss the *punctum*: here, the entanglement of the visual and the textual, the surprise of the fleeting emotion conveyed by the reminisced familiar sight of a domestic object, or the shape of a tree pro-vide (they bring something to *see*, literally) a creative, even 'peaceable' arrangement. This arrangement is in fact intensely *poietic*, in that it involves more than the artist's (the photographer's or the writer's) intentional, creative will and processes of creation, as philosopher Derek H. Whitehead notes in terms close to those of McGahern in 'The Image':

> [...] poiesis is something very much 'in process' contemporaneously, that it remains an 'undercurrent' striving toward the light of day. As such it is likely to surface in rather surprising forms, not least in 'found objects', 'ready-mades', 'assemblages', or 'installations' where the artist's intuitive faculty – in the selection and compositional arrangement of freely chosen elements – appears uppermost.[39]

In that sense, Butler's photographs are not only a tribute to McGahern's literary depictions of County Leitrim. For the visual artist, the text lies at the root of what Whitehead has called his 'inner creative seeing', much as McGahern's writing hinges on visual undercurrents. Both mediums offer a fruitful interaction that brings the viewer/reader with them into a new 'clearing', where the international will of the artist (or praxis) meets poiesis and, Whitehead says, 'bring[s] about a transforming encounter between the artist and his or her work in the unfolding conditions of art-making, which itself communicates a *poietic* world-view to art's recipients'.[40]

> The artist is one for whom the poverty of his or her materials is all that remains in this unveiling of things. It is an inner creative seeing that regathers the things of the world. However, as Heidegger has argued, the 'created work' is not something adjunct or accidental to an artist's being; it is integral to it. A work comes to be that it may be un-concealed or brought into 'the clearing' in the light of *aletheia*, the unveiling of truth. It is this unconcealedness which gives a work of art its authenticity as a self-presencing thing. A work of art comes into visual, aural or tactile view by invading the spaces and textures of the sensible world, by becoming the unveiling (or *aletheic*) reality it means itself to be.[41]

It is thus as a recipient of both McGahern's texts and Butler's images that I can return to the more practical[42] reading I was searching for, as a light-hearted and respectful artisan[43] who has been ushered into the numinous world of the artist.

Chapter 9

—

A Dub in Leitrim: McGahern as Seen Through the Camera Lens

—

Paul Butler

My first introduction to John McGahern was on a sun holiday back in 1990. After rapidly chewing my way through a series of end-of-the-world action hero thrillers, I quickly ran out of reading material and a friend passed me a copy of *Amongst Women*. I must admit that it was very far removed from my usual reading material. However, while intrigued with the main character, Moran, it was McGahern's strong descriptive language that really drew me in. His minute description of the landscape fired my imagination. I visualised through his words the changing seasons, the wildlife, hedges, colours, weather; all leapt from the page and took root in my psyche.

'To leave the ever-present tension of Great Meadow was like shedding stiff, formal clothes or kicking off pinching shoes.' *Amongst Women* (London: Faber & Faber, 1990), p. 33.

I became immersed in his precise detail, especially the way he evoked the countryside, the customs of the people, the striking landscapes and house interiors. I had never been to this part of Ireland and yet I could easily visualise McGahern's literary universe. His collected short stories became a well-thumbed book that followed me through college and spoke to me in a particular way. Living in small, tungsten-lit damp rooms, I would read his books over and over until they ended up as film scenes in my mind, opening up the possibility of wonderful back stories. Being a penniless mature student, I could certainly relate to some of the settings.

I have a lifelong interest in photography and the outdoors. However, Leitrim and the north-west more generally were not on my radar. Growing up in the Dublin suburbs, it was always enjoyable to escape to the great outdoors with the camera on my shoulder; however, normally I headed east or south. But at the beginning of the millennium my wife, son and I moved from Dublin and set up home in Farnaght which is close to Mohill in County Leitrim, bang in the middle of McGahern country. The move to Leitrim allowed me to marry my interest in McGahern with my passion for images. As already mentioned, I always considered McGahern a visual writer and when I ventured out around my new surroundings with camera in hand I stepped into his world. Very quickly the images started to unfold in this magical setting, a place untouched by time. It was as if John McGahern and his characters had simply got up from the kitchen table, grabbed their coats and walked away. The further I ventured out to explore, the more this beautiful world opened up to me.

Pictures grew before me, moody trees peering through the early-morning mist, the golden light permeating ancient woodland bordering the lakes, the big black-blue clouds rolling across an April sky, abandoned dwellings sitting in a boggy field. McGahern's descriptions of interiors, the real smells and sounds of houses, his careful, minimal use of words to set up a scene – it was all so deliberately scripted that I could not fail to think of it in photographic or filmic terms.

There was no end to this magic; the inspiration from McGahern's world was definitely influencing my view through the lens. I really enjoyed exploring the many derelict and abandoned cottages dotting the countryside; they are a treasure trove of remnants from a fading world. It was amazing to step inside and find the curtains still framing the windows, or religious memorabilia fixed to the walls, or the old kitchen utensils left in place. I found myself, out of respect, recording these scenes, as if I was a photographic archaeologist, recording a scene for posterity.

'She was determined to grasp at a life of her own desiring, no longer content to drag through with her repetitive days, neither happy nor unhappy, merely passing them in the wearying spirit of service; and the more the calls of duty tried to tie her down to this life, the more intolerably burdened it became.' *The Barracks* (London: Faber & Faber, 1963), p. 15.

'Within the deep walls on the lake, a butcher's calendar of the year before was hung. Above the tables of the months and days was a photo of two boys wheeling bicycles while driving sheep down a country lane between high stone walls. Helping them were two beautiful black-and-white collies. High-class beef, mutton and lamb at best prices. Large and small orders equally appreciated.' *That They May Face the Rising Sun* (London: Faber & Faber, 2002), p. 17.

'Somewhere, outside this room that was an end, he knew that a young man, not unlike he had
once been, stood on a granite step and listened to the doorbell ring, smiled as he heard a
woman's footsteps come down the hallway, ran his fingers through his hair, and turned the bottle
of white wine he held in his hands completely around as he prepared to enter a pleasant and
uncomplicated evening, feeling himself immersed in time without end.' 'The Wine Breath', in
Creatures of the Earth: new and selected stories (London: Faber & Faber, 2006), p. 120.

'He took down the plain wooden box that held his shaving kit from the top of the medicine press
and opened it on the sewing-machine to get his cut-throat razor and he stroked it over and back
on a strip of fine leather tacked to the side of the press. After he'd tested its sharpness he laid it
carefully on a newspaper in the window and searched the box for the brush and stick of soap.'
The Barracks, p. 43.

When a person passes away in Leitrim, I am astonished by the number of people who arrive to offer condolences; it's as if the whole county is there. The soothing sound of the bell from our local church in Gortletteragh carries across the fields, while in the local shop the radio presenter reads out daily death notices.

Little did I realise that all the stories from McGahern I had read many years earlier were now overlapping with my photographic ideas and technique through a postgraduate thesis I had embarked on.

My initial impression of Leitrim, before we relocated there, was of an empty place, damp and full of trees. No doubt this was related to the advertisements that appeared regularly back in the eighties of acres for sale, or tree-planting. However, I was relieved that my fears were totally unfounded. That said, the land is poor and marshy, but it nevertheless displays a stunning beauty in all seasons.

McGahern's description of how the fields and laneways burst into life during the spring and summer months sums up beautifully the magic of this place. Due to less intensive farming, the fields are quite small and are bounded by a wonderful array of hedgerows. The seasons matter here; in fact, they determine everything, and I find myself noting what jobs the farmers are

'It was so beautiful when she let up the blinds first thing that 'Jesus Christ', softly, was all she was able to articulate as she looked out and up the river to the woods across the lake, black with the leaves fallen except the red rust of the beech trees, the withered reeds standing pale and sharp as bamboo rods at the edges of the water.' *The Barracks*, p. 170.

'The fields between the lakes are small, separated by thick hedges of whitethorn, ash, blackthorn, alder, sally, rowan, wild cherry, green oak, sycamore, and the lanes that link them under the Iron Mountains are narrow, often with high banks. The hedges are the glory of these small fields, especially when the hawthorn foams into streams of blossom each May and June.'
Memoir (London: Faber & Faber, 2005), p. 1.

doing in the area at a particular time. I have always felt that because the N4 merely skirts the lower part of the county, the people and environment have mostly been left to their own devices.

Though the heavy, grey days of November with head-height sagging grey cloud can make you feel quite melancholic, the effect of this neutral light on the falling leaves and leaf litter carpeting everywhere is an annual treasure. October through to May are my favourite months, with the light and colour ranging from suppressed to riotous. Spring gives you the big sky months, monstrous cloud formations rolling across the land. Captured on a wide-angle lens and printed in black and white, they evoke a deep and touching experience.

When you wander through the dark state forests close to our home, devoid of activity save for badger sets and a mattress of neutral brown pine needles, stillness befalls you. Venture further and step out into the bright light of old native wood for a spellbinding sight.

A few years ago Coillte moved into the area around where I live and within a couple of days, forty years of growth was felled and shipped off. The devastated area quickly became populated with natural growth. The one (very)

'When you're in danger of losing a thing it becomes precious and when it's around us, it's in tedious abundance and we take it for granted as if we're going to live forever, which we're not.' 'Catholicism and National Identity in the Works of John McGahern', interview between Eamon Maher and John McGahern, in *Studies: an Irish quarterly*, vol. 90, no. 357, Spring 2001, pp. 72–83, at p. 75.

'There was no longer the dripping on the dead leaves, the wood clamped in the silence of white frost except for the racket some bird made in the undergrowth.' 'Christmas', in *Creatures of the Earth: new and selected stories*, p. 19.

'The weak winter sun had thawed the fields soft enough to course the hare on, and though it still hung blood-orange above the hawthorns on the hill, the rims of the hoof tracks were already hardening fast against their tread.' 'All Sorts of Impossible Things', in *Creatures of the Earth: new and selected stories*, p. 90.

'[...] the best of life is life lived quietly, where nothing happens but our calm journey through the day, where change is imperceptible and the precious life is everything.' *Memoir*, p. 80.

positive from the wood harvest is the amount of light that now floods into the area.

When localised fog sits close to the ground it creates the most atmospheric scene: everything slows, delicate moisture coats the grass and hedgerow, and when that fog is accompanied by a freeze the senses heighten to the sound of a crunch underfoot, or the squawk of a jay as it bolts from the trees, flying low over the high field beside the access road close to my home. Recently, while moving the car out of our drive, a large hare ran in front of me, pounding through the fog as if laying down a challenge, while in the cleared wood a buzzard sat perched on a tall stump watching proceedings. What a way to start a Wednesday morning! Landscape and nature go hand in hand in this photographer's paradise.

People have asked me why I moved to Leitrim. It is hard to put into words, but I will try. When you arrive home from work after a long drive and step out of the car, you see an autumn mist rising from the fields. The dogs rush over to greet you. Looking up at a bright, clear, starry sky you let out a breath, and the wisps float upwards towards the faint steep call of a high-flying redwing migrating to our shores for winter. Life is not so bad for this northside Dub living in Leitrim.

SECTION 3

Friendship, Anger and Sexual Repression

Chapter 10

—

'My sweet guide': Friends and Friendship in the Fiction of John McGahern

—

Máire Doyle

The concept of friendship, and its place in the sphere of human relationships, has been subjected to varying degrees of interest since its earliest manifestation in the field of moral philosophy where it commanded a prominent position, a position it has struggled to maintain. Writing in the late 1950s, C.S. Lewis claimed that the modern world is not interested in friendship. From its previously exalted status in the medieval and ancient world when 'nature and emotion and the body were feared as dangers to our souls, or despised as degradations of our human status',[1] to its position as a peripheral relationship, friendship is no longer deemed essential to humankind and its ethical life. While Lewis acknowledges that most people admit to having friends, these are mere acquaintances when compared to the *philia* that Aristotle wrote so forcefully about in the *Nicomachean Ethics*, and which he deemed essential for the attainment of happiness. According to Lewis, the diminution of friendship is attributable to its being an entirely unnecessary component within human relationships, for 'without Eros none of us would have been begotten and without affection none of us would have been reared; but we can live and breed without friendship. The species, biologically considered, has no need of it.'[2] Lewis set out to challenge this modern disinterestedness in friendship by making a vigorous case for it as one of the 'four loves' in his 1960 work of that title.

In addition to Aristotle's expansive treatise, the classical writings of Plato and Cicero also demonstrate high regard for friendship which they considered a vital component of the 'good life'. Its status as a central element in the moral development of character and the attainment of a satisfactory ethical life continued into medieval times, but its prominent position in the hierarchy of human affairs was gradually eroded as the nature and practice of relationships altered with the advance of the modern world. As the notion of the individual became prominent and traditional ideas of kinship declined, romantic love and domestic relationships were privileged above external intimacies. Thought-provoking essays from Michel de Montaigne, Francis Bacon, Ralph Waldo Emerson and Lewis attest only to sporadic interest in the qualitative aspects of friendship, while maintaining its position in the moral sphere of activity. In the academic world, the development of sociology as a discipline saw the study of friendship re-positioned, as philosophers seemed to become largely silent on the topic.[3]

A recurring feature of most reflections on friendship is the inclusion of the notion of a 'perfect' friendship. Aristotle's perfect friendship is not so much a friendship of self and other as a friendship of two selves where one mirrors the other: such friendships are rare and develop over a long period of time. This notion of the rarity of the perfect or 'true' friendship persisted. Montaigne considered it so rare that it was likely to occur on average only every three hundred years. Subsequent essayists inclined towards the view that real friendships are formed between those that either acknowledge the same truth in the world, or recognise that they are both seeking the same truth. Emerson considered truth one of the two main elements that comprise friendship – tenderness being the other – and, like Montaigne, thought that the 'great conversation' of friendship 'requires an absolute running of two souls into one'.[4] Lewis suggested that the discovery of friendship, or at least of the possibility of friendship, often occurs in an epiphanic moment when the 'typical expression of opening friendship would be something like "What? You too? I thought I was the only one"'.[5] Implicit in all of these concepts of true or perfect friendship proposed by Aristotle and subsequent essayists is an almost narcissistic relationship in which the two are so alike in attributes and purpose that the friendship functions as a relationship of self with self. The intensity of the perfect friendship, the idea of the same 'other self', runs counter to romantic love and its promise of uniqueness. Whether the two can co-exist harmoniously is one of the questions that arise in John McGahern's work.

McGahern's final novel, *That They May Face the Rising Sun*, is distinguished by the characters' openness to the world and the others that inhabit it. The relationships that the Ruttledges develop with members of the local community, and in particular the close friendship with Jamesie and Mary that is of primary importance in this novel, reflect McGahern's representation of a new, more expansive and inclusive social world. Or is it new? What place did these 'others' occupy in previous novels and short stories? These questions prompted an exploration of the concept of friendship in McGahern's earlier work and in particular the relationship between self and the external world and how they merge with apparently unprecedented ease in the final novel.

This examination of friendship explores its role as part of the need to find a way to be in the world and asks whether friendship, where it does exist, helps or hinders the desire for knowledge of the self. As many of McGahern's characters struggle to make the transition from self-absorption to a more ethically rigorous way of being, does the role and function of friendship change? This exploration of friendship takes place against the backdrop of McGahern's belief that society in Ireland was underdeveloped. McGahern often repeated his view that the 'narrow development of proper society' in Ireland meant that there is 'no system of manners in this country'.[6] The lack of a fully developed society allowed the family to become the dominant unit, the kind of dominance he explores in particular in *Amongst Women*. The absence of manners, which for McGahern was a moral void, meant that people had no communal understanding of the ethically proper way to develop relationships with others. There was no guide.

While there are friendships, it is not an exaggeration to say that McGahern's characters are not serial befrienders. From a largely 'friendless' first novel (*The Barracks*) to a final novel that is generally regarded as an unequivocal celebration of community (*That They May Face the Rising Sun*), friendships of varying hues emerge and disappear. Different narratives expose friendships of varying intensity in a way that suggests that the kinds of friendships one has depends on the kind of person one is, and that the sort of life one creates determines the kinds of friendships one has. Attempts to locate friendship within the trajectory of McGahern's moral vision are informed by the thinking of Hannah Arendt, and her ideas on the public and private realms. This exploration of friendship will suggest ways in which Arendt's ideas contribute to an understanding of the acute absence of friendship in Elizabeth Reegan's world in *The Barracks,* and its seemingly vigorous presence in *That They May Face the Rising Sun.*

In the intervening novels and short stories, friendship, with notable exceptions, seems not so much absent as much as peripheral, although never irrelevant. The short story 'All Sorts of Impossible Things' renders a particularly delicate and sensitive portrait of male friendship in which the inertia of *timor mortis* is confronted by the imminent reality of death. The struggle of the young agricultural instructor to move ahead with his plans in spite of ailing health seems to anticipate Maggie in the much later 'Love of the World', who also carries on with life in the face of overwhelming adversity, explaining: 'What else could I do? I was – in life'.[7] Other short stories recall past friendships in a way that acknowledges their contemporaneous importance while accepting the transient nature of relationships forged at different stages in life. The protagonist in 'Bank Holiday' reflects on a friendship of years, interrupted by a colleague's transfer, and which is now reduced to passing pleasantries as if there was 'some deep embarrassment: that they had leaned too heavily on [their meetings] once and they now seemed like a lost strength'.[8] Friendship often seems forged out of the uncertainties of youth, only to become redundant with the surefootedness of maturity. In 'Doorways', the revival of a youthful friendship helps the protagonist return to a pre-ennui stage, and renewed optimism leads to hope of the 'recovery of amazement'[9] through love. In *The Leavetaking*, Patrick Moran's best friend Lightfoot, not without a touch of irony, rejects the title of 'friend', 'since he found friendship disgusting', and he goes on to quote Proust's assertion that it [friendship] is the 'halfway house between physical exhaustion and mental boredom'.[10] Later, when questioned by Isobel, Patrick is unsure about whether the beloved can be both friend and lover: 'Maybe the instinct is too strong to allow for friendship'.[11] The conditional 'maybe' leaves the question open to the test of experience.

In contrast to Patrick, the narrator-protagonist of *The Pornographer* has no friends – only loyalties. The novel retains a Proustian scepticism about friendship but it is less playful than that depicted in *The Leavetaking*, and points to this character's overall existential anxiety, in which fear of interdependence is primary. The pornographer sees the enthusiasm of his lover Josephine for friendship as an extension of her neediness and dependence, which she then focuses on him. Yet, in an almost comic moment at the outset of their boat trip on the Shannon, he responds to her expression of delight at being away from other people with the retort, 'People are all right'.[12] It is difficult to decide whether the moment is epiphanic, ironic or even prophetic, as it is the conception of the unwanted child on this trip and the consequences of this pregnancy that lead to his contemplation of a return to the place of his own birth and to a connection with a local community. The author's creation of a character who is an orphan, nameless, and self-employed in a marginalised and illegal industry reinforces the isolation of the human being both from himself and the world, but it also raises the question as to how, in the absence of familial and filial ties, the individual situates himself in the world.

In contrast, Michael Moran in *Amongst Women* demonstrates a definite antipathy towards friendship, and chooses to anchor himself firmly within the family. The one friendship he has, that which he developed with his junior officer McQuaid, is, like the relationship with his family, characterised and sustained by the exercise of control over his former lieutenant. Theirs was a relationship born in the hierarchy of the army, and Moran's senior position meant it was always unequal. His role as McQuaid's benefactor and his hosting of their annual reunion perpetuates his sense of patronage. When McQuaid finally relinquishes his role as protégé, Moran reflects that 'after years he had lost his oldest and best friend' but he also admits that 'in a way he had always despised friendship'.[13] Moran's attitude towards friendship is unsurprising and is characteristic of his feelings towards the external world in general. Representations of friendship in other texts point to its different roles. Where romantic love is privileged, friendship is either absent or maintains a mute presence, while the experience of James Sharkey in 'All Sorts of Impossible Things' anticipates its pedagogical potential.

But Moran is not the first of McGahern's central characters to actively resist friendship. In this regard, Elizabeth Reegan in McGahern's first published novel does not so much demonstrate an antipathy towards friendship as exhibit a fear of it, or more specifically, a fear of its female version. Her phobic response to relationships with the women around her acts as a counterpoint to discussions of female friendship that produce a set of similar responses that assume women have some special gift in the field of friendship. Women are considered to be better at friendships because they are generally held to be 'more articulate and emotionally accomplished', while male emotional reticence is often attributed to fear of homoerotic overtones.[14] Gendered stereotypes represent female friendships as 'intimate relationships in which sharing feelings and talk are the most prevalent activities', whereas 'men's friendships are represented as ones in which sharing activities [...] dominate interaction'.[15] In the Victorian era, women emerged from the newly established domestic sphere as 'specialists of the heart', for whom friendship 'helped mitigate the disappointments of marriage'.[16] Sharon Marcus points to a more complex reading in which bonds between women are 'structured by the opposition between women and men, and therefore women must either be rivals for men or comrades in the fight against patriarchy'.[17] Elizabeth is loathe to share feeling, to see friendship as an antidote to marriage or to seek comrades in the fight against patriarchy.

Despite her many disappointments, Elizabeth Reegan strenuously avoids establishing relationships with others, believing that her consciousness is more advanced than theirs: 'She feels such sympathy for people and yet she denied them – but this thinking only made bad worse, she wished she was blind as they'.[18] Of course she cannot know how blind (or otherwise) to the futilities of life her near-neighbours are and her sympathy does not generate any active curiosity. She remains within her own mind. Elizabeth yields to an acute consciousness of the disappointments of her existence, believing that she is different to those around her. This is both her hubris and part of her tragedy. In this novel, as he does later in *The Pornographer*, McGahern exposes the dangers of living too much in your own mind – a habit which becomes a form of narcissism for some characters. In *The Barracks*, he employs the character of Teresa Casey, the only other woman that Elizabeth seems (barely) able to tolerate, to articulate these dangers. Anxious always to offer help and to fill her days outside of herself, she observes that 'it's when you have nothing to do and start thinkin' that's the worst' (*B*, 167). However, Elizabeth wants *only* to think. McGahern's warning is not of course about reflection itself, but about the tendency to excessive self-absorption and the denial of others.

In searching for a way to be in the world Elizabeth resolutely tries to find the answer in passionate love. In this, his first novel, McGahern establishes a pattern that other characters, both male and female, will follow with varying degrees of success. This pattern involves the fetishisation of love to the exclusion of all other relationships, leading almost inevitably to loss or disappointment. Elizabeth's particular attitude to love is partly a reaction to the tragic end of an emotionally and intellectually challenging relationship with a doctor while nursing in London. Already beginning to self-educate, she craved the knowledge that the erudite doctor offered – he seemed to be holding open the door to a world that Elizabeth desperately wanted to enter. The 'big questions' (*B*, 64) he was asking, the intellectual discourse she desperately wanted to be part of, led her to believe that they were both seeking 'the same truth'. In its tragic wake, Elizabeth distilled but deepened her expectations. The outside world became irrelevant. In the course of her retreat from the world, Elizabeth fails to realise that she is one of the 'other people' that she so desperately wants to deny. Both Elizabeth and her husband are emotionally paralysed by their respective disappointments with the world and fail to develop a friendship component within their marriage. Their mutual rejection of the external world means they are dependent on each other, yet they are unable to convert their reliance into companionship. Elizabeth fails as a confidante when Reegan shares his hopes for the future while she becomes imprisoned in the frustrated expectation that he too will open a door, not to the outside world but to a world of emotional intimacy – the only world in which she thinks she wants to reside. Thus, Elizabeth deprives herself of an external world in which alternative relationships can be formed and nurtured. She retreats into marriage and a small rural community that at first charms her and then terrifies her.

Of that period in Ireland, that is the 1950s in particular, McGahern has said: 'People did not live in Ireland then. They lived in small, intense communities and the communities could vary greatly in spirit and in character, even over a distance of a few miles […]'.[19] The intensity of the community experience is exacerbated for Elizabeth because of the 'community within a community' that she must inhabit. As home, workplace and site of public access, the barracks represents a space in which the public, private and domestic vie for attention and distinction. What emerges from this fusion (or even confusion) of space and activity is a kind of group portrait of connected but disparate characters: arguably a more claustrophobic and distilled version of the kind of community depicted in *That They May Face the Rising Sun*.

While Elizabeth participates in the formalities of neighbourly relationships with her husband's colleagues and their wives, hers is a passive participation and she does not actively seek either the help or company of the other wives. In her sociological study *Women of the House*, Caitríona Clear discusses the prominence of neighbourly relations in both urban and rural areas of Ireland in the early to mid-twentieth century. In rural areas neighbours were often needed for 'provisioning and basic amenities' while also stepping in to help in times of illness or childbirth.[20] In effect, women provided services that the state did not. In *The Barracks*, Teresa Casey steps in as willing housekeeper during Elizabeth's illness, welcoming the opportunity to feel 'needed', a desire often expressed by Elizabeth but only in the context of her relationship with Reegan. While neighbourliness for men meant sharing physical and material resources at busy times of the year, the domestic sphere was constantly busy. Clear's study reveals that this constancy of need and the absence of boundaries between women's work and living space meant that female exchanges were more likely to be fraught with tension. Some of this tension was reflected in the tendency for women to refer to each other as 'Mrs' rather than by first name – a tendency that Clear suggests may have been an attempt to 'keep neighbours at what was at least a symbolic distance'.[21] While there are three other Garda wives in *The Barracks*, we only learn the first name of Teresa Casey, with the others referred to as Mrs Mullins and Mrs Brennan respectively. Teresa Casey's distinction reflects her childless status but also her role as a possible alter ego to Elizabeth.

However, Elizabeth's resistance to forming relationships with other women goes beyond not liking some of her neighbours. She views the women in her immediate and local community – indeed, almost all women – with a caustic eye, and her observations of her own sex suggest that women are constantly vying for position and status. Her rejection of the local priest's invitation to join the Legion of Mary is based on her belief that it serves not only as a ready source of labour for the church but also as a 'legalised gossiping school for women' (*B*, 163). These negative constructions of women are echoed in McGahern's later novel *The Pornographer*, when a young woman comments that she 'can't stand women who are lady-like and fragile, never sniffing at a fact of life, while they'd carve you up in small pieces without batting an eyelid' (*P*, 170–1). This, an echo of Elizabeth's mental comparison of a conversation among her companion patients in hospital to the memory of seeing greyhounds attempt to devour a weaker dog: 'How the first poor bitch would be suffering scalds of vanity now. They had her by the heels. They'd drag her down' (*B*, 137). Elizabeth remains mute: 'She had her private life and her dreams [...]' (*B*, 138). These acerbic observations follow from the earlier revelation that she had 'such a horror of the domestic talk of women that she felt she must be lacking somehow, she got frightened sometimes, it could make her feel shut in a world of mere functional bodies' (*B*, 75). Elizabeth desperately wants her relationships to be defined by more than the commonality of the domestic experience and its apparent domination of female discourse.

The Elizabeth who is trying 'to gather the strewn bits of her life into the one Elizabeth' (*B*, 72) fears any identification with a world of 'mere functional bodies' lest she become defined by that world. In her search for the 'one Elizabeth' she denies the possibility of different selves. Her quest, and the allusion to women as 'functional bodies', echoes the anxiety of those held in slavery: that the obscurity of their position would render them so invisible that no trace of their existence would remain after death.[22] Elizabeth seems to fear that even in life there might be no trace of her existence. The position that Elizabeth adopts in relation to the women that form part of her daily social circle and these temporary interactions clearly alienates her from any society to be found in the world she chose to inhabit when she decided to marry Reegan. As she oscillates between feelings of superiority and rebuking herself for harbouring such sentiments, it can be difficult to discern whether she distrusts the manifestations of female life that surround her and the roles that society seems to have thrust on all women, and longs for a more authentic version, or whether she is in fact rejecting a gendered notion of daily existence.

So, how do we explain this rejection of female society, this apparent mistrust of women? Are there simply obstacles to female friendship that are not of Elizabeth's making? Janice Raymond has argued that 'the most blatant obstacle to female friendship is the prevailing patriarchal adage that 'women are each other's worst enemies'. 'This theme', she says, has many variations, and a chorus of male voices through the centuries has echoed Jonathan Swift's words: 'I never knew a tolerable woman to be fond of her own sex'.[23] Raymond argues that it would be 'easy to dismiss this chorus by virtue of its sex or to emphasise the unintended clue given in Swift's remark that the women whom men find "tolerable" are not fond of their own sex'.[24] This suggests that women disidentify with other women in order to make themselves 'tolerable' to men. Garda Mullins' remark to Elizabeth, 'You're the only person anyone can have real talk with about here. You're the only one who understands anything' (*B*, 150), points to Elizabeth's capacity to connect and understand, and perhaps she does find it easier to talk to men because she is not expected to identify with them. Ironically, Mullins' observation also suggests that he may have the same problems relating to his wife as Elizabeth does to Reegan. However, Raymond's research suggests that many women have absorbed this anti-female message and that 'by blaring the hetero-relational message that "women are each other's worst enemies", men have ensured that many women will be each other's worst enemies'.[25] In this context it could be argued that as Elizabeth observes women behaving as each other's worst enemies but is not a participant, her observations may also be read as McGahern's critique of both an ill-developed society and a developed but wasted consciousness where, to quote Patricia Bourden, the passive Elizabeth is 'victim of her own paralysis, incapable of self-transcendence, capable only of gestures towards self-assertion'.[26] While Elizabeth fails to achieve transcendence, she also fails to recognise that the attitudes of the other women whom she views so harshly are symptoms of a society still in the process of formation. The group of women in the hospital can be seen as a microcosm of this society, a society characterised by insecurity and uncertainty of position, an uncertain and embryonic structure with no accepted system of manners. Even where there is a yearning for friendship, it can only emerge where the conditions for friendship exist. If friendships, of any kind, are to emerge, then McGahern suggests they require some sort of code of manners.

But McGahern's portrayal of Elizabeth is also a critique of retreat from the world and its consequences. The world, in this context, is understood as Arendt's 'public realm', the realm that constitutes the common discourse of humanity: the discourse of concerns that are shared by all.[27] In her desperation, Elizabeth has blinded herself to the consequences of her choice to opt out of that world. Raymond argues: 'Women who dissociate from the world either by political choice or involuntary derivative status must put something in place of that world'.[28] Difficulties arise for women when this worldlessness, or 'dissociation' from the world, becomes 'a prominent mode of existence' in situations where women 'derive much of their meaning and reality from husbands, lovers, fathers, or males bosses', thereby 'seldom experiencing the world directly'.[29] Elizabeth, having voluntarily retreated into worldlessness, fails to put anything in its place. She refuses to experience the world directly, instead hoping to experience it through her love for Reegan, having previously abdicated responsibility for her worldliness to Halliday.

Love, argues Arendt, by 'reason of its passion, destroys the in-between which relates us to and separates us from others'.[30] Passionate love belongs exclusively to the private and it cannot be brought into the public realm. This does not involve a rejection of passionate love but requires action to move beyond it. This action takes the form of interaction with others outside of the intimate, self-absorbed world of passionate love. Arendt's argument proposes that when one is 'in love' one is 'out of' the world. Elizabeth expects love to create a world which will satisfy all her needs. When it fails to do so, she dissociates not just from her husband, but from all who surround her. Raymond argues that: 'Dissociation gives women the illusion that they can retreat into an undisturbed time and space where a semblance of freedom can be preserved'.[31] While Elizabeth imagines herself as a kind of slave to her chosen circumstance, a 'shackled [...] thieving animal' (B, 51), she also imagines that her determination not to give way to her emotional needs helps her stay 'in some measure free' (B, 71). The irony is that her idea of freedom is limited. She views the other women as domestic ciphers, itself a form of passive collusion in the construction of female stereotypes. Even the connection she establishes with Mullins is only superficial as she admits that rather than be honest, she would satisfy him with 'the mirage of flattery' (*B*, 149). Through the tragic character of Elizabeth Reegan McGahern explores the consequences of dissociation from the world – it is an exploration that he returns to most specifically in *The Pornographer*. But the narrative of dissociation, and the conflicts it generates, has its most achieved exposition in the hermetically sealed world of Michael Moran in *Amongst Women*. Thereafter, the final novel looks, if not to resolution, at least to its possibility.

While *The Barracks* privileges the consciousness of Elizabeth Reegan, and all interaction is enclosed within the claustrophobic atmosphere of the police barracks to construct a physical and metaphysical worldlessness, McGahern's final novel is astonishing in the stark contrast it establishes between the interiority or paralysis of almost all the previous works and the blatant exteriority evident from the opening page. This exteriority is achieved through the openness of domestic space, the exterior location of much of the action, the constant presence of nature, but also through the almost unrelenting dialogue – almost everything is literally 'out in the open'. Despite the sharp contrasts, both texts are concerned with the consequences of inaccessibility, self-imposed or otherwise, to the world. While Denis Sampson describes this as a 'closed community',[32] it seems so only in the sense that there are no new applicants (the Ruttledges being somewhat of an aberration) and there is no generation of children to replace the ageing population. Where familial relationships and/or a yearning for a beloved other dominated previous work, this narrative privileges a commitment to friendship and this commitment sustains what would otherwise be fragile and volatile connections between such a disparate group of people. The book makes the transition from the Ireland whose only society was the family, to a 'family-less' society where inter-dependence, reviled by other McGahern characters, is essential to human existence, particularly the qualitative aspect of daily experience. The exigencies of life in the isolated rural community are such that there can be no debate on relationships of equals – everybody is equal in their essential need of others just to get by. The key ingredient in this particular kind of friendship is respect, the kind of respect articulated by Arendt:

Respect, not unlike the Aristotelian philia politikē, is a kind of 'friendship' without intimacy and without closeness; it is a regard for the person from the distance which the space of the world puts between us, and this regard is independent of qualities which we may admire or of achievements which we may highly esteem. Thus, the modern loss of respect, or rather the conviction that respect is due only where we admire or esteem, constitutes a clear symptom of the increasing depersonalization of public and social life.[33]

Implicit in this concept of respect is the notion of tolerance, and survival of this small community described by McGahern is dependent on allowing even the sometimes intolerable its space in the world around the lake. The lake not only connects and divides the variety of characters that populate the text but also, in its calmest of days, serves to reflect their human frailties.

Juxtaposed with this larger, or macro, idea of community friendship are the personal friendships essential to the quality of existence of some of the characters – most particularly Joe and Kate Ruttledge and Jamesie and Mary. There is no fetishisation of the family in this novel because the few families that exist are separated and fragmented. The friendship between the Ruttledges and the Murphys has its source in a traditional neighbourliness – a reciprocity of time, labour and hospitality – a mutual generosity of spirit that each couple recognised in the other. The necessity of forced neighbourliness, often part of poverty and general hardship as discussed by Caitríona Clear, has diminished with time and economic progress and in this new friendship the two couples can enjoy its benefits without the tension of material interdependence. Joe's friendship with Jamesie, whose willingness to share knowledge about the locals and his openness of self, enables Joe to establish relationships with the broader community. There is a strong pedagogical aspect to this relationship, as there is in general to the Ruttledges' experience of life around the lake. This is an element of Joe Ruttledge's return that Margaret Lasch Carroll foregrounds by pointing to how the Shah, Patrick Ryan and Bill Evans all teach Joe 'appropriate' behaviour.[34] In good student fashion, Joe learns his lessons and makes judicious use of his knowledge when required. McGahern's remarks to Hermione Lee following the publication of this text that, 'We'd be lost if we didn't have other people. In fact, I think that the only true journey to the self, the only true knowledge of the self, is through others and the knowledge of the world. Otherwise one is looking at the pool of Narcissus',[35] can be understood as an endorsement of the concept of friendship as a route to Arendt's principle of worldliness. It also contains within it the recurring motif of the wheel as the individual moves beyond self-consciousness to the consciousness of others and the external world, and returns to better understand the self. In this context, the experiential repetitiveness of the human condition is illuminated through interaction with others. The self that moves into a world of shared consciousness is strengthened with each return journey.

While the two couples obviously share similar values, as evidenced by their generous hospitality, manners, respect and altruism, combined with a healthy dose of occasional cynicism, theirs is not a friendship of mirrored selves. The reference to James as 'my sweet guide'[36] subverts theories of the 'perfect' friendship as one with 'another self'. Instead, this is a friendship where Jamesie's guidance illuminates the world for Joe Ruttledge, and the success of the friendship is dependent on Joe's willingness to allow himself to be guided and to reciprocate when appropriate. This willingness, along with a strong sense of ethical responsibility, is central to the Ruttledges' successful integration into the community. While McGahern employs an omniscient narrator, the Ruttledges and their home are at the centre of most of the activity, and the reader meets all of the characters through their interaction with them. The excesses of other characters – their sometimes extreme responses – are tempered by Joe's seemingly mild-mannered and judicious approach to difficult situations. Some of the ethical perspectives on friendship that were touched on in McGahern's earlier work are more fully explicated here. Proustian scepticism about friendship and existential fear of interdependence are absent in the lives of the main characters. While some characters –particularly Patrick Ryan and John Quinn – generally eschew specific friendships and make erratic appearances, they remain very much part of the local community. John Quinn's self-absorption makes him an unlikely candidate for the kind of public friendship that Arendt promotes, while Patrick Ryan seems to relish the freedom of unreliability.

McGahern establishes an association between role playing and friendship in the relationship between Patrick Ryan and Jamesie's brother Johnny, who both met and became friends when they were involved in the local drama group many years earlier. The 'play-acting' resumes when Johnny comes home for his annual visit. Patrick, unable to sustain the role of caring friend, cruelly points to his friend's mistake in emigrating. Joe rebukes him and, in a scene that points backwards to the pornographer's refusal to adopt sentimental poses, Patrick claims: 'I tell the truth and ask no favours'. Joe's response that 'Kindness ... sympathy ... understanding' (*RS*, 79) are sometimes more helpful than truth reintroduces the importance of the moral imagination in relationships with others. The same view is later echoed by Jamesie when he says: 'There are times when the truth is the wrong thing' (*RS*, 98). The pornographer's admission that 'Broken in love, I had turned back, let the light of imagination out' (*P*, 251) is a recognition that his moral imagination had been disabled: its importance is reclaimed by Joe Ruttledge.

While these manifestations of friendship and a participatory connectedness to the public realm are evident, the reason for the shift is not quite as obvious. As the Ruttledges are unobtrusive but pivotal forces in the dynamic of this lakeside community, their motivation in choosing to settle there, to return from London, is central to understanding why they are a subtle but vital (human) force in the novel. The Ruttledges' decision was based on a desire to live in a way that demanded more of them, that felt more 'real' and that involved feeling 'responsible or fully involved' (*RS*, 20) in the world of human affairs, a desire for a more ethically rigorous relationship with the world.[37] Of reality, Arendt says: 'Since our feeling for reality depends utterly upon appearance and therefore upon the existence of a public realm into which things can appear out of the darkness of sheltered existence, even the twilight which illuminates our private and intimate lives is ultimately derived from the much harsher light of the public realm'.[38] The openness of the Ruttledges, epitomised by the always-open doorway of their home, functions as an invitation to the world/the public realm to enter and shine a light on the shadows of their existence. In a sense the Ruttledges are willing to collapse the distinction between their private and public worlds. The key to this illumination is discourse. For Arendt, friendship is not a private matter, but is demonstrated and activated through shared discourse – and, as already mentioned, this is a text that privileges conversation. The Ruttledges' entry into the public world is through conversation and mutually understood action. They no longer wish to live solely in a private world and choose instead to respond to the demands of the external world, from which intimate love, as an intrinsically private emotion, expels the couple 'in love'.

Arendt is emphatic that while friendship is a significant and beneficial force in the public sphere, '[romantic] love [...] destroys the in-between which relates us to and separates us from others':

As long as its spell lasts, the only in-between which can insert itself between two lovers is the child, love's own product. The child, this in-between to which the lovers now are related and which they hold in common, is representative of the world in that it also separates them; it is an indication that they will insert a new world into the existing world. Through the child, it is as though the lovers return to the world from which their love had expelled them.[39]

The Ruttledges are childless. In the novel, Patrick Ryan pointedly questions the absence of children but receives no explanation, while in an essay on children in McGahern's fiction, Patrick Crotty wonders if the Ruttledges' 'emotional self-sufficiency' explains their childless status.[40] The scene during the lambing season when a small black lamb is found dead suggests the contrary. Joe Ruttledge's observation that, unlike humans, the mother will have 'completely forgotten him in another day' (*RS*, 262) points to personal experience. The death of the lamb prompts a response that 'reached back to other feelings of loss and disappointment' (*RS*, 263). The scene suggests that their emotional self-sufficiency is more likely hard-won: the absence rather than the presence of children making them long for other kinds of responsibility outside their private world.

When Jamesie and Mary's son migrates to the city and establishes his own family, their openness to developing a friendship with the Ruttledges mirrors that couple's need to be useful in a world outside themselves. The reciprocal relationship that develops between the two couples is not the kind of intimate friendship in which they remain 'unmolested by the world and its demands',[41] speaking only of each other to each other. The kind of friendship that McGahern advocates in this text, the kind that Arendt proposes, is the kind in which the things of the world become human only when they are discussed between people.

The tentative, fearful and sometimes sceptical attitude towards friendships that characterised the earlier narratives was part of a distrust of the world and an inability to respond to its ethical demands, to set the self aside. Finally, the individual's resistance to others and to a shared experience is replaced by an alternative discourse that seeks to strengthen the connection with the public sphere. Whatever form friendship takes, it yields most when understood as a moral activity that offers ethical substance to the lives of its participants. This 'painful becoming of ourselves' (*P*, 20), the journey to knowledge of the self (to the 'one Elizabeth'), is incrementally achieved through association with others so that 'we [learn to] humanize what is going on in the world and in ourselves only by speaking of it, and in the course of speaking of it we learn to be human'.[42]

Chapter 11

—

McGahern's Rages

—

Joe Cleary

'Rage is the face of life before its own death'[1]

I

There is something in the way in which McGahern's oeuvre develops from those rather bleakly purgatorial novels of the early career towards the apparently hard-won sense of overcoming attained in *Amongst Women* or *That They May Face the Rising Sun* that suggests that the author had wrestled with demons, eventually exorcising or taming them. McGahern's career, that is, traces an arc broadly similar to that, say, of the careers of T.S. Eliot or Patrick Kavanagh. After the desolation and neurosis of signature works such as 'The Love Song of J. Alfred Prufrock', 'Gerontion', or *The Waste Land*, Eliot strives in his later career for some equivalent of Dante's *Paradiso*; the nearest he comes to it is *The Four Quartets*. And after the splenetic bromide of the career-defining *The Great Hunger*, Kavanagh repudiates satire and strives instead for a language of consolation, acceptance, even celebration; where *The Great Hunger* excoriated, the Canal Bank poems bless. McGahern's late works eschew the overtly religious registers of the late Eliot or Kavanagh, but the liturgical cadences are there all the same as the very titles *Amongst Women* or *That They May Face the Rising Sun* suggest, and even if they do not aspire to the condition of Christian grace and submission that Eliot's or Kavanagh's late works seek after, these novels appear nonetheless to have some secular equivalent of these qualities.

McGahern is one of the more complex individuals and accomplished writers in recent Irish letters and his work, though uneven, is rightfully held in high esteem. My object here is not to challenge that esteem but to suggest that there is much in McGahern that still needs to be fathomed, much still to be teased out. The irenic image of John McGahern suggested by the later works and burnished in much of the criticism published since his death conceals more than it reveals and what that image occludes particularly is the degree to which hurt and rage remained a consistently animating force in the work, and even in *Memoir*, McGahern's valedictory address to the reading public. The figure with which rage will be most readily associated in McGahern is the father: Old Mahoney in *The Dark* and Michael Moran in *Amongst Women* are grimly memorable portraits of tantrum-tormented fathers who visit their rage in unpredictable physical or psychological violence on their children, and who compound this abuse by their clamant insistence that their children should love and honour them despite such abuse. The father, as I have written elsewhere, may provoke a sense of terror and dread in these novels, but he is also the figure that compels everyone's attention; it is the unpredictable rhythms and riddles of the father's rage that power the plots in *The Dark* and *Amongst Women*, the dark materials that lend these works their fascination.[2] Why are these fathers so persistently, so self-thwartingly angry? What on earth is bugging them? Do their sudden and outlandish transports of rage have a source or an object? Or is it because they can never discover their source or object that those transports are so volatile? Still, while the father in McGahern's world is the figure most obviously possessed by an ungovernable rage, it would be a mistake to conceive of rage in his oeuvre only in these terms. As well as the foul weather tantrums of the father, there is also throughout McGahern's work a son's stubborn and steely if much more muted resentment of and rage against the father, a force equal and opposite to that of the paternal rage and in its own way possibly as implacable. This is a more difficult rage to decipher or write about, but if it is ignored there is much that we will miss about McGahern's work, much that we will suppress or sentimentalise.

'Daddy, Daddy, you bastard', wrote Sylvia Plath in a poem written in 1962 and published in her posthumous collection *Ariel* in 1965, the same year that *The Dark* was published.[3] When Plath wrote 'Daddy' her father had already been dead twenty-two years; the poet herself would be dead by suicide a year later in 1963. When McGahern published *The Dark*, however, his father was still very much alive and in *Memoir* McGahern records that he had sent him a copy of his first novel *The Barracks*, commenting only that his parent seems at least to have read the first page. McGahern does not say if he also gifted his father the works that followed, but he does note that by the time

The Dark was published he must have acquired in his home county 'some underground reputation as a poet of domestic violence',[4] and towards the end of *Memoir* he records a tense reunion with his father in the course of which the latter queries whether McGahern is not worried that other Irish writers seem to have more visible success than he, and then asks his son what his object as a writer might be were it not to attain success. 'To write well, to write truly and well about fellows like yourself', a stung McGahern retorts. Pat, McGahern's maternal uncle and the writer's companion on the visit, shakes with laughter at the reply, his response invoking the Irish fear of the writer as satirist when he tells the father, Frank McGahern, 'Now, Frank, you'll have to look out. You'll have to watch yourself' (*M*, 263). Later, when they are alone, Agnes', McGahern's stepmother, admonishes the writer for his reply, telling him, 'You should let those things go with your father.' 'It seemed like war to me, Agnes,' McGahern replies. 'Sometimes, unfortunately, you have no choice but to meet fire with fire' (*M*, 263). 'Meeting fire with fire', or answering paternal aggression with literary counter-aggression, appears in many respects fundamental to McGahern's writing. The invocation of war – 'It seemed like war to me' – coming at the end of *Memoir* appears telling and it is hard to wage war without rage. It is the import of that lifelong emotional guerrilla warfare conducted without truce between father and son that will bear investigation in what follows.

II

'It is the fate of all of us, perhaps, to direct our first sexual impulses towards our mother and our first hatred and our first murderous wish against our father'.[5] Contemplating the parricidal tragedies *Oedipus Rex* and *Hamlet*, Freud wrote this line in *The Interpretation of Dreams* (1899), surmising that every child's primary erotic attraction is to its mother, that the father therefore first appears to the child as a powerful rival for the mother's affections, that rivalry provoking on every infant's part its 'first murderous wish'. 'King Oedipus, who slew his father Laius and married his mother Jocasta', Freud continues, is no aberration but rather a type or everyman who 'merely shows us the fulfilment of our own childhood wishes' (*ID*, 262). But because we view Sophocles' play as socialised adults and thus come to it at a time when we have long since learned to detach primal sexual attachments from our mothers and to forget our murderous jealousy of our fathers, the audience's reaction to Oedipus' murder and incest is, Freud suggests, one of shock and repugnance rather than pleasure. 'Here is one', Freud writes, 'in whom these primeval wishes of our childhood have been fulfilled, and we shrink back from him with the whole force of the repression by which those wishes have since that time been held down within us. While the poet, as he unravels the past, brings to light the guilt of Oedipus, he is at the same time compelling us to recognize our own inner minds, in which those same impulses, though suppressed, are still to be found' (*ID*, 262–3). For Freud, Sophocles' play, like his own work of analysis, compels adults to recognise something from their buried pasts that they would prefer to disown, to consign to amnesia. 'Like Oedipus', he concludes, we all 'live in ignorance of these wishes, repugnant to morality, which have been forced upon us by Nature, and after their revelation we may all of us seek to close our eyes to the scenes of our childhood' (*ID*, 263). In this reading, Oedipus' final anguish reminds us that our failure to recognise the abiding force of infantile impulses, to pride ourselves that we have safely left behind all of that messy emotion on attaining adulthood, is to risk a hubris that will sink us, like Oedipus, in seas of anguish. Feminist critics have long since pointed out the male-centredness and phallocentrism of Freud's writings on the Oedipus complex and the concept generally was controversial in psychoanalytic circles from the outset. Nevertheless, the conception of that complex, and of the castration complex, continued to preoccupy Freud and remained fundamental to his work. And since we are primarily concerned here with father–son animosities, it is worth pursuing a little further Freud's deliberations on that topic.[6]

Later in his *Introductory Lectures on Psycho-Analysis* (1915–17), Freud will ponder whether in fact the erotic attachments of childhood are triggered by the parents rather than stemming from the child: 'Incidentally, children often react in their Oedipus complex to a stimulus coming from their parents, who are frequently led in their preferences by differences of sex, so that the father will choose his daughter and the mother her son as a favourite, or, in case of a cooling-off in the marriage, as a substitute for a love-object that has lost its value'.[7] Here, Freud speculates whether the Oedipal attachments might be more contingent than universal, and more top-down than bottom-up in origin, the attachments prompted by parents in an unhappy relationship who divert a disappointed erotic attachment to their partner onto a child of the opposite sex. But Freud is ultimately reluctant to abandon a commitment to the typicality of the Oedipal complex; in the case of unhappy marriages, he concludes, the parents bring an added stimulus or surplus intensity to a pre-existent drama that would have to be negotiated in any case by the usual arduous processes of psychic development.

Developing the ideas broached in *The Interpretation of Dreams* in his essay on 'Infantile Sexuality' published in *Three Essays on the Theory of Sexuality* (1905), Freud argued that infants are capable of emotions of which as adults they retain only fragmented recollections, though those early emotions, he insists, are not so much negated as consigned to an amnesia similar to that experienced by neurotics, or, in other words, withheld from consciousness via their repression. This amnesia, Freud holds, turns everyone's childhood into something like a prehistoric epoch and conceals from subjects the beginnings of their own sexual life, a forgetting that leads to the common belief that children have no sexual life before puberty. However, in Freud's view, the sexual life of children usually becomes accessible to observation around the ages of three or four, but during this period of latent development, when the physical reproductive functions have not as yet been developed, the forces of education and socialisation divert these impulses either by repressing them by means of feelings of disgust or by sublimating them via the claims of moral or aesthetic ideals. In these early stages, Freud notes, the sexuality of the child is not yet genitally affixed but rather auto-erotic – the subject obtains pleasure from the erogenous zones of his or her own body. Sucking and the lips that suck constitute the primary modes and zones of erotic activity: 'No one who has seen a baby sinking back satiated from the breast and falling asleep with flushed cheeks and a blissful smile', Freud writes, 'can escape the reflection that this pictures persists as the prototype of sexual expression in later life'.[8]

Fundamental to Freud's theory of sexual development, then, is his proposition that children behave from a very early age as though their dependence on the people looking after them were sexual in nature. As such, the simplest course for the child would be to choose as her or his sexual object the same person whom she or he has first loved because she satisfies the child's first needs for care and nourishment, namely the mother. However, the interval between the latent sexuality of childhood and the fuller development of the sexual instincts and capacities in puberty allows society the time needed to inculcate in the child the incest taboo which debars familial self-enclosure and prioritises the higher needs of social reproduction. As part of this process, Freud writes, society makes strenuous efforts to loosen the connection of children to their family, and does this with particular force for adolescent boys. Nevertheless, Freud also insists that the development and the later suppression and dissolution of the Oedipus complex is achieved not just by way of external socialisation – by extra-familial interventions such as religious instruction or education – but is also facilitated by painful sexual dramas transacted within the family itself. As children learn to distinguish between male and female genders, and as the genitals become the primary erogenous zone, the male child directs his libido upon his mother, with the result that feelings of intense jealousy and emotional rivalry are directed against his father, a competitor who claims primacy in her affections. The boy's id makes him want to kill his father to overcome this obstacle, but the pragmatic ego knows the father is the stronger of the two competing males and thus inhibits direct displays of this murderous hostility. The resultant tensions manifest themselves as fear of castration, meaning that the boy will feel himself rendered impotent by being deprived of his sexual object by the stronger father or that he will be punished by him should he stubbornly fail to accept that the mother is prohibited to him. 'The Oedipus complex', Freud writes, 'offered the [male] child two possibilities of satisfaction, an active and a passive one. He could put himself in his father's place in a masculine fashion and have intercourse with the mother as his father did, in which case he would soon have felt the latter as a hindrance; or he might want to take the place of the mother and be loved by the father, in which case the mother would become superfluous'.[9] In Freud's theory, the crucial turning point in the dissolution of this Oedipal deadlock comes when the boy-child realises that women lack the male phallus, thus confirming the real possibility of castration, hitherto experienced as a threat but disregarded. (For the female child, the discovery of her lack of the phallus means, Freud contends, that her love is transferred to the father, this leading to an even deeper repression of mother-love.) However, once the male child recognises that castration is no empty threat but a reality, the Oedipal rivalry with the father begins to wane because no matter which path he chooses now, the boy seems confronted with loss. Should he choose the dominant masculine position and persist with his desire for the mother, he will be met by the wrathful punishment of the father; should he want to take the place of the mother and be loved by the father, this will entail an assumption of the feminine position now also associated with castration. Stymied, the boy has no option but to surrender the primal object-cathexes; the authority of the father or parents is introjected into the ego, new erotic objects are sought after, and the libidinal attachment to the parents is cooled and sublimated into affection. But though the elemental force of the infantile Oedipus complex is dissolved in such cases, the repressed impulses and antagonisms are never abolished; this is why, Freud speculates, the antagonism between the son and the father so often reappears with renewed turbulence during adolescence. And, Freud remarks, 'If there are quarrels between the parents or if their marriage is unhappy, the ground will be prepared in their children for the severest predisposition to the disturbance of their sexual development or to a neurotic illness' (*TETS*, 94).

I have offered this rather lengthy summary of Freud's account of infantile sexuality and identity formation because McGahern's larger oeuvre, both the major novels and the *Memoir* that rounds off the career, re-inscribe a drama of this sort with not only an uncanny literalism but also a terrific intensity. If we take *Memoir*, written in the face of the author's own death, to begin with, we can hardly fail to note how closely it traces the contours of the core Freudian psychodrama, not only at the level of content but also at that of compositional form. The opening lines of *Memoir* begin not immediately with the author's mother but with an invocation of the poor soil of Leitrim, 'in places no more than an inch deep', and then with a verbally ornate account of the abundantly rich flower and animal life that blooms in the hedges that 'are the glory of these small fields', moving on then to describe the maze of tree-roofed country lanes that run like a 'green tunnel pierced by vivid pinpoints of light' until they come to main roads. Then, changing verbal tack, the vocabulary becoming more terse, McGahern informs the reader that he had returned to this landscape some thirty years earlier, buying a small farm between two lakes, his father expressing his disapproval of the acquisition with the remark: 'My eldest son has bought a snipe farm in behind the Ivy Leaf Ballroom' (*M*, 2). This paternal disapproval, the memoirist notes, was motivated partly by his father's sense that for his son to choose to live there was to step down from the professional middle class to which McGahern Senior belonged as well as to settle 'too close to where my mother's relatives lived and to where I had grown up with my mother' (*M*, 2). The very name of the Ivy Leaf Ballroom, McGahern speculates, would probably have provoked his father's disapproval, this remark then opening an anecdote about Patsy Conby, a local man who made money in America and who built the ballroom, generating local employment and facilitating a flush of rural romance such that 'there wasn't a haycock safe for a mile around in the month of July' (*M*, 2–3). Like McGahern's father, the Catholic clergy had disapproved of the ballroom, but, McGahern notes with evident approval, 'Patsy was more than able to hold his own against the pulpit' (*M*, 3).

Memoir's opening passages establish strong lines of readerly identification and dis-identification and serve as a leitmotif to the composition as a whole. The soil of Leitrim, like that of Kavanagh's Monaghan, is thin, but it can nonetheless support on its verges a surprisingly rich flora and fauna and by extension, we surmise, the region's apparent social and cultural thinness (Henry James' or Seán O'Faoláin's 'thin soil' that disabled the nineteenth-century American or twentieth-century Irish novel[10]) may also yield to the properly attuned writer a human drama sufficient in its own right. To this natal landscape, agriculturally poor and backward but thereby preserving intact its verdantly tree-matted and womblike 'green tunnels', the author had returned as an adult, accompanied by his wife, and resettled near to his mother's family, paternal disapproval notwithstanding. To that father, who belongs to the world of 'civil servants, teachers, doctors, nurses, policemen [and] village inspectors' (*M*, 2), his adult son's choice of home serves as a rebuke, but the son clearly relishes his home's proximity to his maternal line and indeed to Patsy Conby's Ivy Leaf Ballroom. The note of authorial identification with Patsy, returned emigrant, purveyor of romance and sexual pleasure, and 'more than able to hold his own against the pulpit', clearly expresses, without direct declaration, McGahern's sense of satisfaction that he too, like Conby, had challenged a culture of sexual puritanism and had also been able to hold his own against the pulpit. In this overture, the writer-son strikes a note of defiance against disapproving fathers, familial and clerical, takes repossession of the childhood territory of the mother, and declares allegiance to a stubborn pleasure principle that will persist in even the most penurious natural landscape and the most puritanical social world. This opening passage registers a bluff resentment against fathers, familial and clerical, and a subdued yet almost cocky sense of pride in defying them.

Only when he has taken adult repossession of the maternal landscape does McGahern return in *Memoir* to the world of childhood proper and begin to unspool a chronological formation narrative. In his case, the separate spheres of the father and mother had been unusually distinct, his father living as a police sergeant in the barracks of Cootehall, his mother working as a national schoolteacher and occupying a separate house about a mile outside Ballinamore, later moving to another house in Aughawillan. In this scenario, the father is associated by profession with the authority of the law and the coercive power of the state, the mother with the comparatively softer power of education and enculturation. But given the atypical family living arrangement, the father appears not as resident domestic magistrate but as an intermittent interloper in the mother's house, visiting his wife and children two days per month, with the family as a whole spending the summer holidays in the Cootehall barracks. Consequently, the young McGahern as firstborn son occupies in early childhood an exclusive possession of his mother, noting that: 'I was a single star till the twins [his sisters Breege and Rosaleen] arrived, and I became insanely jealous of the natural transfer of attention' (*M*, 6). This sibling resentment, he recalls, led him once to release the brakes from the twins' pram, causing it to run downhill and overturn, though in this anecdote culpability for this misdeed is transferred from the jealous self to the paternal McGahern grandmother, who lives with his mother, and who displays a callous violence apparently innate to the McGahern side of the family when she watches the boy commit this act without any intervention on her part. Eight pages later, this unloved paternal grandmother vanishes without any sense of regret, and it is clear that even after his sisters' arrival the eldest boy child continues to enjoy confident command in his mother's world, so much so that he informs the reader: 'I haven't a single memory of my father staying in the bungalow, though he must have come many times in the Baby Ford he owned' (*M*, 9).

This drama's starkly obvious Freudian register is not, of course, lost on McGahern; indeed, he himself draws laconic attention to it: 'That I have not a single memory of my father in the house, and that the lane to Liscarn was walked alone with my mother', he observes, 'conforms to a certain primal pattern of the father and the son. The first memory I have of him in all that time', he adds, 'seems to reinforce that further' (*M*, 9). This then leads immediately into a classic castration anecdote that unfolds, interestingly enough, not in the mother's house but in the paternal barracks:

> I had a head of curls like a girl. My father decided to remove them in spite of my frightened protests, made worse by my mother's and grandmother's obvious distress, which served only to strengthen his resolve. In his uniform with the three silver stripes of his rank on the blue sleeve, he took me out into the long hallway that ran along the stairs to the dayroom. He took a chair and newspaper and the small silver shears from the green box and locked the two women in the living room [...]. The chair was

set down on the newspaper and it did not take long to remove the curls. He carried the curls in the folds of the newspaper. 'Weep not for me, O children of Jerusalem, but for yourselves and for your children,' he quoted triumphantly. (*M*, 9–10)

The filial castration dramatised here constitutes the son's first and abiding memory of the father; it is the Ur-scene of their relationship. Shears-yielding, bearing the stripes that signify his legal authority and rank, McGahern Senior wrenches his son from his place amongst women, then returns the shorn child to them, satirically citing scripture as he does so. His lost curls, McGahern notes, 'came to resemble for me John the Baptist's severed head borne into the room on a silver plate' (*M*, 10). Here, McGahern's father is at once a punitive son-sacrificing God the Father and a women-rebuking Christ figure; John McGahern at once a mutilated John the Baptist and a sacrificed Christ-like son. Domestic and scriptural narratives knot in a confused tangle and issue not so much in the son's separation from the mother as in a bitter disavowal of the father, this leading to an even more determined cleaving to the female parent.

Still, despite that attachment to the mother, her physical power nevertheless begins to wane, that waning as theorised by Freud again uncannily literalised in McGahern's family narrative in the form of her breast cancer. Even if the son refuses the dominant masculine position by identifying with the father, Freud argues, he will in time be forced to confront the fact that in patriarchal societies women are associated with castration and after such realisation most male children begin gradually to surrender their primary libidinal attachment to the mother, because to remain so attached now risks not only the father's punishment but also the castration and attendant abjection associated with male effeminacy. In *Memoir*, the account of the mother's cancer and physical deterioration runs concurrent with the period, between three and the onset of puberty, when boys, according to Freud, experience the dissolution of the Oedipus complex and are socialised as males. In McGahern's case, we might speculate, the actual death of the mother when he was aged nine, and thus still prepubescent, completes this process of emotional separation in a particularly stark and brutal way. And yet by the same token that trauma arrests matters at this stage of attachment because the mother's departure takes place before the son could reach the second stage of pubertal sexuality, at which time he would himself have broken the bond and replaced his mother with another sexual object. It is worth recalling in this context that it is the mother's, not the father's, desire that the son become a priest or father figure. Her fantasy, reluctantly entertained by the son, was that she should come to live with him after his ordination in the celibate domesticity of the presbytery. The early death of the mother in this sense prematurely severs a bond that sexual maturity would eventually have diminished in any event because the son always felt that there was something amiss with her presbytery fantasy. Nevertheless, his mother's tragically early death also means that the boy is spared any active adolescent repudiation of the mother because she is wrenched from him by her fatal illness before he could ever detach from her of his own volition.

The language that describes this painful process of mother–son separation is deliberately and overtly sexualised in *Memoir*. When the mother returns from hospital in Dublin to Aughawillan the son recounts joyously: 'My beloved was home and I was alone with her. The evening was clear and dry, the leaves yellow and fallen, and there was a burning red sun on the rim of the sky. We looked at the upstairs rooms, the two small bedrooms of the narrow landing, the larger bedroom where we would sleep that night' (*M*, 62). The 'burning red sun' and the son incandescent with delighted repossession of his mother in the house they will occupy alone, without father or siblings to hinder their reunion, radiate a lyrical intimacy. A walk with the mother in the moonlight that night is remembered as 'so intense that it brought on lightheadedness' (*M*, 64). Meanwhile, the repudiated father tries to win back his son, the idiom of his efforts to do so also sexualised: 'At this time my father began to court me' (*M*, 76). 'It must be hard for you to live in a house of women', his father tells him on a visit to Cootehall. 'Could you say *piss* or *shit* in front of women?' (*M*, 64) he demands, invoking a masculine roughness of language and infantile pleasures in micturition and defecation as inducements to come live with him. At this anxious juncture in *Memoir* it is as though the son has to fend off both earthly and heavenly fathers, each threatening to separate him from the childhood bliss of mother possession. When his ailing mother tells him that God can take people to Himself at any stage, the child is terrified and angered: 'I saw too clearly what she was saying. Its unfairness enraged me. God had all the angels and saints and His own blessed Mother in the company of the Faithful in heaven, and I but the one beloved. She was all that I had' (*M*, 101).

On the day of his mother's funeral, when God the Father has finally wrested her to Himself from his grasp, the weeping boy, clutching a clock to his breast, mourns his mother in the womblike tunnel of trees while in his mind he imagines his father attending her funeral service. However, as he thinks of his father and her brothers bearing her coffin from the church to the grave, the boy reaches the river where two men with phallic rods are departing for a day's fishing and he begs them to take him with them. They refuse as it would be disrespectful for the boy to go with them while his mother is being interred, and the bereaved son thinks: 'I was ashamed of my quick desire to go on the river. She was hardly buried when I was willing to abandon her to my own selfish pursuit of life and pleasure. I was unable to watch even one hour with her'[11] (*M*, 134). A disciple of little faith, a Gethsemane sleeper in the anguished hour, the death of the mother opens nonetheless to the boy-child a new world of pleasures figured here by fishing the river, though first the son will have to weather the wintry years of adolescence in his father's house. Eventually, we know, the grown McGahern will also separate himself from that paternal house and marry twice, first to the Finnish Annikki Laaksi, and then the American Madeline Green. Both non-Irish partners receive respectful mention in *Memoir*, but each remains a penumbral presence, ringside spectators only to the more intense family romance that dominates from first to last.

Memoir opens with McGahern reclaiming the world of his mother despite his father's disapproval; it closes with a somewhat cursory and dispassionate naming of his siblings and their fates, bids his un-comprehended father to the care of an unfathomable God, then reclaims, one final time, his mother for his own exclusive repossession. When the writer reflects first on his reactions to his father's death in these last pages the tone is one of muted bafflement, exorcism and leavetaking:

> When word of my father's death reached me, the intensity of the conflicting emotions – grief, loss, relief – took me unawares. I believe the reaction was as much for those years in which his life and mine were entangled in a relationship neither of us wanted as for the man who had just met the death each of us must face. He made many demands but gave little and always had to dominate. A life from which the past was so rigorously shut out had to be a life of darkness. Though I have more knowledge and experience of him than I have of any other person, I cannot say I have

fully understood him, and leave him now with God, or whatever truth or illusion or longing for meaning or comfort that word may represent. (*M*, 270–1)

Earthly and celestial fathers are consigned here to each other's company, the one almost as unknowable as the other, the word 'love' appearing with reference to neither. As though setting its back to both fathers, *Memoir* then turns towards the mother one last time. She, it is recalled, had great love and trust in God, the difference between her faith and his father's representing a wider split in 'the violent history of Catholicism' between a domineering, repressive fortress church and a spirit-elevating one of windows and spires that gestures towards 'love and light' (*M*, 271). The tense then switches from the past tense characteristic of memoir as genre to the future conditional of a wistful 'would' and the writer imagines a post-death reunion with his mother, not in heaven, but in the summer lanes of his childhood. He would, he tells us, bring his mother to the lake's edge to show her the home of the otter who 'whistles down the waters for the male when she wants to mate and chases him back again to his own waters when his work is done; unlike the dear swans that paddle side by side and take turns on their high nest deep within the reeds' (*M*, 272). The imagery here is overtly of sexual mating, the solitary otter-mother recalling his own mother's separateness from his father, the dear swans perhaps a harmony that had escaped her or maybe the serener coupling with the child that separation from her husband had once allowed. In this last reclamation, *Memoir* represents a victory over the world of fathers, earthly and divine, that had taken the mother from the son, and an incestuous retaking of the mother through the power of writing. This is a narrative retaking that refuses to respect, even as it never breaches, the incest taboo: refuses, because in this narrative the mother romance carries a far more powerful erotic charge than anything else and is the secure union that writing works to recover; unviolated, because writing is not after all the same as sex and there is no actual intercourse involved.

Like many memoirs, and like 'misery lit' to which it is generically first cousin, *Memoir*, to borrow Robert Stollers' phrase, 'converts trauma into triumph'.[12] Like McGahern's fiction generally, this last work does so by exposing the father's appalling domestic brutality to the world, thus breaching the abuser's codes of family secrecy and transgressing the etiquette of filial respect. In so doing, the writer-son becomes, in his words, 'a poet of domestic violence' and returns the domestic humiliation that he had visited on others to the father, recuperates the lost mother to himself, and at the same time transmutes a world of pain and damage into a burnished narrative form. Given the trauma involved, the process seems in some ways astonishingly successful, but in other respects the dividends are thinner than one might expect. Though mother-love suffuses *Memoir*, McGahern's mother in this final testament remains a surprisingly elusive figure, more an imago or benign ambient presence than a richly created or deeply explored person – as though McGahern had never experienced, perhaps because she had died too soon for this to develop, Susan McManus as a separate individual with her own intimacies with others besides him, or as if he wanted to share her as sparingly with readers as with his father or siblings. We learn the rudimentary details of her life, but little of her emotional or mental world. How did she make sense of her marriage? Was she as fixated on the eldest son as he on her or was her love distributed more evenly across her children? How did her other children, McGahern's brothers and sisters, regard her? How on earth did such a woman ever come to marry a man like Frank McGahern?

Memoir does not, perhaps cannot, press such questions. His mother's people, the writer observes, were resourceful, thrifty, careful and abhorred extravagance or self-indulgence. 'The single aberration seems to have been the girls' choice of husbands. All three McManus girls essentially married vain, self-indulgent men who were essentially childish, as if the sexual instinct craved a rougher cloth' (*M*, 44). This hints at sexual masochism on the part of the McManus girls, and the inelegantly repeated 'essentially' in this sentence imposes an insistent certitude that may merely varnish a lack of any such sureness, but the reference to 'childish men' suggests a disposition on the sisters' part perhaps to be mothers rather than wives. Similarly, though the father's appalling mental and physical brutality is brought vividly to life, explanations for his behaviour are never vigorously pursued. *Memoir* records that there was something masturbatory in the father's physical intimacy with the son and that there was something even more coarsely sexual in his physical beatings of his children (*M*, 188, 190). Elsewhere, it is noted that Frank McGahern drank heavily as a young man, then, disposed to extremes, renounced alcohol entirely to become a Pioneer of Total Abstinence. Catholicism's insistence on authority and disdain for sexuality generally, it is observed, cultivated a mix of severity and sexual frustration that were licensed and vented as domestic violence.

As insights go, these seem sensible, but scarcely sufficient to account for a man who seems so exorbitantly harassed and harassing, and who apparently beat one daughter with a spade and clattered another into a cataleptic fit. However, we learn at one point that Frank McGahern was an only child, possibly illegitimate, and that his mother never mentioned her husband, and the she must, the writer imagines, have wished her son to be a priest. This implies a certain parallelism between McGahern father and son, each sole or would-be sole possessors of mothers who both wished them to be priests, father and son alike refusing that destiny. But despite these intermittent speculations, none ever properly developed, McGahern for the most part insists less on knowledge than on inscrutability: 'I knew him better than I knew any living person, and yet I had never felt I understood him, so changeable was he, so violent, so self-absorbed, so many-faced. If it is impossible to know oneself, since we cannot see ourselves as we are seen, then it may be almost as difficult to understand those close to us […]. We may have an enormous store of experience and knowledge, psychological or otherwise, but we cannot see fully because we are too close, still too involved' (*M*, 226). There is an intellectual agnosticism here and an apparent disinclination to judgement that seems to indicate an emotional need not so much for closure as to keep things open – when Frank McGahern is consigned to his God, John McGahern refuses to play God by either condemning or forgiving. Either would constitute a verdict or summation and thus a finality of sorts. However, *Memoir* suspends intellectual (if not emotional) judgement as though in some sense it is as impossible to let go of the unfathomable nature of the father's malevolence as it is of the mother's love.

III

'Daddy, Daddy, you bastard', When Sylvia Plath wrote these lines in 1962 they had a bravely iconoclastic ring of daughterly impiety, a clamant register of anti-patriarchal hurt and anger that would soon be taken up by second-wave feminism. Plath's poem wears its rage on its sleeve, risking the accusations – soon enough to follow – of hysteria or tantrum, linguistic excess and emotional overkill.[13] 'Daddy, Daddy, you bastard' is an imprecation that courses through John McGahern's work too, and *Memoir*, his valedictory opus demonstrates that the anger had not been exorcised by *Amongst Women* or *That*

They May Face the Rising Sun. Despite the sense of release and recovery that issues from the decline and death of the ageing father recounted in the one novel and the sense of autumnal serenity and coming to terms with terminal life in the other, real anger abides. However, unlike Plath's, McGahern's work rarely wears its anger on its sleeve, rarely allows rage loud release. Indeed, McGahern's writing gravitates in a contrary direction to Plath's: his style disdains storminess and showiness and serves to massage or assuage anger into a stoic calm. Whereas Plath, with her Nazi imagery and Holocaust metaphors and barbed-wire lines, is always deliberately upping the verbal ante of domestic family romance towards public history, McGahern's work as deliberately takes matters in the opposite direction and mutes its rage and seeks after serenity, as though rage were the cantankerous other of wisdom and dignity. Part of the reason for this, surely, is that by indulging her rage Plath was courageously defying the convention that women should not be publicly angry; she unapologetically brings the madwoman down from the attic and lets her loose in the then male-dominated world of poetry readings. However, for McGahern to vent his rage in any like manner would be to become a version of the writer as 'Angry Young Man' and thus to slide into the place of the father, to become, like Daddy, another raging bull. If, as Freud argues, the Oedipus complex requires the boy to surrender the mother and either to become a masculine father-like creature himself or to put himself in the place of the mother and to court the love of the father, McGahern's reflex response seems to be an adamant 'No' to both options. As a writer, he rarely if ever indulges in father-like ventings or tantrums and he is typically cautious of strong expression, even when recounting painful episodes such as his sacking from his teaching position when he married a divorced woman; as a man, he would never apparently become a father, either clerical or familial, but, as *Memoir* demonstrates, neither would he ever reconcile with Daddy.[14]

What are we to make of all this? In an essay on rage as fine in its own way as anything to be found in McGahern, David Lloyd has written that:

> Rage, as sheer manifestation, has in fact neither subject nor object. It stands *before* the law- and subject-making moment of violence; indeed, its archetype is the infantile protest at the violence that splits one into subject and object, the no to an ineluctable process of differentiation and subordination to the law. […] If violence is agential, destructive of its objects, transitive, and, in its way, subject-forming in the very transformation of the other into its

object, rage is a most un-Hegelian moment of suspension or stasis whose vertiginous oscillations are set in motion by a reciprocal annihilation – the annihilation of the subject in the one who rages and the disappearance of the subject in the one who witnesses the obliterating gaze of the enraged. To be enraged is to be beside oneself, out of oneself; it is to be possessed of a force that is indifferent to the subject in oneself and to the subject in another by a force that is in another. Hence the one who witnesses rage witnesses the enraged as a lack of subject and knows that in the absence of subjecthood, his or her own subject is no less annihilated. The enraged does not see the other as subject or even as object; in the sheer transport of rage, differentiation is undone. Rage, therefore, can be neither founding nor destructive, though it may give way to either. It neither institutes nor destroys; it is resolutely non-narrative and gives rise to nothing out of its stasis, and though, indeed, it may give way almost immediately to violence, it remains another moment with another logic. It is sheer manifestation, but of nothing.[15]

Lloyd's prose is very different to McGahern's: the one idiom is as expressive of a drive to grasp and articulate the complex as the other is laconic and expressive of a will that refuses to imagine one could ever finally know or explain. Nevertheless, this makes the convergence of subject matter the more remarkable. Rage, Lloyd posits, is not completely to be identified with violence. Instead, it belongs to an occult zone of frenzy that stands almost out of time, that belongs to a non-time of 'suspension or stasis' when both the enraged and the subject towards which rage is directed have each had their subjectivities obliterated and know only a furious immediacy of anger and terror. 'Rage', Lloyd writes, 'is sheer manifestation, but of nothing'. Violence inaugurates, it founds and regulates subjects and states and laws; rage, full of sound and fury, is a surplus that violence disowns, but is also what continues to haunt the subject, the state, and the law as the remainder and reminder of their formative fallibility.

Will this explain McGahern for us? Perhaps not, or at least not entirely. But in the figure of Frank McGahern, the dashing IRA hero in his youth who in later life dons the Garda uniform of the new Irish state and becomes a sullen and cantankerous magistrate of the law, and who would vest the law of the *pater familias* and the law of the state in the higher sanction of Catholicism, despite disliking priests, McGahern *fils*, always *fils*, proffers his readers an unforgettable compound image that overlays atop each other the psychic traumas of bourgeois male subject formation, the political trauma of state formation, and the ontological trauma of mortality as such. McGahern's writing, that is, never ceases to remind its readers of the violence and rage inherent to each of these processes, a violence that no coming of age, no maturity, can anneal. The liberal critic may be content to read in the tealeaves of this vision a socio-political critique of post-independence Ireland, its crude patriarchy, its unholy complicities of church and state, its half-hidden savageries of social and domestic violence. Such readings are not mistaken, but involve only a partial remembering and in many ways another form of forgetting and disowning because all of these processes of subject, state, legal and personal formation remain, in however modified a form, as indispensable to the new neoliberal Ireland as to the Ireland of the founding fathers. The whole character of the state, the family, parenting, and the socialisation of children would have to be changed more radically than reformism typically recognises to fundamentally change the grimmer Irish family narratives so familiar to us.

Perhaps this fixation with the violence and rage of the father is why there is so little interest in any new Ireland in McGahern, so little interest indeed in contemporary politics, hardly any investment in futurity even, and so much investment in retreat, writing and the calm clock-tick of quotidian quietude as their own reward. In McGahern's work, the majesty of the law is a terrifically cold majesty, its rule unimaginable without violent displays and sudden tantrums of rage. In this vision, the father and his law always have power but also always lack authority and the wisdom necessary to secure authority. Unreconciled, father and son confront each other in a lifelong and unmitigated standoff, the son, abused and bereft, nevertheless through writing always working patiently to attain the composure and authority the raging father will never possess. In what seems a secular conversion of the mother's uncomplaining religious submission to God's will, McGahern as writer cultivates an ethic of secular stoicism and calm dignity in the face of death that some have called existential, but that might equally be termed quietist, a withdrawal from conflict: 'I am sure it is in those days that I take the belief that the best of life is lived quietly, where nothing happens but our calm journey through the day, when change is imperceptible and the precious life is everything' (*M*, 80). 'Quiet', 'calm', 'imperceptible change', 'precious life' – there is something Zen-like here, the all-too-understandable craving of the traumatised survivor to retreat from agitation, to win through to the farther shores of restfulness. This is the ethos nursed into accomplished form in *That They May Face the Rising Sun* and reaffirmed one last time in the richly evoked Leitrim landscapes of *Memoir*. Whether in a world as outrageously violent and self-destructive as ours is, this stoic ethos, this association of wisdom with 'quiet' and 'calm', is an achievement of wisdom or a form of reversion from conflict, or a mixture of both, we may wonder.

Chapter 12

—

Sins of the Flesh: Problematic Sexuality in McGahern and François Mauriac

—

Eamon Maher

It is common practice, perhaps as a result of his themes and settings, to view John McGahern as a distinctly 'Irish' writer. This is undoubtedly the case, but there are times when it can be useful to undertake a comparative reading in order to underline the extent to which he was indebted to other writers, many of them French. Denis Sampson's *Outstaring Nature's Eye* (1993) underlines McGahern's diverse reading tastes and states that he took inspiration from Irish figures such as Beckett and Kavanagh, as well as the French writers Albert Camus, Gustave Flaubert and Marcel Proust; in a similar vein, David Malcolm's *Understanding John McGahern* (2007) makes reference to the impact of Beckett, Chekhov, Flaubert and Tolstoy among others on McGahern's artistic evolution. The tenth anniversary of the writer's death saw three new monographs published, each of which introduced different lenses through which to profitably explore the oeuvre. Stanley van der Ziel underlines how canonical writers like Shakespeare, Austen, Wordsworth, Joyce and Beckett offered nourishment for McGahern's literary imagination. Richard Robinson's *John McGahern and Modernism* explores how McGahern, contrary to what a number of critics have suggested, was both aware, and made use of, certain modernist themes and techniques – Joyce, Yeats, Chekhov, Beckett and Nietzsche are evoked in an attempt to prove this thesis. Frank Shovlin's study of McGahern's classical style brings some interesting new figures to light in relation to how they acted as 'touchstones' for McGahern, namely Matthew Arnold, Stendhal, Horace, Douglas Stewart, William Blake and Dante. Shovlin also mentions several of the aforementioned writers and makes a very strong case for Yeats as an abiding influence.[1]

So it is clear that there is nothing really new about considering the way in which McGahern's aesthetic may have been moulded by various literary figures at different stages in his development. That said, in the case of all those just mentioned, we know from comments he made in articles and interviews that McGahern had actually read them. The person to whom I wish to compare him, the French Nobel laureate François Mauriac (1885–1970) and one of the foremost writers of the twentieth century, is not someone whom McGahern ever mentioned publicly as a possible influence. However, in *Young John McGahern: becoming a novelist*, Denis Sampson, citing various French writers whom McGahern admired, observes:

> Notable in his absence is François Mauriac, prominent apologist for a Catholic and conservative France at this time, but the lack of reference to him is not clear evidence that McGahern did not read any of his novels; on the contrary, it is more than likely that he did.[2]

While the presentation of Mauriac as an 'apologist' for 'a Catholic and conservative France' is at best dubious, given that he excoriated the failings of the French church on numerous occasions in his novels and journalism, it is hard to disagree with Sampson's contention that McGahern in all likelihood read at least some of Mauriac's fiction.[3] After all, what aspiring Irish writer of the early 1960s would have been unaware of someone on whom the Nobel Prize for Literature was bestowed in 1952? Also, an Irish writer whom McGahern respected hugely, Kate O'Brien, openly admitted a predilection for Mauriac, as did his contemporary Brian Moore and his distant cousin John Broderick. The stifling Catholic environment of the rural district of Les Landes, near Bordeaux, where most of Mauriac's most successful novels are set, along with the strained family relations and problems associated with burgeoning sexuality that they evoke, would have definitely struck a chord with McGahern.

The type of reading I am undertaking in this chapter does not, in fact, require that McGahern should have read Mauriac, as what I seek to highlight are the similarities in the portrayal of sexuality in the fiction of the two writers. They were both exposed to a puritanical form of Catholicism during their youth which emphasised the sinfulness of the human body – an attitude ingrained particularly in Mauriac's mother, whose faith was moulded by Jansenism, and in McGahern's father who appears to have bought into the morbid distrust of the flesh that characterised Irish society in the 1940s and '50s. In the fiction of the two writers, many characters feel obliged to repress their sexual urges, a decision that can have severe psychological consequences, as is pointed out by Michel Foucault:

If sex is repressed, that is, condemned to prohibition, nonexistence and silence, then the mere fact that one is speaking about it has the appearance of a deliberate transgression. A person who holds forth in such a language places himself to a certain extent outside the reach of power; he upsets established law; he somehow anticipates the coming freedom.[4]

I will use Foucault's notion of 'transgression' in my exploration of the presentation of sexuality in Mauriac and McGahern. Prohibiting discussion of sex inevitably leads to its being driven underground, to its being viewed as unsavoury or sinful. In the fiction of Mauriac and McGahern, sex is more often than not portrayed as problematic, a taboo subject about which one must be silent so as not to upset the 'established law', to use Foucault's phrase. This silence can result in heightened feelings of shame and guilt for those who actively engage in sexual practices, or dwell on them mentally. In Jean-Luc Barré's recent biography of Mauriac, in which he speaks openly about the writer's struggle with '*la tentation homosexuelle*' (homosexual temptation), he notes how the notion of sin was imbued in the writer from a young age:

And what sin could be more fearsome than the one about which you merely had to think in order to be 'separated from God', the sin of the flesh, the privileged domain of evil, the home of corruption and the fall from grace?[5]

In a similarly forthright manner, McGahern made regular reference to the damage caused to people like himself by the Catholic Church's insistence on linking sex with sin, a teaching that left its mark on the psyche of generations of Irish men and women. In an interview he gave in November 2000, McGahern made the following comments:

I would think that if there was one thing injurious about the Church, it would be its attitude to sexuality. I see sexuality as just a part of life. Either all of life is sacred or none of it is sacred. [...] And I think it [the church] made a difficult enough relationship – which is between people, between men and women – even more difficult by imparting an unhealthy attitude to sexuality.[6]

When McGahern wrote about sex, he did so from the perspective of someone who believed that sexuality was sacred, as opposed to the traditional church teaching that urged people to think of it as sinful, except when, within marriage, it was open to the possibility of conception. In *The Leavetaking*, the male protagonist Patrick Moran is shocked at his American wife Isobel's admission that as a young woman she had an abortion after discovering she was pregnant. What surprises him even more is her lack of remorse afterwards: 'No, I felt great', she tells him.[7] The contrast between this carefree attitude and what Patrick would have felt in similar circumstances is stark. He muses: 'The true life was death in life. The sexual life was destruction; the sweet mouth, ruin. In my end was my beginning' (*L*, 156). Patrick does manage to break away from such a fatalistic view of sexuality, thanks in large part to the healthy physical relationship he enjoys with Isobel, but it is clear that such liberation is not easily won.

The historian Diarmaid Ferriter detects a change of attitude towards sex in Ireland from the start of the 1960s. In *Occasions of Sin: sex and society in modern Ireland*, we read: 'At the personal level, many people were also challenging their religion and rejecting teaching they regarded as conditioning them to equate flesh with sin.'[8] This more enlightened approach can be seen in some of McGahern's later work, particularly *The Pornographer* and *Amongst Women*, where the younger generation often turn their backs on the restrictive sexual mores of their parents in order to pursue their bodily inclinations more freely. But there remain residual traces of their religious upbringing in some of their attitudes, as shall become evident later in this chapter.

Discussion of sex, particularly within the family circle, is often occluded by McGahern's characters. Consider for example the reaction of Moran's daughters in *Amongst Women* on the night of his wedding to Rose, when the newlyweds make their way to the bedroom: 'They [the daughters] tried not to breathe as they listened. They were too nervous and frightened of life to react or to put into words the sounds they heard from the room where their father was sleeping with Rose.'[9] Presumably the discomfort experienced by the girls is due to their unspoken realisation that Moran and his new bride were not, in fact, 'sleeping' in the room below. The impossibility of 'putting into words' what is happening serves to intensify the stigma associated in their minds with sex. Later in the novel, another pair of newlyweds, Sean and Sheila, leave the meadow where the Morans are working at the hay to return to the house hand in hand. The resentment felt by Sheila's siblings is palpable:

'No one spoke in the tense uneasiness, but they were forced to follow them in their minds into the house, how they must be shedding clothes, going naked towards one another [...]. They hated that they had to follow it this way. It was more disturbingly present than if it were taking place in the meadow before their very eyes' (*AW*, 165–6). Silence is once more the response demanded of the family members. Michael, no novice in the sexual domain himself, captures the anger of the Moran children at what they consider selfish absorption, when he says: 'You'd think they could have waited' (*AW*, 166). The feeling that Sean and Sheila are somehow destroying the 'inviolability' of Great Meadow, the family home, is connected to the way the children see this place as a type of monument to an unchanging world that should not be despoiled by anything as depraved as sex.

Mauriac's personal struggle with sexuality was traumatic. From an early age, he believed himself to be hideous and incapable of inspiring love. Photographs of him as a boy show a slight, anxious-looking child who seems to have many of the world's problems on his shoulders. One of the best commentators on his work, Charles du Bos, in a complimentary review of *Le Désert de l'amour*, noted that there are only two important things in life, sexuality and God, and God often assumes prominence for the simple reason that sexual passion can never be fully satisfied. He added that the subject matter of Mauriac's novels was provided, not by personal experience, but by the things that the novelist would never allow himself to experience.[10] This refusal to live out his sexual yearnings may partly explain the sometimes risqué topics Mauriac covered in his novels. His approach was occasionally a source of scandal to Catholic readers, who found it hard to accept the lasciviousness that characterises some of his most memorable fictional characters. Donat O'Donnell (a *nom de plume* for Conor Cruise O'Brien) captures the mood well in his exemplary study, *Maria Cross*:

> The real charge against Mauriac was that his tone, and the images he evoked, suggested a secret sympathy, a connivance with sin, instead of the uncompromising detestation of sin which Catholic critics felt they had a right to expect from a Catholic novelist.[11]

Indeed, when one considers his oeuvre as a whole, it is noticeable how few of Mauriac's characters have a positive view of sex. If he was prone to homosexual longings and felt unable to give in to them, as would appear to have been the case, the frustration and unhappiness that this caused may logically have found an outlet in his creative writing. But being a husband and father meant that it was important to keep the truth under wraps in order to protect his family, something that was not as easy as it might first appear. In *Le Roman-cier et ses personnages*, for example, he wrote: 'Behind the most objective fiction [...] can always be found the real-life drama of the novelist, the deep personal struggle with his demons and sphinxes.'[12] While it is never advisable to assume that events from a novelist's life can be directly transposed into fiction, there can be little doubt that a link exists between the two. McGahern regularly revealed his discomfort with critics who saw his work as autobiographical, claiming that he was a novelist first and foremost, not a memorialist or jour-nalist. That is a fair point, but Mauriac was equally right in asserting that a novelist cannot prevent his or her innermost struggles from appearing in some form, whether veiled or unveiled, in fiction. And because his novels describe things that so closely resemble events in his own life, such as the death of his mother, the spiteful violence of his father, attendance at religious rituals, the struggle with the land, emigration, sexual frustration, in settings that are remarkably similar to areas in Roscommon and Leitrim where McGahern spent the majority of his life, it is reasonable to conclude that at the very least the life informed the work. In his Introduction to *Commencements d'une vie*, Mauriac made the following revelation: 'Fiction alone does not lie; it shines a light into a writer's soul that reveals things that he does not even recognise in himself.'[13] Using the fictional form, for Mauriac, did not therefore automati-cally remove the writer from the danger of self-revelation.

Having provided some background with regard to the novelists' mindset in relation to sexuality, I think it would be useful at this point to see how this translated into their fiction. Initially we will look at two early works, McGahern's unpublished first novel 'The End or the Beginning of Love', and Mauriac's *Le Baiser au lépreux* (1922), both of which are revealing of the approach the two writers adopted to this theme. The manuscript of 'The End or the Beginning of Love' is available in the McGahern Archive in the Hardiman Library in NUI Galway. It opens with the scene of a mother and her young son Hugh discussing whom he loves most of all in the world. The reply, 'You, Mammy', earns him a rebuke and he is obliged to repeat the usual formula about loving God most of all, then his mother and father equally. This is territory to which McGahern returned in both *The Leavetaking* and *Memoir* and it takes its inspiration from the writer's childhood memories.

Denis Sampson rightly observes: 'McGahern's lifelong preoccupation with this material is a clear indication that in it he discovered the central spiritual issues of his work and also its stylistic challenges.'[14] The devout mother is keen that Hugh should one day become a priest, and to his plea that she must not die and leave him, she replies:

> But I'll be up in heaven praying for you. When you grow up, you'll say Mass for me and I'll still watch over you so that you can come to no harm. One day we'll meet in Paradise and we will be with each other for all eternity.[15]

The broken promise made to his mother about his priestly vocation leaves an indelible mark on Hugh as he progresses through adolescence to early adulthood. After his wife's death, Hugh's father derives sexual excitement from beating his children. One incident, narrated through the eyes of his son, reveals Mahoney Senior's reaction when administering a punishment to his daughter Maura: 'Even in the dim light he saw by his father's trousers that he was sexually aroused. Mahoney's face was horrible with passion' (p. 143). Another example is when Hugh goes to visit his cousin Fr Gerald who, in keeping with the behaviour of the man of the same name in *The Dark*, comes to his room in the middle of the night under the pretext of discussing his vocation and ends up showing the boy the scars on his stomach.

For all that the father's abuse and the inappropriate behaviour of Fr Gerald are interesting manifestations of McGahern's early preoccupations as a writer, it is the romantic relationship that develops between Hugh and a trainee teacher Kathleen Lynch that is most revealing of the transgressive nature of sexual relations in this narrative. Whenever the couple allow passion to take hold of them, they end up loathing each other afterwards. We are told: 'There was little kindness or tenderness in the lust of their love' (p. 265). Kathleen is particularly puritanical: 'You shouldn't kiss me like that', she declares on one occasion. 'It's wrong, it's sinful, it's passionate kissing' (p. 242). At times, especially when the thought of death and the Final Judgment fill him with terror, Hugh is forced to agree with his girlfriend. He goes to Sunday mass simply because it is easier to go than not to go, and he can see the influence of his sentimental education on his psyche: '[…] he was by no means free of the religion of his childhood; he would never be fully free' (p. 252).

Kathleen's character is devoid of any real endearing qualities. She blows hot and cold and leaves Hugh doubting where he stands with her. One day she announces her desire to enter a convent and 'leave all this passion and sin' (p. 292) behind her. Even within marriage, she considers sex evil: '[…] there's something dirty and disgusting about sex, something', she shuddered with repulsion, 'unclean' (p. 293). Hugh and Kathleen are portrayed as being victims of the unwholesome approach to sex in Ireland, an approach of which McGahern was outspokenly critical in many of his interviews and non-fiction writing. This is particularly clear from the following line from the unpublished novel: 'They all seem to have inherited the idea of the horrible ugliness and sewer filth of sex' (p. 293). This negative attitude is by no means unique to McGahern: it is manifest also in the work of Kate O'Brien, Walter Macken, Edna O'Brien, Brian Moore and many other Irish writers of the middle decades of the last century. McGahern was clearly intent on bringing to the fore the crippling effect a repressive social and religious regime can have on people's view of sexuality. Something that is natural and beautiful, something that should be embraced and cherished, is reduced to hideousness for people like Hugh and Kathleen, who cannot escape what they view as 'the sewer filth of sex'. Hence we encounter unpalatable descriptions like the following emanating from the disturbed mind of Hugh:

> It had come up before his own mind: black blood splashed against the pale skin of the loins, the stench of rotting fish, blood matted in the hair that twisted like a pile of worms, the rough edges of a tapeworm moving in the blood it fed on […]. He passed his hand across his eyes in horror. Their minds were diseased, blasphemous against life, the horrible smell of decay before death from them. (p. 293)

Such a stark representation of the aftermath of the sexual act is a good point of departure for a comparative discussion of McGahern's unpublished novel and Mauriac's *Le Baiser au lépreux*. Published in 1922, this depressing tale of the doomed marriage of the repulsive Jean Péloueyre, the only son of a wealthy provincial widower, to the beautiful Noémi d'Artiailh, provides a good illustration of Mauriac's skill at depicting human relationships. Jérôme Péloueyre, anxious that his possessions should not fall into the hands of his sister Félicité Cazenave and her son Fernand, conspires with the local curé to arrange a meeting between Jean and the seventeen-year-old beauty Noémi.

Intensely aware of his ugliness, Jean apologises to the woman who is to become his wife, stating he knows how unworthy he is of her. Noémi is described as belonging to a race of people 'who do not look for any carnal pleasure in marriage; a woman of duty, subservient to God and to her husband'.[16] It is one thing to acknowledge that her destiny is unavoidable – '*on ne refuse pas le fils Péloueyre* / one cannot refuse a Péloueyre, after all' (p. 461) – but quite another to share her life and bed with a man as repulsive as Jean is. She experiences the full horror of her plight on their wedding night:

> Jean Péloueyre had to fight a long time, firstly with his own lack of passion, then with his lifeless partner. At dawn, a faint groan marked the end of a struggle that had lasted six hours. Soaked in sweat, Jean Péloueyre did not dare to move, more gruesome than a worm beside this corpse which had finally succumbed to him. (p. 466)

After this interlude, Noémi resembled 'a sleeping martyr', the victim of an appalling attack by the monster to whom she was now married. Jean is named twice in this description and the vocabulary used by Mauriac conveys the cancerous effect this man has on his wife: she is the 'corpse', he the 'worm' that eats away her insides. Note how similar the language is to the last quotation we read from 'The End or the Beginning of Love': in both instances, we have reference to worms that suck the lifeblood out of their hapless victims. As the months pass by, Jean Péloueyre cannot help noticing the deterioration in Noémi's appearance and realises that he is draining the life out of the young woman with whom he is hopelessly in love: 'What victim was ever more loved by her executioner?' he muses (p. 469). Jean resolves to give his suffering spouse some respite by heading to Paris for a few months: '[…] he was fleeing from her so that she could blossom once more' (p. 473). This is what happens, in fact. Noémi, left on her own, rediscovers her former beauty and attracts the attention of a handsome young doctor newly arrived in the area, whom she observes passing by the Péloueyre residence during the steamy summer afternoons. The deep desire she feels for this stranger fills Noémi with guilt and so Jean is summoned home before something untoward might occur. On descending from the train, his ghastly appearance is a huge contrast to his wife's flowering, a discovery which seals Jean's decision to begin daily visits to a local tuberculosis victim, *le fils* Pieuchon, in the knowledge that he will most likely contract the serious disease and die.

Jean Péloueyre empowers himself by choosing death as a means of securing his wife's enduring devotion. Because Noémi is aware of the heroic sacrifice he makes for her, she bestows on him the types of kisses that saints reputedly lavished on the lepers for whom they cared (from whence the title of the novel). Having lived like a dead man, Jean's death releases him from his torment, whereas Noémi is compelled to remain a widow or forfeit the family inheritance: '[…] no path was left open to her, apart from self-denial' (p. 499). As is customary in Mauriac's novels, there is no fairytale ending, no resolution of life's cruel dilemmas. The writer's acute awareness of his own physical unattractiveness obviously influenced his portrayal of Jean Péloueyre. But the depressing account of sexual incompatibility, of the lack of real communication between a man and wife, gives *Le Baiser au lépreux* a special place in Mauriac's work. Like McGahern's 'The End or the Beginning of Love', the tragic story of Jean and Noémi reveals a decidedly unwholesome depiction of sexuality that owes much to Jansenism. Malcolm Scott summarises the impact of this theology on Mauriac in the following terms:

> [H]e [Mauriac] was prone to anxieties that brought him to the brink of the theological pessimism inherent in this theory of grace. One was the view of sexual love as the greatest obstacle to the love of God, irredeemable even within marriage – a notion rooted in Mauriac's own sexuality and given support by Pascal's view of 'holy wedlock' as 'the most perilous and base condition of the Christian state'.[17]

In the concluding part of this paper, we will examine how McGahern never went as far down the road of Jansenistic pessimism and scrupulosity as Mauriac did by examining one of his less well-known novels, *The Pornographer*, alongside Mauriac's chef d'oeuvre, *Thérèse Desqueyroux*.

Published in 1979, *The Pornographer* does not attract the same degree of critical attention as the early and late novels. This may be because it is part of what I term McGahern's 'experimental' phase, a period when he was searching for the type of style that would allow him to become more detached from his material. We know that he rewrote sections of *The Leavetaking* during the same period for reasons that he spelt out in the Preface to the 1984 edition:

> The crudity I was trying to portray, the irredeemable imprisonment of the beloved in reportage, had itself become blatant. I had been too close to the

'Idea', and the work lacked that distance, that inner formality or calm, that all writing, no matter what it is attempting, must possess. (*L*, p. 5)

The 'beloved', his mother, was the wellspring of his writing and he found it difficult to be detached when evoking her death. Whether or not he actually managed to achieve 'that inner formality or calm' in the second version of *The Leavetaking* is dubious in my opinion, but what is significant is the now mature writer's awareness of the need for distance when evoking experiences that have a resonance in real life. (It could have been this reticence that led to his decision not to publish 'The End or the Beginning of Love'.) Sex was another area that informed McGahern's philosophy in a substantial manner and he sought the same type of detachment when writing about it as when treating all other aspects of life. *The Pornographer*, he admitted in an interview with this author, was 'a deliberate attempt to see if sex could be written about'. He went on: 'The pornography was a kind of backdrop to see if the sexuality in its vulnerability and humanness could be written about. My own view is that it probably can't.'[18] It was definitely not possible to write about sexuality in a sensitive way through the medium of pornography, but McGahern did achieve something akin to his stated ambition in his depiction of the relationship between the nameless pornographer and Nurse Brady, whom he meets when visiting his dying aunt in hospital. Whereas callous and manipulative in his treatment of his mistress Josephine, a bank official whom he cynically uses to assuage his sexual needs and from whom he seeks to distance himself as soon as she becomes pregnant, with Nurse Brady he is a completely different person. Making love to her transports him into a type of mystical state:

> This body [the nurse's] was the shelter of the self. Like all walls and shelters it would age and break and let the enemy in. But holding it now was like holding glory, and having held it once was to hold it – no matter how broken and conquered – in glory still, and with the more terrible tenderness.[19]

The nurse's body is described as 'the shelter of the self', a refuge from the storms of life which will be diminished by age, but without losing its power to inspire awe and wonder. This is one of the few unequivocally positive descriptions of sex in McGahern's fiction, and it is found in a novel where pornography holds centre stage most of the time. The disillusioned poet Maloney, who publishes the pornographer's fictional accounts of the sexual exploits of Colonel Grimshaw and his partner Mavis, offers the following advice to his protégé: 'Above all the imagination requires distance [...]. It can't function close up' (P, 21). In many ways, this is as good a summary as you will get of McGahern's own conviction about the importance of impartiality in literature. Maloney sees his publishing work as a way of bringing some enlightenment to a country that is wrapped up in a Victorian past. His refrain, 'Ireland wanking is Ireland free' (P, 25), shows a desire to shock, to divest himself of all the customary traits associated with orthodoxy. And yet in his personal life, we learn that Maloney allowed himself to be walked into marriage by a woman who mistakenly thought she was pregnant and he is critical of the pornographer's decision to leave Josephine in the lurch when she finds herself in the same condition. Josephine, in spite of a strict religious upbringing, is open about her need for, and enjoyment of, sex and repeats on several occasions that she doesn't feel guilty afterwards. Josephine is a strange mixture of hedonism and conservatism and is representative of a different outlook on sex among McGahern's characters.

The Pornographer is a philosophical novel which treats of several existential dilemmas. Numerous passages allude to the links between sex and death. On one occasion the orgasm is compared to the last gasp of a dying man: 'Death must sometimes come in the same way, the tension leaving the body, in pain and not in sweetness and pride, but a last time, the circle completed' (P, 57). And then there is the memorable analogy drawn between 'the womb and the grave': 'The christening party becomes the funeral, the shudder that makes us flesh becomes the shudder that makes us meat' (P, 30). All of which reveals a yearning to come to terms with the true meaning of sex. When evaluating whether McGahern is successful or not in portraying sexuality in 'its vulnerability and humanness' in this novel, one would have to say that there are definitely glimpses of such an achievement. Nevertheless, love is constantly linked to pain, loss and futility: 'Having drunk from the infernal glass we call love and knowing we have lived our death, we turn to love another way, in the ordered calm of each thing counted and loved for its impending loss' (P, 97). In spite of this distrust, at the end of the novel the pornographer decides he will return to live on his deceased parents' farm in the west of Ireland with Nurse Brady, if she will have him. There is some hint of hope in such a scenario.

Mauriac's *Thérèse Desqueyroux*, published in 1927, at a time when the author was undergoing a crisis of faith that may well have been triggered by the strong attraction he felt for the Swiss cultural attaché, Bernard Barbey, was a daring undertaking for a man so strongly associated with the 'Catholic novel'. The book recounts how a woman, finding herself in a loveless marriage to a wealthy landowner, Bernard Desqueyroux, sets about poisoning him. Nothing too daring in that, you might say, but Mauriac was not merely content to describe Thérèse's homicidal attempts; he also displayed a secret empathy, even a connivance, with her. In the Foreword, he anticipates readers' disquiet at his giving life to 'a creature more odious than any characters in my other books'. He explains that virtuous characters do not interest him, whereas he possesses a deep knowledge 'of the secrets of the hearts that are deep buried in, and mingled with, the filth of the flesh'.[20] Undoubtedly novelists tend to be more interested in evil or criminal characters than in virtuous ones, as they offer more scope for dramatic representation. Indeed, some would argue that saints are, by virtue of their other-worldly nature, almost beyond literary depiction – Georges Bernanos was one of the few to successfully bridge that particular gap. Mauriac is renowned for the psychological probing of his characters' subconscious. With Thérèse, he had a particular empathy, perhaps because she, like him, finds it difficult to tolerate the hypocritical attitude of her conventional husband and his family, whose primary concern is always the preservation of the reputation and wealth of the family. Her close friendship with Bernard's half-sister, Anne de la Trave, was one reason why Thérèse chose him as her future husband. The other, stronger, reason was that the land of the families 'seemed made for fusion' (p. 25), a definite motivation for someone like Thérèse who had 'the sense of property in her blood' (p. 31).

Mauriac's heroine is lucid and pitiless when it comes to analysing her own actions and those of others. She accepts that Bernard was probably an inherently decent person, superior in many ways to countless men of his background and education. Their relationship was not helped by sexual incompatibility. Indeed, Thérèse quickly developed a profound dislike of sexual intercourse, which in her view brought about an irredeemable loss of innocence: 'Everything which dates from before my marriage I see now as bathed in a light of purity – doubtless because that time stands out in such vivid contrast to the indelible filth of my wedded life' (p. 22). Note how close Mauriac's 'indelible filth' is to the phrase employed in McGahern's unpublished novel, 'sewer filth'. To describe the sexual act in these stark terms betrays an incapacity on the part of the characters to view it as being anything other than prurient. One of the qualities Thérèse finds so attractive in Anne is her air of innocence, her seeming total ignorance of evil. Certain critics have argued that Thérèse's unspeakable lesbianism is the reason why she finds heterosexual relations so unpleasant – could this have been in some way a veiled admission by Mauriac of his own unsettling feelings for Bernard Barbey? Certainly some of Thérèse's evocations of Anne show an undisguised desire that is in sharp contrast to the following description of her husband's sexual antics:

> I always saw Bernard as a man who charged head-down at pleasure, while I lay like a corpse, motionless, as though fearing that, at the slightest gesture on my part, this madman, this epileptic, might strangle me. (p. 35)

Early pregnancy drives an ever-greater wedge between them, especially the way Bernard now proudly looks on her as 'the woman who bore within her the future master of unnumbered trees' (p. 44). Then Anne falls madly in love with Jean Azévédo, whose family is reputed to be of Jewish origin and whom Bernard suspects of being a consumptive. The letters she writes Thérèse during the latter's honeymoon fill her with angry jealousy. Why should Anne have the benefits of this grand passion, while Thérèse languishes in a state of bemused frustration? She resolves to ensure that the liaison comes to an abrupt end and she follows up that action by systematically poisoning her husband.

There are many ingredients in *Thérèse Desqueyroux* that McGahern would have admired. The huge attachment to the land; the horror at the prospect of a local fire spreading to the Desqueyroux pine trees; the image of Bernard hypocritically walking at the head of the Corpus Christi procession, 'doing his duty'; the family tensions that flare up when it comes to finding a suitable partner for Anne; the detailed descriptions of nature – all this would have appealed to the Leitrim writer. Mauriac made a significant admission during an interview with Cecil Jenkins:

> *Thérèse Desqueyroux* was indeed the novel of revolt. The story of Thérèse was the whole of my own drama, a protest, a cry [...]. And I could well say, even though I have never contemplated poisoning anyone, that *Thérèse Desqueyroux* was myself.[21]

Note that, like Flaubert's similar assertion in relation to *Madame Bovary*, it is the work, and not the heroine, to which Mauriac refers in this instance. One could say the same about McGahern's work, that it is the purest version of himself that you will find. His various secrets, obsessions, hopes and fears are captured in a style that was carefully shaped throughout a long literary career. He sought objectivity and detachment in the manner of Flaubert, whose comment he often quoted or paraphrased: 'The writer should be like God in the universe, always present but nowhere visible.' So while not being so naïve as to suggest that the portrayal of sexuality in Mauriac and McGahern is a direct transposition of the writers' personal experiences, there is nevertheless a strong connection between the two. Their characters, however liberated and enlightened they might be in relation to the Catholic mores which shaped their youth, never fully manage to escape from the haunting guilt that lingers around sexuality. I will conclude with a final quote from Foucault which sums up the theme I have been attempting to explore in this paper:

> How does one account for the displacement which, while claiming to free us from the sinful nature of sex, taxes us with a great historical wrong which consists precisely in imagining nature to be blameworthy and in drawing disastrous consequences from that belief?[22]

Sex and sexuality are clearly not easy to come to terms with in the normal routine of life, but when one adds a heavy dose of Catholic indoctrination, it takes on the disturbing and disorienting guise of transgression that is such a prominent feature of the work of Mauriac and McGahern.

AFTERWORD

From out of *The Dark*: John McGahern and Truth[1]
Donal Ryan

I

There is a particular type of silence that precedes the creative process: unbroken, empty of struggle, imbued with a very temporary immaculateness. All silences except the final one are broken eventually. This silence allows the extension of human empathy to a point beyond its natural limit, so that it surpasses its own potential for connection, and allows a glimpse of the truth of the human condition. There is a particular type of darkness that attends this silence: where the light that's required to see isn't refracted or prismed or compromised by ambient conditions; this is a darkness that allows worlds to be imagined that don't exist, for them to be cast in the sharpest relief. John McGahern, I imagine, existed for much of his creative life in this fecund place of silence and darkness of a particular quality, beyond the limits of empathy, beyond the boundaries of easy explanation, beyond the reach of his peers.

We live in a world that demands a lot from language. As malleable and pliable as language is, it can still be broken. There are a million words that humans use, and therefore, as good as an infinity of ways of saying any one thing. Language can be twisted and tortured into any shape, to any end. The obfuscatory language of politics is used daily to encourage us to swallow all sorts of unpalatable things; the closed, joyless, terminal language of rationality is used to denigrate faith in God; the language of macro-economics is used to parse humanity into mathematical units of various values; the strident, trenchant language of dogma is used to build prisons of faith.

John McGahern was one of the rare writers who manned the breach between the language of truth and beauty and the language of control, dogma and power. His work allows his readers a profound relief. His pristine sensibility is a beacon for writers. Here is life, portrayed in words, where each unit of language is used for its ideal purpose, for its intrinsic meaning; here is literature set to its highest task, in its most immaculate form, fuelling a flame that casts light, not just on the parts of us most in shadow, but on all the open plains and occluded crevices of the quotidian, on the terrain we all negotiate. Here is existence, in the place where ink meets paper, without abstraction or wilful opacity, without agenda or trick. Here is ease to our minds and our souls.

II

I read *Amongst Women* in 1995 or 1996. It almost finished me as an aspiring writer. How could a book be this good? Existence is inchoate and incoherent and senseless. How could this representation of existence feel so resolved, so correct, so like it hadn't been written at all, but alchemised from flesh to paper and ink; how could this Moran character have seared his mark so indelibly on my consciousness? Why could I still see Rose months later in my mind's eye, and hear her gentle voice? Michael 'out in the front garden among his flowerbeds', Luke, and the terrible chasm that couldn't be bridged. And worse: I had thought of my idiotic young self as 'a fella who was well able to do a nice description of landscape' – until I came across this subtle, perfect, achingly beautiful description of the morning of a day when hay could be saved:

> […] a white mist obscured the dark green shapes of the beech trees along the head of the meadows and their sandals made green splashes through the cobwebbed pastures. A white gossamer hung over the plum and apple trees in the orchard. A hot dry day was certain. Not even by evening would there be a threat of rain. No work could be done until the sun burned the mists away and dried the swards.[2]

I resolved there and then never to try to match John McGahern. To put him away. He was dangerous to my brittle sense of myself and my abilities. His bar was far too high. It took me years to shake off the sense that there was no point in trying; that McGahern had said already all that needed to be said, had created art of such clarity and pristine beauty that no paltry offering of mine could or should share the same shelves.

And yet I'm grateful for every sentence he left in this world.

The Dark was, for many, almost unbearable to read. For many it still is. Lines like the following strike a chord, with their description of a son anxiously awaiting the arrival of his widowed father, with whom he shares a bed:

The worst was to have to sleep with him the nights he wanted love, strain of waiting for him to come to bed, no hope of sleep in the waiting – counting and losing the count of the thirty-two boards across the ceiling, trying to pick out the darker circles of the knots beneath the varnish. Watch the moon on the broken brass bells at the foot of the bed. Turn and listen and turn. Go over the day that was gone, what was done or left undone, or dream of the dead days with her in June.

The dreams and passing of time would break with the noise of the hall door opening, feet on the cement, his habitual noises as he drank barley water over the dying fire, and at last the stockinged feet on the stairs.

He was coming and there was nothing to do but wait and grow hard as stone and lie.[3]

The Dark caused John Charles McQuaid, then Archbishop of Dublin, to denounce John McGahern, labelling him a man who 'had an obsession with dirty books'. And yet from *The Dark* springs nothing but hope. The hope that writers have and will follow in McGahern's wake and push and push towards the truth of things. That fiction serves a noble purpose, to oust secrecy, to obliterate shame, to stand as mirror to the soul of man and reflect him back to himself; to delineate his terrible propensity for violence and abuse and to use narrative as a blessed valve to relieve the awful pressure of the ignored, pent-up, unspoken pain of existence. John McGahern had the guts to write of people 'stripped down to the last squalor' and for his pains was sacked, censored, censured and exiled. He endured this with stoicism. He took care of his sentences. He was a hero in the truest sense, and never sought to be seen as such.

To be tongue-tied should be no burden for a writer. To be unable or unwilling to take part in exhaustive, intensive interrogation of one's own work. To be unable or unwilling to justify oneself in public, to give reasons for writing what one has written. A literary work should need no accompaniment, no scaffold, no re-enforcement. As the great poet Michael Hartnett said of Dylan Thomas in 'Poets Passing':

> By a perverted act of will
> the poet injects limelight in his veins
> till what was exhilaration
> has become the poet's opium.

Soon in some public place
he must explain and must reshape
the very gift he has
as if the public were the giver,
refine his accent, modify his speech,
must jingle literary cap and bells
and end with insulted brain and liver
far from Wales on a mortuary slab
or with an exhausted heart
in a New York taxi-cab
or out of human reach
in the last of his self-inflicted hells,
by the Mississippi river.[4]

John McGahern, I think, would have concurred with the sentiment so powerfully expressed here. Writers should be allowed to choose public silence in the spaces between works. What purpose does a work of art serve if its creator must stand beside it, explaining its elements? A thing dismantled and exposed and reassembled repeatedly loses some of its integrity each time, and will eventually be sundered completely, rendered useless.

My mother and father met John McGahern once, in the mid-1990s, in a guesthouse on Achill Island. He was having supper with his wife and my father noticed him and was struck by a most uncharacteristic attack of shyness. John McGahern was one of his great heroes. He finally worked up the courage to strike up a conversation and John told him he was reading that evening in a converted church down the road. 'You should come along', he said. But Dad's alien shyness persisted and he felt embarrassed and self-conscious and so they didn't go to the reading, believing it to be for 'a different kind of set'. To this day he regrets his strange refusal to take up the author's kind suggestion, and often speaks of it. 'What got into me at all', he wonders. 'What in the hell got into me?' I think if they'd met again afterwards that John McGahern would have understood. That sometimes it's difficult to be easy and free. It's difficult to cast off doubt and fear, even of the most unreasonable kind.

To be happy with the truth of oneself is an aspiration now, overtly expressed in all sorts of media. There are people, and businesses, and all kinds of mentors and pedagogues and shamans who will assist you on the path to self-knowledge, and self-improvement, and some kind of commercialised version of peace and fulfilment. In *That They May Face the Rising Sun*, Patrick Ryan delivers this pithy philosophy:

> I would not swap with a lord. We all want our own two shoes of life. If truth was told, none of us would swap with anybody. We want to go out the way we came in. It's just as well we have no choice.[5]

Truth, of course, is a nebulous concept. All fiction is guesswork; each portrayal of a human transaction is created with no real certainty, because certainty cannot survive in the cold vacuum of human experience; each of us experiences the world in our own unique way and none of us can be certain of the quality of the next person's experience. We are all, essentially, unknowable. It's the privilege of poets to wait for the muse to alight on their shoulder and whisper encouragement. The novelist has to force it, has to take an extended, elliptical route towards resolution, finding when he or she gets there that he or she isn't there at all, that the journey is only starting, that nothing can ever be fully resolved. A writer should never feel he or she has arrived at an indefatigable, unassailable truth. Certainty is terminal. A writer can only take care to listen, to be still and silent and to wait for that soft settling of words, for that moment, however fleeting, of rightness. I've heard writers claim they feel sickened by everything they've written, that they are ashamed of their sentences' imperfections, apparent to them only in retrospect. I've made this claim myself, and I've wondered afterwards how I could forget how important it is to tell people about the joy I feel sometimes, how those small moments of rightness make their pursuit worthwhile, how the world can sometimes seem taut, and balanced, and settled; how existence can seem to have a cause beyond chance. There isn't a line I'd write the same, if I was to start again, but still I'm glad I wrote them as I did.

I lived in a flat once that approximated in my mind a garret apartment on the Left Bank of the Seine. Except my flat was on the outskirts of Limerick city. Which is a better place to be a writer than bohemian Paris, untainted as it is by self-consciousness, by a spiritless presumption that location will somehow magically generate inspiration. There was a ghost there, but I was mostly alone, and I had a broken heart for a little while, and a view of swaying trees. Conditions were perfect then for writing. And still I couldn't write a line. I didn't become a writer until I met my wife, Anne Marie. She has a soft, musical voice, and an artist's heart. She was born and reared in Kilmeedy and in Newcastle West, places where poetry lives in every exchange, where every utterance has a slight twist, a playful cadence, an undertone of gentle mocking, of questioning; where it's hard to be very serious for very long. Where it's impossible to take oneself too seriously. The only ambition I ever had was to be a writer, so for thirty years I did everything except write. The short spaces of time where I did write were darkened by secrecy and shame, and a sense that I'd been given a longing to write and no gift for it; that I'd been cursed. And then my self-generated clouds of doubt and misery rolled back, and there was Anne Marie, and she was laughing at me, and saying: 'Of course you're a writer, stop talking about it, just do it. Stop worrying.'

I told this story to my colleague at the University of Limerick, Giles Foden, after four or five pints of Guinness, and he pointed out these lines to me from Seamus Heaney's *Station Island*, lines that contain the same sentiment that Anne Marie gifted to me, lines that should echo always in the minds of writers:

> His voice eddying with the vowels of all rivers
> Came back to me, though he did not speak yet,
> A voice like a prosecutor's or a singer's,
> Cunning, narcotic, mimic, definite
> As a steel nib's downstroke, quick and clean,
> And suddenly he hit a litter basket
> With his stick, saying, 'Your obligation
> Is not discharged by any common rite.
> What you must do must be done on your own.
> So get back in harness. The main thing is to write
> For the joy of it. Cultivate a work-lust
> That imagines its haven like your hands at night
> Dreaming the sun in the sunspot of a breast.
> You are fasted now, light-headed, dangerous.
> Take off from here. And don't be so earnest,
> Let others wear the sackcloth and the ashes.
> Let go, let fly, forget.
> You've listened long enough. Now strike your note.'
> It was as if I had stepped free into space
> Alone with nothing that I had not known
> Already. Raindrops blew in my face
> As I came to.[6]

It's easy to imagine John McGahern as the subject of these lines. Dreaming the sun in the sunspot of a breast. I imagine John McGahern all the time; his eye and his ear and his heart. I imagine my father, awestruck in his presence, and I feel the same awe, every time I read his faultless, gleaming prose. If the heavens split open and gave me a chance, a moment to speak to this greatest of writers, all I'd be able to say is: 'Thanks, John, for the truth of your words, for the gifts you left behind.'

The final words, I have to give to him, as in *Memoir* he imagines walking again with the woman who gave him life:

> If we could walk together through those summer lanes, with their banks of wild flowers that 'cast a spell', we probably would not be able to speak, though I would want to tell her all the local news.
>
> We would leave the lanes and I would take her by the beaten path the otter takes under the thick hedges between the lakes. At the lake's edge I would show her the green lawns speckled with fish bones and blue crayfish shells where the otter feeds and trains her young. The otter whistles down the waters for the male when she wants to mate and chases him back again to his own waters when his work is done; unlike the dear swans that paddle side by side and take turns on their high nest deep within the reeds. Above the lake we would follow the enormous sky until it reaches the low mountains where her life began.
>
> I would want no shadow to fall on her joy and deep trust in God. She would face no false reproaches. As we retraced our steps, I would pick for her the wild orchid and the windflower.[7]

NOTES AND REFERENCES

Foreword

1   John Killen (ed.), *Dear Mr McLaverty: the literary correspondence of John McGahern and Michael McLaverty, 1959–1980* (Belfast: The Linen Hall Library, 2006), p. 20. The underlined words are in the original.

2   Allan Wade (ed.), *The Letters of W.B. Yeats* (London: Rupert Hart-Davis, 1954).

3   'All Sorts of Impossible Things', in *The Collected Stories* (London: Faber & Faber, 1992), p. 135.

Introduction

1   See Derek Hand, *A History of the Irish Novel* (Cambridge: Cambridge University Press, 2014), pp. 1–13.

2   See Declan Kiberd, 'Introduction', in Stanley van der Ziel (ed.), *John McGahern – Love of the World: essays* (London: Faber & Faber, 2009), p. xvii.

3   'The Image', in van der Ziel (ed.), *Love of the World*, p. 5.

4   Seamus Deane, *Celtic Revivals: essays in modern Irish literature* (London: Faber & Faber, 1985), p. 105.

5   John McGahern, *Amongst Women* (London: Faber & Faber, 1990), p. 183.

6   Ibid., p. 184.

7   For a comprehensive examination of the role of religion in McGahern's work, see Eamon Maher, *'The Church and Its Spire': John McGahern and the Catholic Question* (Dublin: The Columba Press, 2011).

8   van der Ziel (ed.), *Love of the World*, p. 11.

9   See John McGahern, *Creatures of the Earth: new and selected stories* (London: Faber & Faber, 2006), p. vii.

10   John McGahern Symposium: 'Ten Years On: assessing the literary legacy of John McGahern (1934–2006)'. Held on Thursday, 28 and Friday, 29 April 2016, St Patrick's College, Drumcondra.

11   See Stanley van der Ziel, *John McGahern and the Imagination of Tradition* (Cork: Cork University Press, 2016) and Frank Shovlin, *Touchstones: John McGahern's classical style* (Liverpool: Liverpool University Press, 2016).

12   van der Ziel (ed.), *Love of the World*, p. 186.

13   Ibid., p. 114.

14   Deirdre Madden, *Molly Fox's Birthday* (London: Faber & Faber, 2008), p. 90.

15   van der Ziel (ed.), *Love of the World*, p. 9.

16   As an example, see Eamonn Hughes, '"All that Surrounds Our Life": time, sex, and death in *That They May Face the Rising Sun*', *Irish University Review*, vol. 35, no. 1, 2005, pp. 147–63.

17   John McGahern, *That They May Face the Rising Sun* (London: Faber & Faber, 2002), p. 99.

18   Ibid., p. 129.

19   John McGahern, *The Leavetaking* (London: Faber & Faber, 1984), p. 168.

Chapter 1

1   'The "Anonymous Sky" and the "High Ground": John McGahern in the Eighties', my address to the conference organised at Queen's University Belfast in March 2013, has been expanded and edited here; much of 'John McGahern: the enigma of reputation', presented at the conference organised at the University of Swansea in March 2011, has also been incorporated.

2   The phrase comes from Proust's essay 'On Reading'. In *Young John McGahern: becoming a novelist* (Oxford: Oxford University Press, 2012), I attempted to reconstruct McGahern's reading of Proust and others who appear to me to have been crucial in his establishment of his artistic foundations

in the 1950s and '60s. In drawing here on unpublished documentation from archives, etc., I will make reference to this book as a source that may be consulted, the title abbreviated as *YJMcG*. For drafts of fiction and other unpublished work in the NUIG archive of McGahern's papers, I will cite the appropriate manuscript number in the catalogue of the papers prepared by Fergus Fahey. I acknowledge the support of the McGahern Estate for facilitating research on which aspects of this essay and the book are based. The assistance of the Special Collections staff at the James Hardiman Library NUIG is also gratefully acknowledged.

3   Quotes cited in *YJMcG*, pp. 130–2.

4   NUIG P71/28. See *YJMcG*, pp. 152–3.

5   *YJMcG*, pp. 151–2.

6   'Charity Begins …' [Editorial], *Irish Times*, 7 May 1965, p. 11.

7   Editorial, *Irish Times*, 12 February 1966, p. 9.

8   *Irish Times*, 5 June 1965, p. 10.

9   Benedict Kiely, 'The Whores on the Half-doors', in Owen Dudley Edwards (ed.), *Conor Cruise O'Brien Introduces Ireland* (London: Deutsch, 1969), p. 148.

10 John McGahern, 'Censorship', in Stanley van der Ziel (ed.), *John McGahern – Love of the World: essays* (London: Faber & Faber, 2009), p. 68.

11 Maurice Kennedy, review of *Self-Portrait* by Patrick Kavanagh, 27 March 1964; letter from Augustine Martin, *Irish Times*, 2 April 1964, p. 10.

12 Andrew Hamilton, 'McGahern Claims He Was Dismissed because of *The Dark*', *Irish Times*, 7 February 1966, p. 1.

13 Ray Rosenfield, 'John McGahern Gives Insight on Melville', *Irish Times*, 25 November 1967, p. 11. See also Richard Murphy, *The Kick: a life among writers* (London: Granta, 2002), pp. 261–2.

14 Mary Leland [report on reading and Q&A by McGahern at UCC], *Irish Times*, 30 December 1977, p. 8.

15 John McGahern, *Creatures of the Earth: new and selected stories* (London: Faber & Faber, 2006), p. 150.

16 P71/159.

17 Ibid.

18 P71/162.

19 John McGahern, *Memoir* (London: Faber & Faber, 2005), p. 166.

20 P71/757.

21 P71/537.

22 *Irish Times*, 10 January 1985, p. 11.

23 'An Interview with John McGahern', in Eamon Maher, *John McGahern: from the local to the universal* (Dublin: The Liffey Press, 2003), p. 145.

24 Ibid., p. 120.

25 John McGahern, *Amongst Women* (London: Faber & Faber, 1990), p. 130.

26 Ibid., p. 179.

Chapter 2

1   John McGahern, 'The Solitary Reader', in Stanley van der Ziel (ed.), *John McGahern – Love of the World: essays* (London: Faber & Faber, 2009), p. 89.

2   Denis Sampson, *Young John McGahern: becoming a novelist* (Oxford: Oxford University Press, 2012), p. 4. McGahern explains his surprise that his reading in the Protestant library did not spark the expected paternal ire: 'At the time Protestants were pitied because they were bound for hell in the next world, and they were considered to be abstemious, honest, and morally more correct than the general run of our fellow Catholics' ('The Solitary Reader', p. 89).

3 See Richard Gill, quoted in Terence Brown, *Ireland: a social and cultural history* (London: Fontana, 1985), p. 133.

4 Seamus Deane, *A Short History of Irish Literature* (Notre Dame, IN: University of Notre Dame Press, 1994), p. 206.

5 Terry Eagleton, *Heathcliff and the Great Hunger* (London: Verso, 1995), p. 69.

6 W.B. Yeats, 'A Prayer for my Daughter', in *Collected Poems* (Basingstoke: Macmillan, 1985), p. 213.

7 David Malcolm, *Understanding John McGahern* (Columbia, SC: University of South Carolina Press, 2007), p. 98; Otto Rauchbauer, quoted in Belinda McKeon, '"Robins Feeding with the Sparrows": the Protestant "Big House" in the fiction of John McGahern', *Irish University Review*, vol. 35, no. 1, 2005, pp. 72–89, at p. 74.

8 Fredric Jameson, *The Political Unconscious: narrative as a socially symbolic act* (London: Methuen, 1981), p. 20.

9 Ibid., pp. 18–19. Jameson cites Benedetto Croce in the second quotation.

10 Slavoj Žižek, *Living in the End Times* (London: Verso, 2010), p. 84.

11 Jacques Derrida, *Specters of Marx* (New York: Routledge, 1994), p. 25.

12 Elizabeth Bowen, *The Last September* (London: Vintage, 1998), p. 244.

13 Julian Moynihan, *Anglo-Irish: the literary imagination in a hyphenated culture* (Princeton, NJ: Princeton University Press, 1995), p. 244. See also Neil Corcoran's reading of the ruined mill in terms of the political unconscious: *Elizabeth Bowen: the enforced return* (Oxford: Oxford University Press, 2004), pp. 53–4.

14 See R.F. Foster, *Modern Ireland, 1600–1972* (Harmondsworth: Penguin, 1988), p. 594: 'The Protestant population in the Republic decreased by 24 per cent between the end of the war and 1971 – from intermarriage and a declining birth rate rather than emigration.'

15 Derrida, *Specters*, p. 22.

16 John McGahern, *Creatures of the Earth: new and selected stories* (London: Faber & Faber, 2006), p. 252. References to this edition will be hereafter cited in the text as *CE*.

17 James Whyte, *History, Myth and Ritual in the Fiction of John McGahern: strategies of transcendence* (Lewiston, NY: Edwin Mellen Press, 2002), p. 55.

18 Jameson, *The Political Unconscious*, p. 79.

19 William Shakespeare, *Hamlet*, edited by Ann Thompson and Neil Taylor (London: Bloomsbury, 2014), 5.2.197–201, p. 448.

20 Stanley van der Ziel, *John McGahern and the Imagination of Tradition* (Cork: Cork University Press, 2016), pp. 28–9.

21 McKeon, '"Robins Feeding with the Sparrows"', p. 84.

22 Liliane Louvel, 'The Writer's Field: "patrols of the imagination". John McGahern's short stories', *Journal of the Short Story in English*, vol. 34, 2000, pp. 65–85.

23 See Walter Benjamin, 'Theses on the Philosophy of History', in *Illuminations*, trans. Harry Zorn (London: Pimlico, 1999), p. 248: 'There is no document of civilization which is not at the same time a document of barbarism.'

24 Karl Marx, *The Eighteenth Brumaire of Louis Bonaparte* (Moscow: Progress, 1977), p. 10.

25 McGahern, 'The Solitary Reader', p. 88.

26 David Thomson, *Woodbrook* (London: Vintage, 1991), p. 134. References to this edition will be hereafter cited in the text as *W*.

27 McKeon, '"Robins Feeding with the Sparrows"', p. 84.

28 See Arthur Broomfield, 'The Conversion of William Kirkwood', *Journal of the Short Story in English*, vol. 53, Autumn 2009, pp. 217–25.

29 Denis Sampson, *Outstaring Nature's Eye: the fiction of John McGahern* (Washington, DC: Catholic University Press of America, 1993), p. 202.

30 McKeon, '"Robins Feeding with the Sparrows"', pp. 85–6: 'It is as if the equality which was signalled on the horizon in "The Conversion of William Kirkwood" has arrived, and issued fully in the violence that was in that story foreshadowed.'

31 W.B. Yeats, 'In Memory of Major Robert Gregory', in *Collected Poems*, p. 151.

32 Malcolm, *Understanding John McGahern*, p. 96.

33 Quoted in Whyte, *History, Myth and Ritual*, p. 55.

34 Quoted in Eamon Maher, *'The Church and Its Spire': John McGahern and the Catholic Question* (Dublin: The Columba Press, 2011), p. 126.

35 Seán O'Faoláin, 'Midsummer Night Madness', in *Midsummer Night Madness and Other Stories* (Harmondsworth: Penguin, 1989), p. 43.

36 W.B. Yeats, *Purgatory*, in James Pethica (ed.), *Yeats's Poetry, Drama, and Prose* (New York and London: Norton, 2000), pp. 170–1, 174–5.

37 Elizabeth Bowen, *Collected Impressions*, quoted in Moynihan, *Anglo-Irish*, p. 224.

Chapter 3

1 This is for instance what critic Jürgen Kamm wrote about McGahern: 'It is entirely misleading to earmark McGahern as an "experimental" writer as his fictions are realistically told and the narrative tone is clearly indebted to the tradition of Irish story-telling. In fact, McGahern's prose is most effective and assured in his descriptions of the provincial milieu which he knew so intimately'. Kamm, 'John McGahern', in Rüdiger Imhof (ed.), *Contemporary Irish Novelists* (Tübingen: Gunter Narr Verlag, 1990), pp. 175–91.

2 John Cronin, '*The Dark* Is Not Light Enough', *Studies*, vol. 58, Winter 1969, p. 427.

3 Letter from James Joyce to Grant Richards, in Stuart Gilbert (ed.), *Letters of James Joyce*, volume 1 (London: Faber & Faber, 1957), p. 63.

4 Michael J. Toolan, 'John McGahern: the historian and the pornographer', *Canadian Journal of Irish Studies*, vol.7, no. 2, Dec. 1981, pp. 39–55.

5 John McGahern, *The Collected Stories* (London: Faber & Faber, 1993), p. 268. All subsequent references to this text will be noted by the abbreviation *CS* and page number in brackets.

6 Denis Sampson, 'Open to the World: a reading of John McGahern's *That They May Face the Rising Sun*', *Irish University Review*, Spring/Summer 2005, p. 140.

7 John McGahern, *That They May Face the Rising Sun* (London: Faber & Faber, 2002), p. 6.

8 *'Ce qui est sûr c'est que le langage a son champ réservé dans cette béance du rapport sexuel, que sa fonction essentielle est de remplir tout ce que laisse béant qu'il ne puisse y avoir de rapport sexuel'* ['What is certain is that language has its own reserved area in this gaping wound that is the sexual relationship, that its primary function is to fill all that yawning gap which appears when there cannot be any sexual expression']: Jacques Lacan, [...] *Ou pire*, séminaire inédit, séance du 8 décembre 1971. Quoted by Chaboudez Gisèle, 'Le rapport sexuel en psychanalyse', *Figures de la Psychanalyse*, 2/2001, n° 5, pp. 41–64, http://www.cairn.info/revue-figures-de-la-psy-2001-2-page-41.htm [accessed 29 October 2018].

9 Jacques Lacan quoting a poem by Antoine Tudal. Quoted by Jean-Paul Ricœur, 'Lacan, l'amour', *Psychanalyse*, 3/2007, n° 10, pp. 5–32, http://www.cairn.info/revue-psychanalyse-2007-3-page-5.htm [accessed 29 October 2018], DOI: 10.3917/psy.010.0005.

10 Samuel Beckett, *Endgame* (London: Faber & Faber, 2009 [1958]), p. 19.

11 Ibid., p. 8.

12 John McGahern, *The Barracks* (London: Faber & Faber, 1963), p. 18. All subsequent references to this text will be noted by the abbreviation *B* and page number in brackets.

13 John McGahern, *Amongst Women* (London: Faber & Faber, 1990), p. 26.

14 John McGahern, *The Leavetaking* (London: Faber & Faber, 1984), p. 92. All subsequent references to this text will be noted by the abbreviation *L* and page number in brackets.

15 John McGahern, *The Pornographer* (London: Faber & Faber, 1979), p. 37. All subsequent references to this text will be noted by the abbreviation *P* and page number in brackets.

16 'That next Saturday he stayed alone in the room, studying by the light of a bulb fixed on a Chianti bottle': McGahern, *The Collected Stories*, p. 189; 'I turned off the light fixed in the ancient Chianti bottle, for the firelight now flamed on the wallpaper and more softly on the long curtain': McGahern, *The Leavetaking*, p. 93.

17 Adrian Johnston, 'Jacques Lacan', *The Stanford Encyclopedia of Philosophy*, Summer 2014, edited by Edward N. Zalta, http://plato.stanford.edu/archives/sum2014/entries/lacan [accessed 29 October 2018].

18 Richard Robinson, 'An Umbrella, a Pair of Boots, and a "Spacious Nothing": McGahern and Beckett', *Irish University Review*, vol. 44, no. 2, pp. 323–40 [accessed 29 October 2018]; Pascal Bataillard, 'Love and Solitary Enjoyment in "My Love, My Umbrella": some of John McGahern's uses of *Dubliners*', *Journal of the Short Story in English*, vol. 53, Autumn 2009, http://jsse.revues. org/1000 [accessed 6 July 2016].

19 Jacques Lacan, *L'Angoisse*, séminaire inédit, séance du 19 juin 1963. Quoted by Chaboudez Gisèle, 'Le Rapport Sexuel en Psychanalyse', *Figures de la Psychanalyse*, 2/2001, nº 5, pp. 41–64, http://www. cairn.info/revue-figures-de-la-psy-2001-2-page-41.htm [accessed 29 October 2018].

20 John McGahern, *The Dark* (London: Faber & Faber, 1965), p. 30.

21 *'Il est clair que le témoignage des mystiques, c'est justement de dire qu'ils l'éprouvent, mais qu'ils n'en savent rien. […] Cette jouissance qu'on éprouve et dont on ne sait rien, n'est-ce pas ce qui nous met sur la voie de "l'ex-sistence"?'* ['It is true that when it comes to the experience of the mystics they feel things on a deep level but really don't know anything about it. […] This uplifting feeling that is inexpressible, does it not set us on the path of "ex-sistence"?'], Jacques Lacan, *Le Séminaire*, livre XX, in *Encore* (Paris: Le Seuil, 1975), pp. 70–1.

22 Julia Kristeva, 'From One Identity to Another', in Leon S. Roudiez (ed.), *Desire in Language: a semiotic approach to literature and art*, trans. Thomas Gora, Alice Jardine and Leon S. Roudiez (Oxford: Blackwell, 1980), p. 133.

23 Ibid., p. 134.

24 Ibid., p. 137.

25 Ibid., p. 136.

26 John McGahern, *Memoir* (London: Faber & Faber, 2005), p. 123.

27 Stanley van der Ziel, '"All This Talk and Struggle": John McGahern's *The Dark*', *Irish University Review*, vol. 35, no. 1, 2005, pp. 104–20.

28 'The Image', in Stanley van der Ziel (ed.), *John McGahern – Love of the World: essays* (London: Faber & Faber, 2009), pp. 5–6.

Chapter 4

1 Denis Sampson, *Outstaring Nature's Eye: the fiction of John McGahern* (Washington, DC: The Catholic University of America Press, 1993), p. xi.

2 Ibid., p. xii.

3 Edward W. Said, *On Late Style: music and literature against the grain* (New York: Pantheon, 2006), p. 145.

4 https://www.willacather.org [accessed 29 October 2018].

5 http://cootehallbarracks.com/about-us.php [accessed 29 October 2018].

6   http://www.leitrimobserver.ie/news/home/222936/proposal-for-co-leitrim-interpretative-centre-in-honour-of-late-john-mcgahern.html [accessed 29 October 2018].

7   Tim Collins, *John McGahern: a private world* (Dublin: Humingbird/Harvest Films, 2006).

8   http://www.mcclatchydc.com/news/nation-world/world/article24730576.html [accessed 29 October 2018].

9   Ibid.

10 Eóin Flannery, '"Ship of Fools": The Celtic Tiger and Poetry as Social Critique', in Eamon Maher and Eugene O'Brien (eds), *From Prosperity to Austerity: a socio-cultural critique of the Celtic Tiger and its aftermath* (Manchester: Manchester University Press, 2014), pp. 203–17, at p. 212.

11 John McGahern, *Creatures of the Earth: new and selected stories* (London: Faber & Faber, 2006), pp. vii–viii.

12 W.B. Yeats, *The Yeats Reader*, edited by Richard J. Finneran (New York: Scribner, 2002), p. 85.

13 Sampson, *Outstaring Nature's Eye*, pp. 11–12.

14 McGahern, *Creatures of the Earth*, pp. 198–9.

15 Stanley van der Ziel, *John McGahern and the Imagination of Tradition* (Cork: Cork University Press, 2016), p. 14.

16 C.P. Cavafy, *Complete Poems*, trans. Daniel Mendelsohn (New York: Knopf, 2012), p. xvii.

17 Said, *On Late Style*, p. xiii.

18 Katie Roiphe, *The Violet Hour: great writers at the end* (New York: Dial Press, 2016), p. 8.

19 Sampson, *Outstaring Nature's Eye*, p. xi.

20 Eamon Maher, *John McGahern: from the local to the universal* (Dublin: The Liffey Press, 2003), p. 99.

21 Ibid., p. 159.

22 Roiphe, *The Violet Hour*, p. 11.

23 van der Ziel, *John McGahern and the Imagination of Tradition*, p. 55.

24 Cavafy, *Complete Poems*, p. 102.

25 Sampson, *Outstaring Nature's Eye*, p. 188.

26 Roiphe, *The Violet Hour*, p. 8.

27 van der Ziel, *John McGahern and the Imagination of Tradition*, pp. 114–15.

28 John McGahern, *Amongst Women* (New York: Penguin, 1990), p. 3.

29 Ben Hutchinson, 'On Lateness, Late Style and "the Old Age of the World"', *TLS*, 19 February 2016, p. 14.

30 Maher, *John McGahern*, p. 139.

31 Said, *On Late Style*, p. 96.

32 van der Ziel, *John McGahern and the Imagination of Tradition*, p. 55.

33 Said, *On Late Style*, p. 139.

34 van der Ziel, *John McGahern and the Imagination of Tradition*, p. 60.

35 Said, *On Late Style*, p. 140.

36 Ibid.

37 McGahern, *Amongst Women*, p. 54.

38 Declan Kiberd, 'Introduction', in Stanley van der Ziel (ed.), *John McGahern – Love of the World: essays* (London: Faber & Faber, 2009), p. xii.

39 Maher, *John McGahern*, p. 5.

40 van der Ziel (ed.), *Love of the World*, p. 208.

41 Bruce Chatwin, *In Patagonia* (New York: Penguin, 2003), p. 137.

42 Roiphe, *The Violet Hour*, p. 276.

43 Ibid., p. 32.

44 van der Ziel, *John McGahern and the Imagination of Tradition*, pp. 114–15.

45 McGahern, *Amongst Women*, p. 179.

46 van der Ziel, *John McGahern and the Imagination of Tradition*, pp. 114–15.

47 Said, *On Late Style*, p. xix.

48 Maher, *John McGahern*, p. 125.

49 Said, *On Late Style*, p. 145.

50 McGahern, *Amongst Women*, pp. 87–90.

51 Quoted by Nicholas Roe, 'Ireland's Rural Elegist' (*The Guardian*, 4 January 2002), p. 48.

52 Alastair MacLeod, *Island: the complete stories* (New York: Norton, 2011), p. 178.

53 Said, *On Late Style*, p. 148.

Chapter 5

1 Roland Barthes, *The Pleasure of the Text* (New York: Hill and Wang, 1979), p. 53.

2 Lee Edelman, 'The Future is Kid Stuff: Queer theory, disidentification, and the death drive', *Narrative*, vol. 6, no. 1, January 1998, pp. 18–30, at pp. 19, 22, 28.

3 John McGahern, *Memoir* (Faber & Faber: London, 2005), p. 52.

4 Denis Sampson, *Outstaring Nature's Eye: the fiction of John McGahern* (Washington, DC: Catholic University Press of America, 1993), p. 62.

5 Val Nolan, '"If it was just th'oul book …": a history of the McGahern banning controversy', *Irish Studies Review*, vol. 19, no. 3, 2011, pp. 261–79, at p. 261.

6 Quoted in Diarmaid Ferriter, *Occasions of Sin: sex and society in modern Ireland* (London: Profile Books, 2009), p. 402.

7 Peter Guy, 'Reading John McGahern in Light of the Murphy Report', *Studies: an Irish quarterly review*, vol. 99, no. 393, Spring, 2010, pp. 91–101, at p. 91.

8 Creative-Negri, 'Winning Entry: Journey Into Light', http://www.studionegri.ie/index. php/2012/06/winning-entry-journey-of-light [accessed 15 December 2013].

9 Marie Keenan, *Child Sexual Abuse and the Catholic Church: gender, power, and organisational culture* (Oxford: Oxford University Press, 2012), p. 175.

10 See Giorgio Agamben, *Homo Sacer: sovereign power and bare life*, trans. Daniel Heller-Roazen (Stanford, CA: University of California Press, 1998).

11 Colm Tóibín, 'The Use of Reason', *Mothers and Sons* (New York: Scribner, 2007), pp. 1–40, at p. 18.

12 Michel Foucault, *The Order of Things: an archaeology of the human sciences* (Routledge: New York, 2010), p. xxi.

13 Elaine Scarry, *The Body in Pain: the making and unmaking of the world* (Oxford: Oxford University Press, 1985), p. 27.

14 Ibid., pp. 27–8.

15 Ibid., p. 35.

16 Roland Barthes, *Sade-Fourier-Loyola*, trans. Richard Miller (London: Jonathan Cape, 1977), p. 28.

17 John McGahern, 'The Recruiting Officer', in *The Collected Stories* (London: Faber & Faber, 1992), pp. 100–11, at p. 103.

18 Foucault's well-known account of Greek homosexuality in *The Uses of Pleasure* includes the precise caveat that a shame remained attendant upon the receptive, penetrated partner, owing to the proximity of this position and the anatomical predisposition of women.

19 Graham L. Hammill, *Sexuality and Form: Caravaggio, Marlowe, and Bacon* (Chicago: The University of Chicago Press, 2000), p. 25.

20 Foucault, *The Order of Things*, p. 6.

21 Jane Bennet, *The Enchantment of Modern Life: attachments, crossings, and ethics* (Princeton, NJ: Princeton University Press, 2001), p. 3.

22 Michel Foucault, *The History of Sexuality Part 1: The Will to Knowledge*, trans. Robert Hurley (London: Penguin, 1998), p. 60.

23 See Anne Goarzin, 'A Crack in the Concrete': objects in the works of John McGahern', *Irish University Review*, Special Issue: John McGahern (ed. John Brannigan), vol. 34, no. 1, Spring/Summer 2005, pp. 28–41.

24 John McGahern, *The Dark* (London: Faber & Faber, 1965), pp. 7–9.

25 Michael J. Toolin, 'The Historian and the Pornographer', *The Canadian Journal of Irish Studies*, vol. 7, no. 2, December 1981, pp. 39–55, at p. 41.

26 McGahern, *The Dark*, p. 19.

27 Sigmund Freud, 'A Child is Being Beaten: a contribution to the study of the origin of sexual perversion', in James Strachey (ed.), *The Standard Edition of the Complete Psychological Works of Sigmund Freud*, vol. 17 (London: Vintage, 1999). (Italics in original.)

28 See Kent L. Brintnall, *Ecco Homo: the male-body-in-pain as redemptive figure* (Chicago: The University of Chicago Press, 2011), pp. 68–89.

29 Pierre Bourdieu, *Outline of a Theory of Practice* (Cambridge: Cambridge University Press, 1977), pp. 93–4.

30 Slavoj Žižek, 'Shostakovich in Casablanca', www.lacan.com [accessed 13 January 2015].

31 McGahern, *The Dark*, p. 191.

32 John Cronin, '"The Dark" is Not Light Enough', *Studies: an Irish quarterly review*, vol. 58, no. 232, Winter 1969, pp. 427–32, at p. 427.

33 Cronin, '"The Dark" is Not Light Enough', p. 430.

34 Ibid.

35 Leo Bersani, *Arts of Impoverishment: Beckett, Rothko, Resnais* (Cambridge, MA: Harvard University Press, 1993), p. 4.

Chapter 6

1 A summary list of examples would include: Frank McCourt's *Angela's Ashes* (New York: Scribner, 1996); Dermot Healy's *The Bend for Home* (London: Harvill, 1996); Seamus Deane's *Reading in the Dark* (London: Jonathan Cape, 1996); Nuala O'Faoláin's *Are You Somebody? The accidental memoir of a Dublin woman* (New York: Henry Holt & Company, 1996); and John Walsh's *The Falling Angels* (London: HarperCollins, 1999).

2 John McGahern, *Memoir* (London: Faber & Faber, 2005), p. 260. Subsequent citations will be designated by an in-text abbreviation (*M*).

3 Lawrence Buell, *The Future of Environmental Criticism: environmental crisis and literary imagination* (Oxford: Blackwell, 2005), p. 73.

4 Scott Hess, 'Imagining an Everyday Nature', *Interdisciplinary Studies in Literature and Environment*, vol. 17, no. 1, 2010, pp. 85–112.

5 Michael Cronin, *The Expanding World: towards a politics of microspection* (Winchester, UK and Washington, DC: Zero Books, 2012), p. 94.

6 Paul J. Crutzen and Eugene F. Stoermer, 'The Anthropocene' , *International Geosphere-Biosphere Programme Newsletter* (2000), http://www.igbp.net/download/18.316f18321323470177580001401/1376383088452/NL41.pdf [accessed 29 October 2018].

7 Adam Trexler, *Anthropocene Fictions: the novel in a time of climate change* (Charlottesville, VA: University of Virginia Press, 2015).

8   Ibid., p. 5.

9   Timothy Clark, 'Scale: derangements of scale', in Tom Cohen (ed.), *Telemorphosis: theory in the era of climate change* (Ann Arbor, MI: Open Humanities Press/University of Michigan Library, 2012), p. 150.

10 Ibid.

11 Ibid., p. 156.

12 Timothy Clark, *Ecocriticism on the Edge: the anthropocene as a threshold concept* (London: Bloomsbury, 2015), p. 9.

13 Ibid., p. 80.

14 John McGahern, *That They May Face the Rising Sun* (London: Faber & Faber, 2002), p. 1. Subsequent citations will be designated by an in-text abbreviation (*RS*).

15 Denis Sampson, *Outstaring Nature's Eye: the fiction of John McGahern* (Dublin: The Lilliput Press, 1993), p. 7.

16 Ibid., p. 8.

17 Clark, *Ecocriticism on the Edge*, p. 40.

18 Martin Ryle, 'John McGahern: memory, autobiography, fiction, history', *New Formations*, vol. 67, 2009, p. 45.

19 Ibid.

20 Clark, *Ecocriticism on the Edge*, p. 52.

Chapter 7

1   John McGahern, *The Leavetaking* (London: Faber & Faber, 1974) and John McGahern, *The Leavetaking*, 2nd edn, with a Preface by the author (London: Faber & Faber, 1984). All page references in this chapter are to the second edition and are referred to as *L2*.

2   See Gerd Kampen, 'An Interview with John McGahern', in *Zwischen Welt und Text: narratologische studien zum Irischen gegenwartsroman am beispiel von John McGahern und John Banville* (Trier: Wissenschaftlicher Verlag Trier, 2002), pp. 336–42, at p. 341.

3   John McGahern, *Memoir* (London: Faber & Faber, 2005).

4   For a complete collection of McGahern's non-fictional writings, see Stanley van der Ziel (ed.), *John McGahern – Love of the World: essays* (London: Faber & Faber, 2009).

5   As is well known, McGahern's third novel is based on his own experience of losing his teaching post in 1965 after the censoring of *The Dark* and his marriage to the Finnish dramatist Annikki Laaksi. Isobel's character also draws on McGahern's second wife, the American photographer Madeline Green.

6   John McGahern, 'The Image: prologue to a reading at the Rockefeller University', *The Honest Ulsterman*, vol. 8, December 1968, p. 10. Reprinted with revisions as 'The Image', *Canadian Journal of Irish Studies* [special issue on John McGahern], vol. 17, no. 1, July 1991, p. 12. For a conception of McGahern's work as an extended autobiography and the search for the Proustian lost image, see Denis Sampson, *Outstaring Nature's Eye: the fiction of John McGahern* (Dublin: The Lilliput Press, 1994), and Dermot McCarthy, *John McGahern and the Art of Memory* (Oxford: Peter Lang, 2010).

7   Eamon Maher, *John McGahern: from the local to the universal* (Dublin: The Liffey Press, 2003), p. 3. See also Eamon Maher and Declan Kiberd, 'John McGahern: writer, stylist, seeker of a lost world', *Doctrine and Life*, vol. 52, no. 2, February 2002, pp. 82–97, at pp. 91–2.

8   John McGahern, *Getting Through* (London: Faber & Faber, 1978); John McGahern, *The Pornographer* (London: Faber & Faber, 1979).

9   See Sampson, *Outstaring Nature's Eye*, p. 13, and Marianne Koenig Mays, '"Ravished and Exasperated": the evolution of John McGahern's plain style', *Canadian Journal of Irish Studies* [special issue on John McGahern], vol. 17, no. 1, July 1991, pp. 38–52, at p. 38.

10 John McGahern, *Journée d'adieu*, trans. Alain Delahaye (Paris: Presses de la Renaissance, 1983). For an in-depth analysis of the differences between the two versions of the novel, see my article 'A Fruitful Exchange: a comparative study of the different versions of John McGahern's *The Leavetaking* and its French translation *Journée d'adieu* by Alain Delahaye', in Werner Huber, Sandra Mayer and Julia Novak (eds), *Irish Studies in Europe. Volume 4: Ireland in/and Europe: cross-currents and exchanges* (Trier: Wissenschaftlicher Verlag Trier, 2012), pp. 127–36.

11 McGahern, *L2*, p. 5.

12 Most critical comments on *The Leavetaking* are based on the second edition. The few existing reviews of the first edition can, therefore, provide us with interesting insights. Broderick, for example, praises McGahern as the greatest writer of his generation, and the first *Leavetaking* for its 'poetic truth and strength' and 'perfection'. But he distinguished clearly between '[t]he first hundred pages […] so brilliantly written that they constitute a triumph' and 'the last eighty pages I am not so sure', an opinion he reiterated three times in only a four-page-long article: John Broderick, 'Memory and Desire', in Madeline Kingston (ed.), *Stimulus of Sin: selected writings of John Broderick* (Dublin: The Lilliput Press, 2007), pp. 57–60, at p. 59. See also Julian Jebb, 'The Call of the Deep', *Times Literary Supplement*, 10 January 1975, p. 29; and Denis Sampson, 'John McGahern's *The Leavetaking*', *Canadian Journal of Irish Studies*, vol. 2, no. 2, December 1976, pp. 61–5.

13 Denis Sampson, 'A Conversation with John McGahern' (Feb. 1979), *Canadian Journal of Irish Studies* [special issue on John McGahern], vol. 17, no. 1, July 1991, pp. 13–18, at pp. 15–16.

14 McGahern, 'The Image'.

15 John McGahern, *Creatures of The Earth: new and selected stories* (London: Faber & Faber, 2006), pp. vii–viii.

16 McGahern, 'The Image'.

17 Michael O'Regan, 'A Long Pursuit of an Ideal World' (interview with John McGahern), *Irish Times*, 10 January 1985.

18 Ibid.

19 Liam Harte (ed.), *Modern Irish Autobiography: self, nation and society* (Basingstoke: Palgrave Macmillan, 2007), p. 1. See also Claire Lynch, *Irish Autobiography: stories of self in the narrative of a nation* (Oxford: Peter Lang, 2009), pp. 1–2.

20 See Paul Ricoeur, *Time and Narrative* [1983] (Chicago and London: The University of Chicago Press, 1988) (English translation by Kathleen Blamey and David Pellauer). See also Michael Böss, 'Relating to the Past: memory, identity and history', in Hedda Friberget et al. (eds), *Recovering Memory: Irish representations of past and present* (Newcastle: Cambridge Scholars Publishing, 2007), pp. 20–33, at pp. 22–3.

21 See Linden Peach, *The Contemporary Irish Novel: critical readings* (Basingstoke and New York: Palgrave Macmillan, 2004), p. 38; and Michael Kenneally, 'The Autobiographical Imagination and Irish Literary Autobiographies', in Michael Allen and Angela Wilcox (eds), *Critical Approaches to Anglo-Irish Literature* (Gerrards Cross: Colin Smythe, 1989).

22 Bertrand Cardin, *Miroirs de la Filiation: parcours dans huit romans Irlandais contemporains* (Caen: Presses Universitaires de Caen, 2005), p. 8.

23 See Philippe Lejeune, *Le Pacte Autobiographique* (Paris: Seuil, 1975), p. 42, quoted in Pascale Amiot-Jouenne (ed.), *L'Autobiographie Irlandaise: voix communes, voix singulières* (Caen: Presses Universitaires de Caen, 2004), p. 42.

24 Paul Ricoeur, *Memory, History, Forgetting* (Chicago and London: The University of Chicago Press, 2006) (English translation by Kathleen Blamey and David Pellauer), p. 7.

25 See McGahern, *Creatures of the Earth*, pp. vii–viii.

26 Sigmund Freud, 'Remembering Repeating, and Working Through' [1914], and 'Mourning and Melancholia' [1917], in James Strachey (ed. and trans.), *The Standard Edition of the Complete Psychological Works of Sigmund Freud*, vol. 14 (London: Hogarth Press, 1958), pp. 147–56 and pp. 243–58, respectively.

27 Eamon Maher, '*The Church and Its Spire*': *John McGahern and the Catholic Question* (Dublin: The Columba Press, 2011), p. 69.

28 McCarthy, *John McGahern and the Art of Memory*, p. 163.

29 McGahern, *The Pornographer*, pp. 20–1.

30 Ricoeur, *Memory, History, Forgetting*, p. 413.

31 Maher, '*The Church and Its Spire*', p. 68.

32 McCarthy, *John McGahern and the Art of Memory*, p. 143.

33 Toolan observed that the alternation of past and present in the novel 'is compelling support for the novel's account of the narrator's long withdrawing tide of nostalgic grief for past deaths being gradually, but surely, supplanted by a present- and future-oriented encirclement by a different sea, that of love and trust': Michael J. Toolan, 'John McGahern: the historian and the pornographer', *Canadian Journal of Irish Studies*, vol. 7, no. 1, June 1981, pp. 39–55, at p. 48.

34 McGahern, 'The Image'.

Chapter 8

1 Paul Butler describes himself as 'a photographer based in County Leitrim, Ireland, exploring the ordinary while documenting the fading'. As time has progressed, *Still* (2013) and *The Deep Well of Want* (2016) have both fallen under the umbrella of 'The Deep Well of Want', http://www.paulbutler. me [accessed 8 November 2018]. *Still* was shown in October/November 2013 at the Redline Book Festival, the Library at the Institute of Technology Tallaght and in September 2013 at Ballyroan Library, County Dublin. *The Deep Well of Want* was shown in March/April 2017 at The Dock Gallery, Carrick-on-Shannon, County Leitrim, from October 2016 to February 2017 at the Library in the Institute of Technology, Tallaght; in June 2016 at the Atrium Gallery, Backstage Theatre, Longford, and in April 2016 at St Patrick's College, Dublin City University for the 10th Anniversary Symposium of the death of John McGahern.

2 John Fanning, 'Branding and Begorrah: the importance of Ireland's nation brand image', *Irish Marketing Review*, vol. 21, nos 1–2, 2011, p. 25.

3 The term was used by Marese McDonagh in 'Entering McGahern Country', *Irish Independent*, 19 May 2013, https://www.independent.ie/lifestyle/entering-mcgahern-country-29276442.html [accessed 21 June 2016].

4 SOFEIR: Société Française d'Etudes Irlandaises; IASIL: International Association for the Study of Irish Literatures; EFACIS: European Federation of Associations and Centers of Irish Studies.

5 Jean Brihault and Liliane Louvel (eds), *La Licorne: numéro spécial John McGahern* (Poitiers: UFL Langues Littératures, 1995); Claude Fierobe and Danielle Jacquin (eds), *Etudes Irlandaises – John McGahern: Etudes sur 'The Barracks'* (Lille: Septentrion, 1994); *Etudes Britanniques Contemporaines: numéro spécial John McGahern* (Montpellier: Presses de l'université de Montpellier, 1995).

6 Laure Adler, *Le Cercle de minuit*, France 2, 12 March 1996, http://fresques.ina.fr/europe-des-cultures-fr/impression/fiche-media/Europe00233/john-mc-gahern.html [accessed 29 October 2018].

7 George-Michel Sarotte, *La Caserne* (Paris: Christian Bourgeois, 1986).

8 In his 'Preface to the Second Edition', McGahern wrote: 'That the second part of this edition of *The Leavetaking* came to be reformed is in part an accident. Several years after its publication, I found myself working through it again with its French translator, the poet Alain Delahaye. The more I saw of it the more sure I was that it had to be changed': *The Leavetaking* (London: Faber & Faber, 1974); *Journée d'adieu*, translated by Alain Delahaye (Paris: Belfond, 1983).

9 Bertrand Cardin, '*Les Nouvelles de John McGahern: une oeuvre autour de la thématique du vide*' (supervisor Prof. J. Genet, Université de Caen, 1993); Sylvie Mikowski, '*La Mémoire et l'imagination dans les romans de John McGahern*' (supervisor Prof. J. Genet, Université de Caen, 1995); Anne Goarzin, '*Représentations du même dans les romans de John McGahern*' (supervisor Prof. Jean Brihault, Université Rennes 2, 1997).

10 Eve Meltzer, *Systems We Have Loved: conceptual art, affect and the antihumanist turn* (Chicago: The University of Chicago Press, 2013), p. 11.

11 Metzer quoting Bruss, ibid., p. 12.

12 Ibid., p. 13.

13 Ibid., p. 12.

14 Ibid.

15 Kathleen Stewart, *Ordinary Affects* (Durham and London: Duke University Press, 2007).

16 Ibid., p. 3.

17 John McGahern, 'The Image' [1991], in Stanley van der Ziel (ed.), *John McGahern – Love of the World: essays* (London: Faber & Faber, 2009), pp. 7–8.

18 Stewart, *Ordinary Affects*, p. 4.

19 Ibid.

20 John McGahern, *The Pornographer* (London: Faber & Faber, 1979), p. 238.

21 Stewart, *Ordinary Affects*, p. 4.

22 John McGahern, 'Playing with Words', in van der Ziel (ed.), *Love of the World*, p. 9.

23 John McGahern, 'The Image' [1991], in van der Ziel (ed.), *Love of the World*, pp. 7–8.

24 Stewart, *Ordinary Affects*, pp. 3–5.

25 Ibid., p. 2.

26 See Gilles Deleuze, 'Immanence: a life', in *Pure Immanence: essays on a life*, trans. A. Boyman (New York: Zone, 2001).

27 Jessica Coleman and Rebecca Ringrose, *Deleuze and Research Methodologies* (Edinburgh: Edinburgh University Press, 2013), p. 10.

28 Ibid., p. 5.

29 Paul Butler, 'John McGahern and The Deep Well of Want: portraits of the artist's world', *Irish Times*, 30 March 2016. http://www.irishtimes.com/culture/books/john-mcgahern-and-the-deep-well-of-want-portraits-of-the-artist-s-world-1.2592043 [accessed 29 October 2018].

30 John McGahern, 'The Wine Breath', in *The Collected Stories* (London: Faber & Faber, 1993), p. 187.

31 van der Ziel (ed.), *Love of the World*, pp. 20–1.

32 John McGahern, *The Barracks* (London: Faber & Faber, 1991 [1963]), p. 51.

33 John McGahern, 'Madness/Creativity', in van der Ziel (ed.), *Love of the World*, p. 13.

34 Roland Barthes, *Camera Lucida: reflections on photography*, trans. Richard Howard (London: Farrar, Strauss & Giroux, 1999 [1981]), p. 25.

35 Ibid., p. 26.

36 Ibid.

37 Stewart, *Ordinary Affects*, p. 16.

38 van der Ziel (ed.), *Love of the World*, p. 26.

39 Derek H. Whitehead, '*Poiesis* and Art-Making: a way of letting-be', *Contemporary Aesthetics*, vol. 1, 2003, http://www.contempaesthetics.org/newvolume/pages/article.php?articleID=216#FN8link [accessed 29 October 2018].

40 Roland Barthes, *L'obvie et l'obtus: essais critiques III* (Paris: Seuil, 1992).

41 Ibid.

42 Coleman and Ringrose, *Deleuze and Research Methodologies*, p. 10 (quoting Deleuze and Parnet's *Dialogues II*, 2002): 'The abstract is given the task of explaining, and it is the abstract that is realized in the concrete. One starts with abstractions such as the One, the Whole, the Subject, and one looks for the process by which they are embodied in a world which they make conform to their requirements.' Empiricism, on the other hand, 'starts with […] extracting the states of things, in such a way that non-pre-existent concepts can be extracted from them'.

43 'The person who participates in world-founding *poiesis* is an artist; whereas the individual who engages in producing things is an artisan. Here poetry and pro-ducing have a common trait; they are both modes of 'disclosure'. As Zimmerman writes: 'Poetry discloses the gods needed to order and found the world, [while] genuine producing discloses things respectfully, in accordance with the vision of the poet. This implies, and as an elaboration of Heidegger's own stance, that a truly visionary poet or artist has the capacity to bring forth things that are in demonstrable accord with world-founding *poiesis*. Thus artisanal things share something of the numinous quality of created works, whether of art or poetry, insofar as they are oriented toward the disclosure of being': in Whitehead, '*Poiesis* and Art-Making'.

Chapter 10

1 C.S. Lewis, *The Four Loves* (London: Geoffrey Bles, 1960), p. 71.

2 Ibid., p. 70.

3 *On Friendship*, a recent study by Alexander Nehamas of Princeton University, is a rare and welcome addition to a limited range of philosophical publications on the subject.

4 Ralph Waldo Emerson, 'Friendship', in *Ralph Waldo Emerson: essays and lectures* (New York: Library of America, 1983), pp. 347–9.

5 Lewis, *The Four Loves*, p. 77.

6 John McGahern, 'The Family as Independent Republic', interview by Fintan O'Toole, *Irish Times*, 13 October 1990, p. 24.

7 John McGahern, *Creatures of the Earth* (London: Faber & Faber, 2006), p. 368.

8 John McGahern, *High Ground* (London: Faber & Faber, 1985) p. 143.

9 John McGahern, *Getting Through* (London: Faber & Faber, 1978), p. 84.

10 John McGahern, *The Leavetaking* (London: Faber & Faber, 1984), p. 30.

11 Ibid., p. 108.

12 John McGahern, *The Pornographer* (London: Faber & Faber, 1979), p. 82. All further references to this text will be noted with the abbreviation *P* and page number in brackets.

13 John McGahern, *Amongst Women* (London: Faber & Faber, 1990), p. 22.

14 M.E. Doyle and M.K. Smith, 'Friendship: theory and experience', *The Encyclopaedia of Informal Education* (2002), http://infed.org/mobi/friendship-some-philosophical-and-sociological-themes [accessed 15 April 2016].

15 Karen Walker, 'Men, Women, and Friendship: what they say, what they do', *Gender and Society*, vol. 8, no. 2, 1994, pp. 246–65, at p. 246.

16 Anthony Giddens, *The Transformation of Intimacy: sexuality, love and eroticism in modern societies* (Oxford: Blackwell, 1992), p. 44.

17 Sharon Marcus, *Between Women: friendship, desire, and marriage in Victorian England* (Princeton, NJ: Princeton University Press, 2007), p. 247.

18 John McGahern, *The Barracks* (London: Faber & Faber, 1963), p. 150. All subsequent references to this text will be noted by the abbreviation *B* and page number in brackets.

19 John McGahern, 'From a Glorious Dream to Wink and Nod', in Stanley van der Ziel (ed.), *John McGahern – Love of the World: essays* (London: Faber & Faber, 2009), p. 130.

20 Caitríona Clear, *Women of the House: women's household work in Ireland, 1926–1961* (Dublin: Irish Academic Press, 2000), p. 179.

21 Ibid., pp. 179–81.

22 Hannah Arendt, *The Human Condition*, 2nd edn (Chicago: The University of Chicago Press, 1998), p. 55.

23 Janice G. Raymond. *A Passion for Friends: towards a philosophy of female affection* (London: The Women's Press, 1986), p. 151.

24 Ibid.

25 Ibid.

26 Patricia Bourden, 'No Answer from Limbo: an aspect of female portraiture', *The Crane Bag: images of the Irish woman*, vol. 4, no. 1, 1980, pp. 95–100, at p. 98.

27 Arendt, *The Human Condition*, p. 52.

28 Raymond, *A Passion for Friends*, p. 155.

29 Ibid., p. 153.

30 Arendt, *The Human Condition*, p. 242.

31 Raymond, *A Passion for Friends*, p. 154.

32 Denis Sampson, '"Open to the World": a reading of John McGahern's *That They May Face the Rising Sun*', special issue of *Irish University Review: a journal of Irish studies*, vol. 35, no. 1, 2005, pp. 136–46, at p. 136.

33 Arendt, *The Human Condition*, p. 243.

34 Margaret Lasch Carroll, 'Prodigals' Dreams: John McGahern's *That They May Face the Rising Sun*', *Estudios Irlandeses*, vol. 3, 2008, pp. 42–53, at p. 48.

35 John McGahern, interview by Hermione Lee, *Lannan Readings and Conversations*, 7 April 2004, https://lannan.org/events/john-mcgahern-with-hermione-lee [accessed 14 February 2016].

36 John McGahern, *That They May Face the Rising Sun* (London: Faber & Faber, 2001), p. 312. All subsequent references to this text will be noted by the abbreviation *RS* and page number in brackets.

37 The desire to experience the world in a way that is 'real' is also linked to the notion of an authentic way of being which, I argue, McGahern suggests can be found through marriage. See 'Love and the World: marriage and McGahern's late vision', in Máire Doyle and Željka Doljanin (eds), *John McGahern: authority and vision* (Manchester: Manchester University Press, 2017), pp. 124–139.

38 Arendt, *The Human Condition*, p. 51.

39 Ibid., p. 242.

40 Patrick Crotty, '"All Toppers": children in the fiction of John McGahern', special issue of *Irish University Review: a journal of Irish studies*, vol. 35, no. 1, 2005, pp. 42–57, at p. 55.

41 Hannah Arendt, *Men in Dark Times* (San Diego: Harcourt Brace Jovanovich, 1968), p. 24.

42 Ibid., p. 25.

Chapter 11

1 David Lloyd, 'Rage against the Divine: in memoriam Jacques Derrida', *South Atlantic Quarterly*, vol. 106, no. 2, Spring 2007, pp. 345–72.

2 Joe Cleary, *Outrageous Fortune: capital and culture in modern Ireland* (Dublin: Field Day Publications, 2007), pp. 162–5.

3 Sylvia Plath, 'Daddy', in *Ariel: the restored edition* (New York: Harper Perennial Modern Classics, 2005 [1965]), pp. 74–6.

4 John McGahern, *Memoir* (London: Faber & Faber, 2005), p. 248. All further references to this edition will be denoted by *M*, and followed by the page number.

5 Sigmund Freud, *The Interpretation of Dreams*, translated and edited by James Strachey (New York: Basic Books, 1955), p. 262. All further references to this edition will be denoted *ID*, followed by the page number.

6 Freud's ideas on the Oedipus complex, its relation to the castration complex, its variation in male and female children, and the role of fantasy in parent–child relations all evolve slowly, change significantly, and provoke difficulties for him, as well as much dispute in early psychoanalytic circles.

For useful essays on this complex topic, see B. Simon and R.B. Blass, 'The Development and Vicissitudes of Freud's Ideas on the Oedipus Complex', in Jermone Nehu (ed.), *The Cambridge Companion to Freud* (New York: Cambridge University Press, 1991), pp. 161–74. I have also found the following of interest: Maynard Solomon, 'Freud's Father on the Acropolis', *American Imago*, vol. 30, no. 2, Summer 1973, pp. 142–56; Iris Levy, 'The Fate of the Oedipus Complex: dissolution or waning', *International Forum of Psychoanalysis*, vol 4, no.1, 1995, pp. 7–15; Peter Hartocollis, 'Origins and Evolution of the Oedipus Complex as Conceptualized by Freud', *Psychoanalytic Review*, vol. 92, no. 2, June 2005, pp. 315–34, and especially Rachel Bowlby, 'Family Realisms: Freud and Greek tragedy', *Essays in Criticism*, vol. LVI, no. 2, April 2006, pp. 111–38.

7 Sigmund Freud, *Introductory Lectures on Psychoanalysis*, translated and edited by James Strachey (New York: W.W. Norton & Company, 1966 [1916]), p. 207.

8 Sigmund Freud, *Three Essays on the Theory of Sexuality*, translated and edited by James Strachey (New York: Basic Books, 2000 [1905]), p. 48. All further references to this edition will be denoted by *TETS*, followed by page number.

9 See Sigmund Freud, *The Standard Edition of the Complete Psychological Works of Sigmund Freud*, vol. XIX (1923–5): *The Ego and the Id and Other Works*, translated by James Strachey (London: Hogarth Press, 1961), p. 176.

10 See respectively Henry James, *Hawthorne* (London: Macmillan, 1879), p. 3; and Seán O'Faoláin, 'The Dilemma of Irish Letters', *The Month*, vol. 2, no. 6, 1949, pp. 375–6.

11 The river is associated with sexuality and sexual life. Towards the very end of *Memoir*, when McGahern visits his mother's sister Katie, he outlines for her (and the reader) what became of his siblings in later life. McGahern recounts that Katie did not seem surprised by his own divorce and remarriage, but when she responds that '"I was certain you'd become a priest"', McGahern replies: '"The pull of life was too great', I said. "I always wanted to go on the river"' (*M*, 270).

12 Robert Stollers, cited by Adam Phillips, 'The Magical Act of a Desperate Person', *The London Review of Books*, vol. 35, no. 5, March 2013, pp. 19–20, at p. 19.

13 On Plath's 'Daddy' and the controversies it has provoked, see Jacqueline Rose, 'Daddy', in *The Haunting of Sylvia Plath* (London: Virago Press, 1991), pp. 205–38. Rose contests those critics who read her work as rhetorically overblown, self-aggrandising or self-indulgent. A more extended comparative analysis of McGahern's and Plath's father figures than this essay allows for would have to engage with issues of male and female formation processes and with the different representational issues generated by poetry and the novel. My point in comparing the two figures is essentially to highlight their different stylistic approaches to the topic.

14 The suggestion that John McGahern had actually fathered a son whom he never acknowledged appeared briefly in some newspaper articles after the writer's death. If true, the rejection might evidence the writer's repudiation of fathers or at least an ongoing and painful difficulty with the paternal role.

15 Lloyd, 'Rage against the Divine', pp. 353–4.

Chapter 12

1 The monographs brought out to mark the tenth anniversary of the writer's death are the following: Stanley van der Ziel, *John McGahern and the Imagination of Tradition* (Cork: Cork University Press, 2016); Richard Robinson, *John McGahern and Modernism* (London and New York: Bloomsbury, 2017); Frank Shovlin, *Touchstones: John McGahern's classical style* (Liverpool: Liverpool University Press, 2016). Each one adds significantly to McGahern criticism and they reveal the extent to which McGahern is increasingly viewed as a canonical writer.

2 Denis Sampson, *Young John McGahern: becoming a novelist* (Oxford: Oxford University Press, 2012), pp. 55–6.

3 The writer's sister Monica confided to me that McGahern gave her a few Mauriac titles to read in the 1950s or '60s.

4   Michel Foucault, *The History of Sexuality: an introduction*, trans. Robert Hurley (London: Penguin Books, 1990), p. 6. I would like to acknowledge Liam Maher's role in first mentioning to me the usefulness of Foucault's work in relation to McGahern. Cf. Liam Maher, 'The Courage of John McGahern in writing *The Dark*', *Doctrine & Life*, vol. 63, February 2013, pp. 49–56.

5   Jean-Luc Barré, *François Mauriac: biographie intime, 1885–1940*, tome I (Paris: Fayard, 2009), pp. 49–50. My translation.

6   'Catholicism and National Identity in the Works of John McGahern', interview between Eamon Maher and John McGahern in *Studies: an Irish quarterly*, vol 90, no 357, Spring 2001, pp. 73–4.

7   John McGahern, *The Leavetaking* (London: Faber & Faber, 1984), p. 116. All subsequent references will be to this edition, designated by *L*, followed by page number.

8   Diarmaid Ferriter, *Occasions of Sin: sex and society in modern Ireland* (London: Profile Books, 2009), p. 335.

9   John McGahern, *Amongst Women* (London: Faber & Faber, 1990), p. 48. Will henceforth be captured as *AW*.

10 Cited by Barré, *François Mauriac*, p. 366.

11 Donat O'Donnell, *Maria Cross: imaginative patterns in a group of modern Catholic writers* (London: Chatto & Windus, 1953), p. 30.

12 'Le romancier et ses personnages', in Jacques Petit (ed.), *François Mauriac: oeuvres romanesques et théâtrales complètes* (Paris: Bibliothèques de la Pléiade/Gallimard, 1979), tome II, p. 855. My translation.

13 François Mauriac, *Commencements d'une vie*, Pléiade II, p. 67.

14 Sampson, *Young John McGahern*, p. 108.

15 There are various versions of 'The End or the Beginning of Love' in the McGahern Archive at NUI Galway. The one from which I quote is catalogued at P71/8. This quote is on p. 15. Page number for subsequent quotes will be given in brackets within the text. Thanks to Fergus Fahey, the person responsible for compiling the McGahern Archive, for his help with accessing this manuscript.

16 François Mauriac, *Le Baiser au lépreux*, Pléiade II, p. 458. My translation. Subsequent references, also translated by me, will be to this edition with page number in brackets.

17 Malcolm Scott, *The Struggle for the Soul of the French Novel* (Washington, DC: The Catholic University of America Press, 1989), p. 184. The translation of the Pascal quote is my own.

18 'An Interview with John McGahern', Appendix to Eamon Maher, *John McGahern: from the local to the universal* (Dublin: The Liffey Press, 2003), pp. 143–61, at p. 149.

19 John McGahern, *The Pornographer* (London: Faber & Faber, 1979), p. 177. All subsequent references will be denoted by *P*, followed by page number.

20 François Mauriac, *Thérèse Desqueyroux*, in Gerard Hopkins (trans.), *Thérèse* (Hammondsworth: Penguin Modern Classics, 1981), p. 9. All subsequent references will be to this edition, with the page number in parentheses.

21 Cecil Jenkins, *Mauriac* (New York: Barnes & Noble, 1965), p. 75.

22 Foucault, *The History of Sexuality*, p. 9.

Afterword

1   This is an edited version of the talk that Donal Ryan gave at the symposium organised in April 2017 in St Patrick's College Drumcondra (DCU) to mark the tenth anniversary of McGahern's death. It appeared in a slightly different form in an *Irish Times* article published on 30 March 2017, http://www.irishtimes.com/culture/books/donal-ryan-on-john-mcgahern-amongst-women-almost-finished-me-how-could-a-book-be-this-good-1.3013523 [accessed 29 October 2018].

2   John McGahern, *Amongst Women* (London: Faber & Faber, 1990), p. 160.

3   John McGahern, *The Dark* (London: Faber & Faber, 1965), p. 17.

4 Michael Hartnett, *Collected Poems: Michael Hartnett* (Oldcastle, Co. Meath: Gallery Press, 2001), p. 197.

5 John McGahern, *That They May Face the Rising Sun* (London: Faber & Faber, 2002), p. 63.

6 Seamus Heaney, *Station Island* (London: Faber & Faber, 1984), pp. 92–3.

7 John McGahern, *Memoir* (London: Faber & Faber, 2005), p. 272.

INDEX

Illustrations are indicated by page numbers in bold.